The
Joan Kennedy
Story

SIMON AND SCHUSTER · NEW YORK

noted that "the pain of defeat was far, far less than the pain of the people I have met while campaigning." He talked about jobs for all as "a moral issue" and defended the idea of government helping the poor: "It is surely correct that we cannot solve problems by throwing money at them, but it is also correct that we dare not throw our national problems into a scrap heap of inattention and indifference. A fair prosperity and a just society are within our vision and our grasp."

Then Kennedy turned to his supporters and said earnestly: "There were hard hours on our journey. Often we sailed against the wind, but always we kept our rudder true. There were so many of you who stayed the course and shared our hope. You gave your help; but even more, you gave your hearts. Because of you, this has been a happy campaign."

Near the end of his speech, Kennedy invited Joan and their children to join him at the podium. Then, flanked by his family, he concluded with the now famous lines: "For me, a few hours ago, this campaign came to an end. For all those whose cares have been our concern, the work goes on, the cause endures, the hope still lives, and the dream shall never die."

The crowd again burst into applause and cheers, and Joan, moving toward her husband, put her arm around his neck and leaned her head close to his. Ted circled her waist with his arm and they faced the crowd, their arms around each other. It was the closest I had ever seen them. And as I watched them from the balcony, it seemed to me that the togetherness that had eluded them throughout the campaign had come at last. Perhaps Joan's hope was still alive. Perhaps her dream would not die.

Caught up in the electrifying emotion Kennedy had created, thousands of delegates and friends, many of them crying, roared their approval and imagined being led back to victory by a Kennedy. For just a moment the burst of "Happy Days Are Here Again" on the grand organ resounded with optimism and hope. But then, when the cheers died down at last, they were left with a depressing irony. Acclaim for the Senator, which had erupted in a twenty-three-minute standing, clapping, stomping ovation—the greatest moments of the 1980 convention—had been elicited by the eloquent farewell of the man who had been defeated. Ironic, too, that in defeat, Kennedy was still victorious, the convention's hero.

Joan had also become a kind of heroine during the campaign. Only a few years before, the press had portrayed her as a pathetic woman who went around in skirts a little too short, talked a little too freely, drank a little too much, and suffered as the second victim of the plunge off the bridge at Chappaquiddick. Later she separated from her husband and family and moved to Boston where she struggled to overcome alcoholism. Ted, after years of trying to help her, became distant and remote. It had been a dark time for Joan, but the last few months had changed all that.

The campaign had been the impetus for Joan's own private victory: she had not touched alcohol for over a year. Shedding the pitiable image of the wronged wife, she had walked out onto platforms to charm curious crowds and skeptical spectators. Refreshed and positive, she inspired the public and the press. Even the most cynical reporters began to fall in love with her, as it dawned on them that Joan Kennedy had courage. It hadn't been easily won. But Joan had found renewed purpose in the campaign because she felt Ted needed her. She was a Kennedy. She was his wife.

I knew Joan hoped that her able campaigning had softened Ted's feelings for her and closed the distance between them. Yes, the campaign had unified her family again. Yes, she looked forward to moving back to Washington. Those were the words she had been encouraged to say in reply to reporters' questions, and I think she must have come to believe them. But with the loss of the nomination, living with Ted in the White House was no longer an option. The question they now confronted was whether they would live together at all.

This campaign was over. But the next few days in New York and Washington, and during the coming weekend on Cape Cod, Joan would campaign for a different cause—the chance to win her husband back.

When the ovation finally subsided, Joan and Ted, their staffs, the Secret Service, and the rest of the Kennedy family went to the Waldorf-Astoria from Madison Square Garden and gathered in the living room of the Senator's suite for a party. Considering the circumstances it was a convivial occasion, with soft lights, flowers, lavish cheese platters, hot hors d'oeuvres in silver chafing dishes, a full bar, and a uniformed bartender. The room resounded with praise for Ted's brilliant address and laughter over campaign blunders. The Kennedys had always drawn talented, committed, highly qualified people around them. Staff members became friends, appreciated each other's hard work, and cared for one another. Some of us had worked together for months on the telephone and only met a few days ago. The Kennedys themselves, all attractive, vital, and charismatic, radiated goodwill and gratitude toward each other, their friends, and staffs. And even though the party might have been difficult for the Senator, it was a way for him to thank those who had given so much of themselves to his campaign. He moved easily around the room talking to everyone, thanking them with genuine warmth and affection.

In one corner of the crowded room, Joan and I talked with Barbara Mikulski, the Democratic congresswoman from Maryland. She advised Joan to prepare herself for a letdown after the hectic weeks and months of the campaign, to allow herself time to accept the defeat, but plan activities to fill the next few empty days. Sipping a soft drink, Joan nodded, but her thoughts seemed to be elsewhere. And sometime later during the party, Ted issued her an unusual invitation—a private lunch with him the next day.

"It could be just like old times," she said breathlessly, pulling me aside to tell me about the invitation. Her eyes sparkled. "You have to come over and help me get ready."

Delighted with her news, I promised to be there the next morning. I knew she had been looking for some sign from Ted that their marriage was still alive, and I hoped this was it. In the music and the warmth of friends' voices, neither Joan nor I could imagine a letdown, only the bright possibilities of Ted's unexpected invitation.

The following morning, a steamy hot August day, my taxi pulled up to the Waldorf's Park Avenue entrance and the doorman nodded to me in recognition as I stepped out. Carrying my briefcase, full of speeches and Q and A sheets we would never use again, I went through the brass and glass revolving door, climbed the marble steps to the spacious lobby, and passed some of the convention delegates gathering political gossip and eating late breakfasts at café tables. A few heads turned as I moved through the lobby. People expecting to see Joan occasionally mistook me for her. We were nearly the same height and had similar blond hair styles. I was a few years younger than Joan, but that morning I felt like her mother.

Arrival on the sixteenth floor invariably promised some kind of high drama. The first sight outside the elevator was often sleeping bags, clothes, coffee cups, and cameras. The national press corps covering the Kennedy campaign had set up its camping grounds in the hall, and there they ate, slept, and waited for a Kennedy—any Kennedy—to come or go. By now, recognizing each other, we exchanged greetings and quips as I stepped my way through their living arrangements.

The hallway doors were heavily guarded, but my small orange-and-brass "permanent staff" pin got me through without a question and with several smiles. Passing the staff room and the security personnel room, I finally arrived at the end of the long corridor and the door to the Kennedys' suite. I walked by the Secret Service agents in the entry hall and glanced into Ted's empty bedroom to the left of the large living room still filled with wilting flowers from last night's party.

On the other side of the living room, the white door to Joan's bedroom was closed. I knocked and she called me in. Sitting on the bed beside a huge stack of that morning's newspapers, she looked up at me and beamed. "It isn't every day," she said, patting the pile of papers, "a girl gets her picture on the front page of The New York Times."

It was a picture of Joan kissing Ted as they left the podium at the Garden the night before, a warm and tender moment that would certainly intensify the public's curiosity about their future relationship.

Still dressed in a robe, Joan stood up and began pacing back and forth, nervous with anticipation. Even so, I thought she looked lovely that morning. At nearly forty-four, something of the fresh innocence of the Catholic schoolgirl remained about her. When she had been drinking, she had gained weight and her appearance changed. Her face became puffy and her smiles forced. But none of that showed now; she was radiant in her new sobriety and health. Her blond hair, her trademark, was once again shaped into the smooth pageboy she had worn as a young mother and the wife of the newly elected Senator from Massachusetts. Her blue-green eyes were clear today and shone with excitement.

She and Ted were to lunch together alone, she told me with a slight quiver in her voice. He had chosen an intimate little French restaurant a few blocks away and—for almost the first time, day or night, in the past hectic year—there would be no one else present. It implied a new beginning with Ted, but Joan hesitated to say it because she dreaded another disappointment.

She had already been dismayed that morning to wake up and find that Patrick had left for their house on Cape Cod. The night before he had made his own flight reservations and arranged for an advanceman to drive him to the airport. Joan was afraid she had lost control of her children's lives.

"I've learned something from this campaign," she said. "I have no responsibility for my children." Then she talked of Teddy, Jr., and Kara and how independent they had become. Perhaps that realization made the private lunch with Ted and her hope of renewing their marriage seem even more important.

Joan sipped a cup of coffee from her breakfast tray and I pulled the draperies to let in the bright morning sunshine. Then we began to prepare her for the big event. Even though Joan looked better than she had in years, she was still insecure about her appearance. She had been a much-acclaimed beauty in the fifties and had appeared on the cover of nearly every woman's magazine since her marriage. Long accustomed to thinking of her looks as a primary asset, she often traveled with five or six makeup cases filled with cosmetics and had an even bigger selection in her Boston apartment. Joan called herself "the original before-and-after-girl." We both had lived through twenty rebellious and liberating years, but when it came to cosmetics, we were still women of the fifties, responding almost automatically to the necessity of looking attractive.

Sitting at a dressing table, Joan applied her makeup with a practiced hand. Then she went to a closet and pulled out a ruffled cotton sundress with short puff sleeves. I wanted to say, "No, not that one," but I caught myself. Now was not the time to suggest a change that might undermine her confidence. Joan dressed and then hurriedly dabbed Opium behind her ears just as we heard voices in the living room. The Senator had arrived.

His presence was usually something of a spectacle. Surrounded by aides and security, charged with energy and purpose, Ted was obviously a forceful man, yet warmth and sensitivity showed in his eyes. Tall and well-built, with thick, dark, wavy hair tinged with gray, he had the magnetic Kennedy personality. Generally good-natured, he joked easily, frequently at his own expense. His face, weathered by tragedy and trauma, made him seem somehow more credible now than the boyish, inexperienced figure he had first cut in the Senate many years ago. At forty-eight he was a handsome man and a dedicated senator who had earned his power.

With a last quick glance in the mirror, Joan left her bedroom to greet him. She smiled sweetly when she saw him, her voice soft and hesitant as she spoke. Watching them leave, I felt like a mother bidding good-bye to a daughter on her first date with the most popular boy in school.

I went to a window and pulled the sheer curtains aside, but the suite was too high up to see much on the street below. I hoped that the Senator's usual princely retinue wouldn't be in constant attendance, that the Secret Service agents, the reporters shouting questions, the photographers trying to get a good angle would give them time to be alone.

Within the next few days, Joan and Ted planned to fly to their home in McLean, Virginia, to host a Washington version of last night's campaign-end party. From there, they would go to their house in Hyannis Port. Before Joan returned from lunch, I wanted to organize all of our current notes, schedules, and briefing materials, and get her packing started. I returned to her bedroom, and as I worked, I silently cheered Joan on, believing that she wanted Ted's respect and love more than anything else. Although in the days of drinking and emotional upheavals, and even in the past few months, there had been other men, I felt certain Joan's dream was to be a part of Ted's life again, to live with her children and resume her role as a member of the Kennedy family.

It was not an impossible dream. She had stopped drinking and she was so proud of her recovery. Just a few days ago as we were packing to come to New York she had said, "It's a wonder I'm not drinking. Any other lady alcoholic going to a national convention where her husband could be nominated for President might drink. . . . We all know Ted might not get it, but what if he does? Oh, my God!" Because my loyalty and concern during the past few months had been for Joan, my thoughts—then as now—were on what she would do if he did *not* win the nomination. Perhaps that's what they would talk about at lunch today.

After two hours I began to listen for the commotion in the outer hall that would signal Joan and Ted's return. But when Joan opened the door to the bedroom, she was alone. She walked quickly across the room and collapsed into an armchair. Her face was drawn and tense.

"Can you believe it?" she said. "A private lunch with the national press corps!" She didn't look at me; she simply stared into space. I put down a pile of papers and sat on the bed across from her.

Then she told me the story. The whole entourage had gone into the restaurant. Photographers had taken turns getting shots of them at their table. Waiters hovered and other patrons peered while Ted traded remarks with the press. Finally, Joan said, she had to admit to herself that it was nothing more than a well-timed media event. Perhaps one of Ted's press aides had decided that a final campaign image of the gallant husband and his supportive wife had to be presented to the public once again.

"He hardly spoke to me," Joan sighed. "We hardly even looked at each other."

I felt her disappointment deeply and suggested that she be patient and wait for the weekend when she would be with Ted and their children on the Cape. "He's under a lot of pressure," I said. "He's still in the political limelight and has a lot of decisions to make. And he's still adjusting to his loss—just the way you are." I tried to sound absolutely confident. "The Cape is the place where you can talk and be alone, not a New York restaurant."

Joan nodded pensively.

That Wednesday night at Madison Square Garden, President Carter claimed renomination on a roll call vote—Carter 2,129; Kennedy 1,146. To end the suspense of whether or not Kennedy would support Carter, a few minutes after midnight Chairman Tip O'Neill read a statement from Kennedy: "I will support and work for the reelection of President Carter. It is imperative that we defeat Ronald Reagan." O'Neill then said optimistically as he looked out to the delegations spread over the hall, "So united we stand."

On Thursday, Carter accepted the nomination while Kennedy watched his address on television. Joan left to go to Virginia, Kara and Teddy went to the Cape, and I returned to Boston. That final night of the convention, Kennedy's carefully orchestrated arrival for a "unity" appearance brought the loudest response from the crowd of delegates. With the Mondales on either side of the Carters, Kennedy shook hands with the President and his wife, Rosalynn, as photographers recorded the brief moment of reconciliation. But Kennedy soon moved apart from his recent opponent and, remaining less than two minutes, returned to the Waldorf. The next day he joined Joan at their McLean, Virginia, home.

The thank-you party for the staff and Secret Service agents took place alongside the pool at their rambling, one-story sixteen-room house overlooking the Potomac River. Its modest gray shingle exterior nestled behind thick shrubbery at the end of a long, curving drive. Inside, it was grander. What Joan called "our Republican living room" was lavish with damask and brocade-covered Sheraton and Hepplewhite antiques. Dozens and dozens of photographs on tables and walls told the story of the Kennedy family. Wings sprawled from either side of the house, one of them containing Joan and Ted's bedroom, bathrooms, and closets, and the other reserved for their children. Joan had not lived in this house for over three years, and I hoped she would not feel like a guest at her own party.

The next day she reached me on the phone in Boston to tell me about the party and her trip to the Cape. As she spoke I pictured her at the other end of the line in Hyannis Port, in her terry-cloth bathrobe, lying on her king-size bed with a pile of lacy white pillows behind her head. Her bedroom was always bright with reflected light off the ocean, pink chintz prints, and light blue carpeting. It was a quiet, cheerful room, but Joan's voice sounded breathless and angry.

Finally she calmed down and I learned what had upset her. Happily, everyone seemed to have paid her gratifying attention at the party. Servants poured tea and coffee, mixed drinks, and served pastries as staff and security laughed and replayed the old game of bungled campaign stops. Joan and Ted were relaxed with each other, Ted dressed in a casual blue denim shirt and slacks, and Joan in a flounced cotton sundress. The music was soothing, the air was cool, and guests flowed back and forth from party room to the patio beside the pool. Joan told me she was having a wonderful time, dancing with one Secret Service agent after another, whom she described as "dolls," when suddenly Ted came in from the patio and went directly to her. She stopped dancing. In a low voice, he said that she must hurry. They were leaving for the Cape right away.

Joan was surprised, she said, because the party was far from over, she was having a good time, and there seemed to be no reason to rush. Still, she didn't object. She gathered her things and once again they were off to the airport—the first time they had gone to an airport together in ten months without the wire services and networks in tow. After all, she thought, the Cape was really what she had been waiting for.

"The plane trip was so strange," Joan reported. "He said nice things. Even though he didn't mention my work in the campaign, he did give me some compliments. It was very nice."

I thought of them flying in a small plane, similar to the ones Joan and I had flown in during the campaign. Joan and Ted would be sitting behind the pilot, their matched luggage piled in the rear compartment. As they flew up the coast, lights below would be twinkling in the night. Ted probably had a briefcase on his lap and pulled something out to read. Joan usually tucked a pillow behind her head and slept on planes—but she probably hadn't slept on this flight.

The trip was uneventful, she told me, until suddenly Ted leaned forward and said something to the pilot. The plane almost immediately slanted toward the east and began a descent. The landing was smooth, and when the plane taxied into a tiny airport, Joan knew they were on the eastern tip of Long Island. Montauk Point.

With a few words of good-bye, Ted climbed out of the plane, jumped into a waiting car, and drove off.

"No, that can't be true!" I heard myself saying. But I knew it was as I listened to the note of desolation in Joan's voice.

"It's true all right. Kendall—the captain of Ted's boat, you remember—had sailed *The Curraugh* from the Cape and was waiting for him in the harbor." There was a long pause and then she said, "He's gone off cruising in the Caribbean with some chick, I think."

I didn't know what to say as I imagined her intense feeling of being abandoned—once again. I knew Joan was the kind of woman who rarely made a scene in front of others—or even demanded reasons or answers. The presence of the pilot and driver would have kept her silent. "Oh, Joan," I said finally.

"And so I came home by myself," she said softly.

Glancing around the front hall of my apartment that I had made into an office, I saw that every surface was covered with correspondence, schedules, indexed speeches, press releases. And that mass of paper represented only a small fraction of the exhausting efforts that Joan had made on Ted's behalf. The campaign had put her under enormous physical and emotional strain, yet she went through with it. And now, only a day after Ted's defeat when she was no longer needed, he had left her.

"It makes me so angry," I said.

Joan, who had become accustomed to accepting that kind of rejection and hardened to the realities of her life, was less upset than I. "Well, I'm not anymore," she said in a resigned, bitter voice. "Kara and Teddy have fifty friends in the house. A couple I know, and the rest are all new faces. They were having a big party out on the lawn when I arrived. I really felt weird. So I sat and talked to Patrick and munched. I kept thinking of what Barbara told us that last evening in New York about expecting the letdown and then having to make plans for myself. I just wish I could let go. I really feel weird."

"After all you've done, Joan," I said, still unable to believe what had happened, "and all the changes you've made in yourself."

"I know," she replied. But then she reminded me, and I can still hear her clear and certain tone as she said, "Remember why I did it. You know and I know the real reason I campaigned. I did it for myself."

2 BECOMING A KENNEDY

I felt extra, no good. When I said I didn't want a baby nurse, we had a baby nurse. Everything was done and taken care of and I didn't do it. I was nobody, nothing, not needed.

—JOAN

I grew up admiring women like Grace Kelly and Joan Kennedy. For me and many others, they represented ideal images of what young women in the fifties were taught to strive for—accomplishment without loss of femininity. The expectations on us were exacting: we were asked to be virtuous, attractive, competent. And we were to pursue careers only as long as it took for a man—the "right" man—to pursue and marry us. Thereafter, we became wives and mothers. It was supposed to be, or so most of us thought, that uncomplicated.

I was still in college when Joan married Ted and became a favorite with the press. Her charmed life as the wife of the youngest of the Kennedy brothers was featured in countless magazines and newspapers. I believed the thousands of words written about her, searched the photographs for hints on how to look or wear my hair, and took comfort in the thought that Joan was beautiful and glamorous and therefore "different from you and me," as F. Scott Fitzgerald once wrote about the rich. I never imagined meeting her, much less that we would ever find something in common. But about seventeen years later, after both our lives had veered dramatically from the courses we were expected to follow, our paths did cross and we became friends.

In the fall of 1976, after my marriage to the "right" man had failed, I decided to return to Boston where I was born and later lived after college as a young teacher and wife. I planned to do graduate work at Harvard, and because my two children were still young, I searched for over a year to find a house near good schools in Brookline or Cambridge. But then a friend introduced me to Dan Mullin, a Boston real estate agent who showed me just one apartment. It was in Back Bay, one of the city's most beautiful neighborhoods, the rooms were large and sunny, and the children loved it. We took it, and almost as an afterthought, the agent mentioned that Joan Kennedy also lived in the building. Two months later we moved in (in fact, we still live there) and I have often thought since how different my life would have been if I had found a house in Brookline or Cambridge.

Several months later, on a cool November evening, I met Joan for the first time at the annual condominium association meeting held in one of the apartments in the building. She was seated across the room from me, looking as lovely as the pictures I had seen of her over the years. But I was struck at once by her shyness. She said very little to those around her and did not talk at all during the business discussion.

As soon as the meeting about management and monthly fees was over, all the residents moved into the dining room and gathered around the bar for cocktails, imported cheeses and more conversation. I glanced back into the living room and saw that Joan had been left by herself. Looking uneasy and alone, she sat at one end of the modern white sofa, her legs crossed, her hands in her lap, just waiting.

I noticed then and several times later that people often did not know how to approach Joan. In an effort to treat her "normally," to be nonchalant about a celebrity, they inadvertently ignored her. Still, these were her neighbors, and I wondered if Joan's reluctance to join the group of more than twenty people in the dining room was because of her own shyness—or discomfort about going near the bar. It was known that she had a "drinking problem," and it occurred to me she might have been self-conscious or nervous that others would be watching her. As I hesitated about what to do, I felt an enormous compassion for her. I knew what it was like to have the eyes of everyone in the room on you, waiting apprehensively, powerlessly, to see if you would take that first drink. I knew, too, what it was like to watch others enjoy drinks—even too many drinks—without suffering anything more than a hangover. I had waged a battle of my own with alcoholism. Joan and I had that in common before we exchanged a single word.

Even though I was one of the newest residents in the building, I finally summoned up the courage to speak to her. I walked back into the living room and introduced myself.

"Hello, I'm Joan Kennedy," she said. Her voice, so gentle and whispery, sounded similar to Jackie Kennedy's, I thought. And when I asked if I could get her something from the bar, she seemed relieved and said, "Yes, please."

I didn't want a drink, and assuming that Joan didn't want one either, I returned to the living room carrying two plastic glasses of soda water embellished with not very deceptive lime wedges. Handing her a glass, I smiled in a way that let her know my drink was no more interesting than hers. And although nothing was said, I think at that moment a bond was established between us.

I don't remember what we talked about, but at the end of the evening, Joan and I made plans to get together again. In later conversations we discovered that we had a great deal in common. Yet that seemed less important at first than knowing that neither of us could drink. I had seen it happen so many times before. There seems to be an immediate empathy between two people who have suffered the torments of alcoholism and have struggled to overcome it. Often this shared experience leads to a special friendship, for it is a gift to be able to talk to someone who understands what no one else can.

The more we learned about each other, the more we were surprised by the similarities in our lives. Besides living on our own without husbands and studying for a master's in education degree, Joan at Lesley College and I at Harvard, we found that we both played the piano, loved the arts, and enjoyed attending concerts and the theater.

But there were differences, too. I was divorced. Joan was merely "living apart" from her husband. Her three children, older than my two, lived with their father. And although no one can claim complete victory over alcoholism, my battles were in the past. Joan's were far from over. Indeed, she spoke very little of her own alcoholism at first, as if she were still reluctant to admit it even to herself.

During the next few months we talked on the phone and met often to sip Perrier, Tab, or tea and to compare memories of our childhoods, our school years, and how similar our parents' hopes and expectations for us had been. From the perspective of the late seventies we saw ourselves as classic examples of the women of our generation. In fact, if Joan and I and our friends had heard of *The Feminine Mystique* when it appeared in 1963, we might have thought it was a new night cream. We never anticipated how relevant it would become to our lives.

If there was a theme that pervaded Joan's childhood and upbringing, it was the obligation to perform, an obligation that followed her through her college years and finally overwhelmed her as Ted's wife and a member of the Kennedy family. The forces that drew her into that particular marriage were, I suppose, largely coincidental. Yet, as Joan told me stories about her life, I was struck by an almost eerie feeling of its inevitability, as if she were a character in a novel.

Joan was born in 1936, at Mother Cabrini Hospital in Riverdale, New York, the daughter of Harry Wiggen Bennett and Virginia Joan Stead, after whom she was named, although she was always called Joan. Her father, who traced his descent from ancestors who had settled in Massachusetts in the 1600s, was Protestant and Republican. Her mother was a Catholic and Joan was raised and educated as a Catholic. It was certainly one of the reasons why she was eligible for marriage into the Kennedy clan. And to a family very self-conscious about its social status, I thought perhaps her impeccable lineage was another.

The Bennetts were not rich. But Joan's father was a successful advertising executive in New York who moved his family, which now included another daughter, Candace, born two years after Joan, to the comparatively affluent suburb of Bronxville where they lived in a Mediterranean-style villa. "Can you imagine?" Joan remembered, laughing. Coincidentally, at about the time the Bennetts moved to Bronxville, the Kennedy family left their very large estate in that same suburb for London, because Joseph P. Kennedy had been appointed United States Ambassador to the Court of St. James.

When Joan talked about her father, he reminded me in some ways of the man she would eventually marry. Harry Bennett was tall, handsome, charming, an actor in neighborhood theatrical productions. Joan described herself as a compliant, sweet, shy little girl who obediently accomplished all that was expected of her. A "goody-goody, too much so," was the way one classmate remembered her, "always doing what the teachers asked. The other children didn't like it at all and so she wasn't very popular in the early years." Joan herself remembered that "I was always told to smile, always to smile—and never to complain. It was the same thing in my marriage." To me, it seemed that she had tried very hard to please her father, as she would later try so hard to please her husband.

She must also have tried to please her mother, who taught Joan to play the piano and insisted that she "behave like a lady." Joan talked occasionally about her father, but she rarely spoke of her mother and I sensed that there were unhappy memories she did not care to recall. I learned why from one of Joan's friends, who told me Joan's mother was an alcoholic.

To me it was a chilling revelation. For it meant that Joan, like so many others, was a victim of the genetic factor that predisposed her to her illness. It also meant that she had grown up as the daughter of an alcoholic.

I never asked Joan about her mother's illness or what effect it may have had on her. But from my own experience, and from the experiences I had shared with other women who were also alcoholics, I knew how hard it was on children. I knew, too, that for Joan's mother, little or no help would have been available to her for a condition that was then considered to be a social stigma, a shameful secret, and a sign of personal weakness, especially for a woman. Children were left to suffer, and if that were true with the Bennetts, Joan may have been deprived of the warm, secure, mother-daughter relationship that provides the basis for self-esteem. That, I thought, would certainly have contributed to the problem she was now trying to resolve. But for her mother, tragically, there was no longer any hope. After years of unhappiness, Joan's parents divorced and her father remarried. Years later, her mother was found dead, and Joan told me it was from the effects of her disease.

All through high school, Joan continued the pattern of her childhood. She was shy and studious, often going right home after school to study or practice the piano. "I was a loner," she told me. "I had no friends in high school. Candy was a lot more popular than I was. She was a cheerleader and went out on dates while I went to the library. I was a late bloomer." Joan may have been a little jealous of Candy, but I don't think there was more than the usual rivalry between them. In fact, Joan told me that she and Candy didn't have half the competitiveness that Ted and his brothers grew up with. "They also had to be up on current events for all meals and to talk about what was going on in the world," she said. "We never did."

Joan's world was very small and very sheltered—perhaps because of Bronxville, perhaps because of her religion, perhaps because of her parents, or perhaps all three. She was expected merely to do well in school and to marry well. In 1954 she graduated from Bronxville High School and that fall entered Manhattanville College in Purchase, New York. "I went right from my father's house to the nuns in college," she recalled.

As Joan and I became closer, I met several of her friends from Manhattanville. They had humorous recollections of wearing hats and white gloves and of what it had been like to learn psychology and European history from nuns in long flowing habits. The curriculum was good and the discipline strict. Still, as one of Joan's friends told me, "It was a marriage mill. Our parents needed a safe place for us while we were looking for husbands."

Her friends also described the emergence of a new Joan at Manhattanville. She indeed began to bloom as if, almost overnight, she discovered she was a talented and beautiful young woman. "Joan used to come home to our house weekends," the brother of

one of her college friends told me, "and she was beautiful and bub-
bly with a wonderful unspoiled outlook on life." "Thank God, my
wallflower days of high school were over," Joan herself said, recalling her official debut into New York society at the Plaza Hotel and
then again in the grand ballroom of the Waldorf at the Debutante
Cotillion and the Christmas Ball. There was a widening circle of at-
tentive young men, college dates, Yale weekends, and theater ex-
cursions into New York. One spring vacation in Bermuda she was
chosen college queen. And toward the end of her senior year, her
proud father introduced her to the owner of a modeling agency and
she posed for advertisements for Revlon and Coca-Cola.

But if Joan seemed to have shed her own personal cocoon, she
was still wrapped securely in the web of her parents' expectations,
the prescribed routines of a Catholic college girl, and the very special circumstances of the social set in which she moved, protected—
as always—from most of life's realities.

Given her sudden popularity, which seemed to surprise even
Joan herself, and given her own conventional view of her future as
a wife and mother, it was perhaps all the more remarkable that she
studied conscientiously and continued her serious interest in music.
"I was always the student," she said. In the fall of her senior year,
she almost missed the Kennedys' dedication ceremony because she
was studying. If she had, she might not have met Ted.

To me their meeting seemed almost predestined. Joan was one
of the loveliest and most popular girls at Manhattanville, a college
the Kennedys might well have considered their own private pre-
serve. Rose Fitzgerald Kennedy had attended school there, as had
her daughter Eunice before she married Sargent Shriver, and her
daughter Jean before she married Stephen Smith. Bobby Kennedy
had found his wife, Ethel Skakel, at Manhattanville. And now Ted,
the youngest of the Kennedys' three sons, was the only one still unmarried. Was it more than mere chance, I wondered, that his sisters might have looked for a bride for him there?

It was, in fact, Jean Smith who introduced Joan to her brother
Ted, just as she had arranged for Bobby to meet Ethel. Joan had
met Jean before and they had friends in common. "But," Joan said,
"I didn't know she was a Kennedy."

The names and faces of the Kennedy family were not then as famous as they would soon become. But then, as later, they appeared for special occasions en masse. Joseph Kennedy had given a physical education building to Manhattanville as a gift, and almost the entire family—Joe and Rose, Bobby and Ethel, Eunice, Jean, and Ted—were there for the dedication ceremony. During the reception that followed, Jean chose Joan out of a crowd of pretty young ladies to meet "her little brother." Ted and Joan talked for a while, and then Joan and her roommate drove Ted to La Guardia for his return flight to Virginia where he was a student at the University of Virginia Law School.

I can imagine that Ted was quickly drawn to Joan. And she to him. But their courtship was very conventional. After their first meeting, "Ted called several times just to talk before he asked me for a date," Joan said. "We had lunch in New York on Thanksgiving weekend." During the next few months, they saw each other for the theater, skiing trips, and sailing. In June of 1958 Joan graduated from Manhattanville, and Ted formally asked her father for her hand in marriage. The engagement was announced in September and the wedding was planned for November.

Joan's father undoubtedly considered Ted the "right" man for his daughter. True, the Kennedys were Democrats, but Ted's father was a self-made millionaire and former ambassador, his brother Jack was the fledgling Senator from Massachusetts and Ted himself was a handsome, charming young man with bright prospects for a career in politics or the law. Joan had more than fulfilled her father's expectations.

Once her credentials had been carefully checked, by Rose in particular, Ted's choice pleased the Kennedys. Joan may not have been as well-bred as Jacqueline Bouvier, nor as wealthy as Ethel Skakel, but she was beautiful and very eager to please. Whatever plans the family had in store for Ted, she would make a suitable consort. And she adored Ted. But she could not—or would not—violate the principles of her own strict upbringing and the equally high standards of the Manhattanville nuns. She was a virgin, and intended to remain one until she married. Even at Harvard, Ted seems to have been accustomed to instant compliance from the women he met. Joan's behavior must have been both a puzzle and a challenge to him. She delighted in telling me how she "caught" Ted. "The only reason he wanted to marry me was because he couldn't get me any other way."

Four years older than Joan, Edward Moore Kennedy was the last born of that large, energetic, and ambitious family. His mother Rose was a Fitzgerald, the pious daughter of a clever Irish-Catholic politician and a former mayor of Boston. His father, Joseph Patrick Kennedy, was the son of a second generation Irish immigrant, prosperous enough as a liquor importer and machine politician to send Joe to Harvard. But that was no guarantee of the social status he sought, and so he set out to make money. Involving himself in a number of shrewd enterprises, from banking to movie theaters and movie production (later he turned to liquor wholesaling and real estate), he eventually accumulated a vast fortune, estimated at 250 million dollars, which survived the stock market crash intact. His ambitions went beyond the amassing of wealth. He sought political power, if not for himself, then for his sons. And he instilled in them the importance of achievement and victory. He encouraged competition and had no tolerance for his children coming in in second place. Joan remembers that Ted often used to quote his father's favorite dictum: "Winning is what counts."

As a boy Ted was adored and spoiled, but still expected to do as well as his older brothers. His family moved often and he was uprooted from one school after another. Finally, in the Kennedy tradition, he went to Harvard, but there the pressure on him to win proved to be too great. Failing in Spanish, he paid a friend to take his place at the exam. They were caught and expelled. After two uneventful years in the army, Ted returned to Harvard in the fall of 1953 and graduated in 1956. Refused admission to Harvard Law School, he considered going to Stanford, but his father decided he should stay in the East at the University of Virginia, the same law school that Bobby had attended. Then, in 1957, he met and fell in love with Joan Bennett, but not, apparently, without some reservations. As the date of their wedding approached, he called Joan to ask if she would consider postponing it. She would not. "If you don't marry me the day we planned," she told him firmly, "you'll never see me again."

Joan and Ted were married on November 29, 1958, in St. Joseph's Roman Catholic Church in Bronxville. All the Kennedys were there—"and there were lots of them," Joan told me with a laugh. "I had no idea what I was getting into. I was just a nice young girl marrying a nice young man." The fashionable ceremony was performed under floodlights and recorded on film, an appropriate symbol to mark the beginning of the years of Joan's new life in which every public act, every private pain, would be held up for scrutiny. It was also the beginning of giving in to Kennedy wishes. Joan wanted to be married by John Cavanaugh, the President of Notre Dame, but Ted's family insisted that the young couple be married by Francis Cardinal Spellman.

There was time only for a three-day honeymoon before they had to return to Charlottesville where Ted continued his law studies. Joan learned to cook, tried to play tennis, and had time to take a few classes. But that period as young newlyweds was almost as brief as their honeymoon. "Politics took over our lives almost immediately," she said.

Ted was still in school when he was enlisted to run his brother Jack's reelection campaign in Massachusetts for the U.S. Senate, even as plans were already underway for Jack's bid for the presidency. Ted received his law degree in 1959, and after spending part of the summer with Joan on a delayed honeymoon in South America, he became Jack's campaign manager for the western states. Ted was gone most of the time after that. Joan was pregnant and went to stay with her parents in Bronxville until their daughter Kara was born. Then a month later she joined Ted on the campaign trail. It must have been difficult to leave her daughter, but her presence was something the Kennedys would expect and she wanted to be with her husband.

The campaign was Joan's initiation into the ways of politics—smiling, waving, shaking countless hands, meeting crowds of people, getting little sleep, keeping up with frenetic schedules—a never-ending performance before the public and a watchful press. It was also her initiation into the demands of being a Kennedy. And it

must have been quite a rude awakening for a shy and sheltered
Catholic schoolgirl, a new wife and mother, to find herself caught
up in the relentless, and sometimes ruthless, pursuit of the family's
political goals. Joan's role was, I suspect, largely decorative—as one
observer remarked, she was treated like a "blond toy"—but she did
what she was told and did it well. The campaign against Richard
M. Nixon was fiercely fought and finally won. Jack Kennedy was
elected President of the United States.

In January of 1960 the family gathered in Washington for inauguration festivities. Following the official ceremony, Joe Kennedy
hosted a lunch for his large family and friends while Jack and Jackie
led a procession up Pennsylvania Avenue. Joan remembers going to
the White House for tea after the parade and then making the
rounds of inaugural balls that night with Ted.

I always loved listening to Joan when she relived the early
years of her marriage, and I could compare her memories to my
own recollections of the glamour and excitement of the Kennedys'
reign in Camelot. "The first five years were the happy ones for us,"
she said. After Jack's election, she and Ted briefly considered moving out West, away from the Kennedy name and influence. But the
family had other plans for Ted, and instead they moved to Boston
where he became an assistant district attorney for a dollar a year.
Meanwhile, a Kennedy friend was appointed to fill Jack's vacant
Senate seat until Ted became old enough to make a bid for it.

Joan said she loved Boston right from the beginning. She and
Ted lived in an apartment on elegant Louisburg Square until they
moved into their first home, a red brick townhouse on Charles
River Square on the flat of Beacon Hill. Soon after, they bought a
house on the Cape, on Squaw Island, a short distance from the Kennedy compound in Hyannis Port. Joan was busy and happy, caring
for Kara and Teddy, Jr., who was born in September of 1961. "I can
remember thinking I was settled for a while," she told me. But as
always, the family's plans came before anything she and Ted might
have planned for themselves.

As soon as Ted turned thirty, he declared his candidacy for the
Senate, and Joan was immediately drawn into another campaign.
But this time her role as the candidate's wife would be much more

important and demanding, and Kennedy aides rallied to assist her. "Ted's administrative assistant, Ed Martin, was handling the press then and he helped me with what to say at coffees," Joan told me. "I don't know what I would have done without him. He's terrific, a real pro. Ted's cousin, Sally Fitzgerald, and I drove all over the state. I'll never forget it. We went from coffee to coffee. I think we were in every town in Massachusetts."

Still, I suspect most people came just to see her, not to hear anything she had to say, and she was so pretty and sweet that she was often scheduled at campaign events to draw a crowd. According to one observer, she never really cared about politics—a sad omen for her future—but she worked hard, did her "homework" as she still called it, listened in at briefings, and read news clippings of the campaign to keep informed. She wanted to help Ted win, but what mattered even more to Joan was pleasing him. "I was so nervous about how I was doing. I wanted to do so well." And when Joan told me that, I thought, there it was again: the obligation to perform—to please her father, the nuns at Manhattanville, and now Ted.

Whatever her misgivings, Joan proved to be an invaluable asset in that bitter campaign, and in 1962 Ted became one of the youngest senators in history and Joan one of the youngest Senate wives. "I remember when Ted was sworn in," she said. "I took Kara and Teddy with me to watch. And Gramma and Ethel were there, too. It was such an exciting time."

Joan and Ted immediately moved children and staff from Boston to a large and beautiful house in Georgetown. And so Ted's political career began while his brother Jack was President and his brother Bobby was Attorney General. Inevitably, he and Joan received nearly as much attention from the press and public as Jack and Jackie and Bob and Ethel. They were at the very center of social and political power. "It was really the big time," Joan said with a note of awe in her voice, as if she found it hard to believe herself.

Beneath the sparkling surface of their lives, however, darker currents began to swirl. From the very first, Joan felt somewhat overpowered by her energetic in-laws. She was later quoted as saying: "Ted should have married my younger sister Candy. She was

always the female athlete. She plays tennis and golf and rides beau-
tifully, while I'm still allergic to horses. . . . But my tennis is getting better and so is my skiing. Anyway, I guess there's no going
back now. Ted met me and not my sister."

She was also overwhelmed by the Kennedy way of doing things.
"The house was always full of cooks, baby nurses, and staff," she
told me. "I felt extra, no good. When I said I didn't want a baby
nurse, we had a baby nurse. Everything was done and taken care of
and I didn't do it. I was nobody, nothing, not needed."

A Washington friend of Joan's remembered a visit to the
Georgetown house one afternoon for tea. "The cook was in the
kitchen, but it was the governess's day off. Teddy, Jr. was sleeping
in his carriage and Joan was busy fussing about him. She seemed
delighted to have this chance to take care of her children herself."

Many women, I thought, would also have been delighted to
have an efficient household staff, and beyond that the even more efficient machinery of the Kennedy family. Joan had only to ask and
it was given—and often, it seemed, given even when she hadn't
asked. But in reality she had few opportunities to use the time and
freedom that was provided, in order to do anything for herself. Her
primary obligation was as Ted's wife and her days were fragmented.
"It was difficult to live in Washington and have a life of my own,"
she later said. "I tried doing various things—starting piano lessons,
taking lessons at Georgetown or American and—and something awfully exciting would always happen. Ted would say, 'Would you
come with me on a trip to Russia for a month?' Or he would say,
'to Saudi Arabia and Iran?' Or many times he'd say, 'Let's go to Europe.' And I'd say, 'Of course, I'd love to go.' Then I'd miss half a
semester; a final exam one time; a midterm paper another. And then
I'd just drop it."

Then there were her obligations as a Kennedy, and the inevi-
table comparisons that Joan made between herself and the other
Kennedy women: first of all, Rose, the matriarch of the clan, whom
Joan described as a "saint." "I never heard her complain about anything. And I was supposed to do the same thing." Jackie, the ethe-
real First Lady, Joan considered the epitome of sophistication. And
Ethel, the epitome of motherhood. Finally, there were the Kennedy

sisters, smart, committed, accomplished. "I just couldn't keep up," Joan told me. "I can remember thinking the Kennedys are so good at everything and I'm a flop."

Her feelings of inferiority, of not being able to perform, were magnified when she later suffered two successive miscarriages. "I always admired Ethel," she said sadly, "and wanted to have as many children as she had."

Ironically, not everyone agreed with Joan's assessment of herself. Her brother-in-law Jack affectionately called her "The Dish," and Art Buchwald put her at the top of his list of Washington's ten most beautiful women, an honor that Joan felt, typically, was hardly an accomplishment. To other observers of the family, Joan was also the best-liked of the Kennedy women. Rose, of course, was in a class by herself. But Jackie was thought to be aloof and unfriendly, Ethel too demanding, and Eunice too reserved. Joan was the girl next door, a "nice chick," shy, but friendly and approachable, and for many her lack of sophistication, her eagerness to please, and her candor were all part of her particular charm. The family, however, was not always charmed, and while the Kennedy organization liked her, they felt she wasn't to be trusted. They were never sure what she would say. Once when she truthfully told the press that Jack was unable to pick up his son John because of his back problem, the family interceded and asked her to issue a denial. Another time when she refreshingly mentioned Jackie's wigs, she was asked to apologize.

Perhaps more ominous for the future was the attitude of the Kennedy men toward their wives—and toward the women who were not their wives. The Kennedys weren't interested in great women, according to one observer. They wanted worship. And they felt that because they were devoting themselves to serving society, it was the responsibility of their wives to serve them. As for other women, Ted followed his father's example. Rose had turned a blind eye to her husband's infidelities. Disrespectful of her real feelings, her sons admired her for that and supposed their wives would do the same. They were also expected to further the family's ambitions in a solid front at political and social events, large or small. But the impression that they contributed in more substantive ways was a myth.

According to the same observer, Rose was virtually picked up by the scruff of the neck and ushered out of the room when the talk got serious. By all accounts, Jackie was the only one who would not tolerate that kind of treatment. In the curious way she had of both seeking and shunning publicity, she refused to stay put on her pedestal and demanded center stage. Joan was content to remain in the background.

Ted was very proud of her, treating her with courtliness and consideration wherever they went. And in photographs of the young couple, Joan was more than once caught looking at him with undisguised adoration. Yet they were, in many ways, an ill-matched pair. Ted was intelligent, tough, and analytical, in short, a politician. Joan was sensitive, serious, and often so ingenuous that she was unaware of the impression she created. Ted was clever and competitive; Joan was neither. Joan was faithful; Ted was not.

One Kennedy-watcher noted that Ted's eye began to rove even before the birth of their first child while he was managing Jack's presidential campaign in the West. But during the years of Camelot, press insiders tactfully refrained from reporting both Jack's and Ted's infidelities. And when the rumors that persistently circulated around Washington reached Joan's ears, she staunchly, if naively, refused to believe them. She acted like Rose.

But Joan had not been bred to accept infidelity. She was not a "saint," like Rose, nor was she a very good actress. Yet that was the role in which she was cast in Washington, hustled on command from one stage to another. As a Kennedy, she was required to be poised and charming—but not to call too much attention to herself. I could imagine that under that kind of pressure she might have sipped a drink to ease the tension and bolster her courage. And when Ted's work kept him away from home until late at night, and often for days at a time, she might have had a drink or two to help pass the lonely hours. That, of course, would not have been unusual, for Joan was as yet unaware of her intolerance for alcohol.

A volley of rifle fire in Dallas on the afternoon of November 22, 1963, ended the life of Jack Kennedy, and became for Joan the first of many disasters that would eventually shatter her own seemingly secure existence.

Ted was in the Senate and Joan was having her hair done at Elizabeth Arden's when word burst forth on the wire services around the world that the President had been shot. Attendants at the salon tried to prevent Joan from hearing the news on the radio until Milton Gwirtzman, Ted's legislative assistant, could pick her up. Gwirtzman drove her home where Ted was waiting for her and trying unsuccessfully to get through to his brother Bobby at the White House. When they learned that the President was dead, Ted and Eunice flew to Hyannis Port to be with their parents.

Joan was left in Washington where that very evening she had planned a dinner party to celebrate her fifth wedding anniversary. With Ted gone, she turned to her own family for consolation. Her sister Candy and Candy's husband Robert McMurrey, there for the party, stayed with her through that terrible weekend while the rest of the Kennedys grieved in Hyannis Port. It was not the first time, nor would it be the last, that she was excluded from the inner circle. She took her place, however, among the other Kennedy women at the state funeral and went through the motions of having a reception in their home, but she was hardly able to believe what had happened. Just a few months before, following the death of the President and Jackie's infant son Patrick, she had gone to their Cape house to talk to and comfort Jack. Now his sudden death overwhelmed her. Unlike the other Kennedy women who were able to withstand the shock and grief, Joan went into seclusion in her bedroom for several days, overcome with sadness.

Even though Joe Kennedy had suffered a severe stroke and could barely communicate with his two remaining sons, politics—and particularly the pursuit of the presidency—was still uppermost in the family's plans. It was Bobby's turn next, and in 1964 he ran for election to the United States Senate from New York while Ted ran for reelection for the Senate seat from Massachusetts. Joan was once more plunged into the demands of a political campaign. Then tragedy struck again.

Defying bad weather, Ted was flying to Springfield on June 19 to accept renomination at the Massachusetts State Democratic Convention when his small plane crashed and two passengers were killed. Narrowly escaping death himself, Ted was rushed to the hospital with a punctured lung and a broken back. Joan rose to the challenge, and for the next several months while Ted remained in a hospital bed, she helped run his reelection campaign. Not just a pretty face this time, she traveled all over Massachusetts, speaking for Ted and shaking thousands of hands. It was probably her finest hour as a Kennedy. To campaign insiders she proved herself to be a "great sport"—the ultimate accolade for a Kennedy. Even her father, Harry Bennett, noticed a change in her. "Joan is becoming more and more like Candy," he was quoted as saying. "Ted has brought her out of herself, helped her to be more outgoing, to participate in things more easily." There was a reason. "Ted really needed me then," Joan told me. He won reelection, and Joan was so proud of her part in his victory that when he made his own bid for the presidency in 1980, she suggested humorously to a group of Massachusetts supporters, "Let's keep Ted in bed for this campaign, too."

They returned to Washington, but it was a very different Washington under Lyndon Johnson, who harbored an active dislike for the Kennedys, and for Bobby in particular. The country was caught up with the youth rebellion, the tension and violence of the civil rights movement, and ever-mounting opposition to the war in Vietnam. For Joan, however, nothing much had changed. She resumed her role as a Kennedy wife, and politics decreed long and lonely hours of separation from her husband. She was no longer needed.

In July of 1967 their third child Patrick was born, and the next year, she and Ted were swept up in another presidential campaign when Bobby announced his bid for the Democratic nomination. On June 4, 1968, just moments after his victory in the California primary, which virtually assured him the nomination, Bobby was gunned down in a serving pantry in the Ambassador Hotel in Los Angeles.

When Joan was told what had happened, she could not cry. The tears came later during Bobby's funeral at St. Patrick's Cathedral in New York and on the train carrying his body back to Washington. Then she fled. So great was her grief that she could not attend the burial at Arlington. She disappeared, and no one knew where she had gone.

•   •

Tragedy can often bring a couple closer together. Ted, however, as the last surviving son, now bore the entire burden of his
family's aspirations and responsibilities. Where had that left Joan,
I wondered? When there was talk of his being next in line for a
presidential bid, she was terrified that he might also be next in line
for an assassin's bullet. There were already signs of strain in their
marriage, fueled by the persistent rumors of Ted's affairs with other
women. Already signs, too, that Joan, as one writer later observed,
appeared to need a drink "badly at times, too badly." "It wasn't my
personality to make a lot of noise," Joan said. "Or to yell or scream
or do anything. My personality was more shy and retiring. And so
rather than get mad, or ask questions concerning the rumors about
Ted and his girl friends, or really stand up for myself at all, it was
easier for me to just go and have a few drinks and calm myself down
as if I weren't hurt or angry. I didn't know how to deal with it. And
unfortunately, I found out that alcohol could sedate me. So I didn't
care as much. And things didn't hurt so much."

The legend of Camelot was taking hold, however, and out of
respect for a family that had already suffered so much, reporters
were discreet about Joan's drinking, just as they continued to ob-
serve a conspiracy of silence about Jack's extramarital affairs. Ted
was not so fortunate. And with Chappaquiddick he found himself
the object of the intense and incredulous attention of the entire
nation.

Joan spoke only with great difficulty of this next tragedy that
came into her life all too quickly. But Chappaquiddick became an
issue once again during the 1980 campaign, as the known events
and unknown answers were relived, reviewed, and reprinted over
and over, with new theories posed and new questions asked. Joan
was again pregnant, and on July 18, 1969, while she was staying at
their Cape house in the seclusion her pregnancy required, Ted attended a party at a rented house on a remote island off Martha's
Vineyard. The six women at the party—all unmarried former assistants to Robert Kennedy—had been invited to a farewell thank-you
cookout by six men, Kennedy staffers and friends, all but one of
whom were married and there without their wives. Ted and Mary

Jo Kopechne left the party in his car, which he drove off the main road onto a narrow dirt road where it plunged over a wooden bridge into a pond. Ted escaped the submerged vehicle. Mary Jo Kopechne drowned. Controversy still surrounds Ted's activities of the next few hours, but the following morning the car was discovered by fishermen, police were summoned to the scene, and Kennedy made a statement to the local police.

From that moment on the efficient Kennedy machine went into high gear: Ted was allowed to leave the island with no further questioning; Mary Jo's body was sent back to her parents in Pennsylvania without an autopsy; and everyone who had attended the cookout was hurriedly whisked away before officials even learned of the party or had a chance to question them. In the strained and tension-filled days that followed, Ted's advisers converged on the Cape house, and Joan stayed upstairs in her bedroom almost the entire time, again excluded from taking any part in decisions that would shape the future course of her marriage and the rest of her life. At some point, amid the myriad of strategies being planned, it was decided that Joan should accompany Ted to Mary Jo Kopechne's funeral. As always, she complied and numbly played out the role of the loyal Kennedy wife standing by Ted's side across the aisle from the grief-stricken Kopechnes. "Before Chappaquiddick," one friend was quoted as saying, "she was only an adornment, but afterward she was the only ally Ted Kennedy had. He needed her desperately, and she knew it, and she rose to the occasion." But for Joan, "It was a terrible experience, one of the worst in my life," she told me. "And it was the beginning of the end for Ted and me." Under enormous physical and emotional strain, shortly after the accident she miscarried again.

In the months following her miscarriage, Chappaquiddick seemed to magnify everything that had started to go wrong with their marriage. Until then, Joan had never really believed that Ted had been unfaithful to her. That was the irony of Chappaquiddick, according to one observer. Ted and Mary Jo Kopechne were not romantically involved with each other in any way. And knowing that her death was simply a tragic accident, Kennedy advisers thought Chappaquiddick would draw sympathy for Ted. It was a terrible miscalculation. He was vilified. To Ted it must have seemed that it no longer mattered what he did. For Joan, the accident seemed to confirm the rumors she had so long denied.

Their relationship would never be quite the same. One journalist noted the change: "There is a Perfect Escort quality about the public attention Ted Kennedy pays to his wife, the emptiness of which, one suspects, carries into their rare private moments." Moreover, with the same recklessness and disregard for the consequences that had characterized the ill-fated flight to Springfield and his behavior at Chappaquiddick, Ted became even more indiscreet in his relationships with other women. Deeply hurt, Joan went to Jackie for advice in handling Ted's highly publicized affair with socialite Amanda Burden. "Jackie said Kennedy men are like that," Joan told me. "It doesn't mean anything." But Joan was very different from Jackie, one friend observed. "She was unused to this kind of behavior and was shattered by it." Joan herself recalled, "I tried telling myself it didn't matter, but I couldn't help wondering who might be with him. What hurt most was finding out about someone I knew." And later, in a published interview, she remarked, "People ask whether newspaper stories about Ted and girls hurt my feelings. Of course they hurt my feelings. They went to the core of my self-esteem. When one grows up, feeling that one is sort of special and hoping that one's husband thinks so, and then suddenly thinking maybe he doesn't. . . . Well, I didn't lose my self-esteem altogether, but it was difficult to hear all the rumors. And I began thinking maybe I'm just not attractive enough or attractive anymore, or whatever, and it was awfully easy to then say, well, after all, you know, if that's the way it is, I might as well have a drink."

There was now just one Kennedy couple left to feed the public's insatiable curiosity about the family. With her marriage to Aristotle Onassis, Jackie now moved in the international social set. Ethel fiercely guarded her privacy at Hickory Hill, her Virginia estate. Only Joan and Ted remained on the firing line in Washington, and while Ted pursued his political career with perhaps greater diligence and commitment than ever before, after Chappaquiddick his stature and credibility were continually on trial. Gradually, the public's perception of Joan also began to change. The long-suffering composure she had displayed at the Kopechne funeral was replaced by the image of a rather silly and shallow woman, and with reports of her troubled marriage and speculations about divorce, a rather pathetic one. Her years in Washington had taken a toll. In fact, Joan herself had changed. She had fallen into the grip of alcoholism.

"I drank socially at first," she later told an interviewer, "and then I began to drink alcoholically. I really did. But at the time I didn't know it. No one really ever does know. I mean, sure, once in a while you have too much to drink and you wake up the next morning and you have a hangover and you think, Oh, I'm not going to do that again. And you say something like that and then a week or two goes by and nothing happens, and then you go and you drink too much again. It becomes a pattern that starts to creep up on you."

Feeling lonely, an outsider, unloved, unneeded, Joan slipped into periods of uncontrolled drinking. A so-called "binge" drinker, she was able to stay completely sober for brief times, and then once more would fall under the power of her addiction. Had she been a daily drinker, her problem might have been more evident to those close to her—perhaps even to herself—but it was not. Family and friends were probably aware that she was drinking too much, but unaware that she was unable to stop. "And I tried seeing a psychiatrist," Joan later said. "I must say a lot of people in the medical profession in this country really don't know much about alcoholism. And so I really got no help there. I tried, and when I gave that up I really didn't know where to turn."

It was a vicious and self-destructive circle. Joan recalled drinking to overcome her feelings of inadequacy and loneliness, only to find when she stopped that she still felt inadequate and lonely. Whether or not Ted understood the nature of her problem, he encouraged her to work for the Kennedy Foundation, but that resulted only in Joan's comparing herself even more unfavorably to his sisters. There was, however, one field in which she could excel—her music—and once again Ted encouraged her to pursue her interest in it.

Joan became a member of the board of the National Symphony

Orchestra and then began to accept invitations to narrate *Peter and the Wolf*, usually under the direction of Boston Pops conductor Arthur Fiedler. "I got some comfort from my music," she told me. "It would keep me involved for a time."

Despite her desperate battle with alcoholism, she was able to perform in public occasionally. "I wouldn't drink. I just made myself practice—but it took a lot out of me." She played the piano at the prestigious Philadelphia Academy of Music and at the Washington Performing Arts Society and occasionally narrated Benjamin Britten's *The Young Person's Guide to the Orchestra*.

But her music was not enough to give her a sense of purpose or restore her shattered self-esteem. Recalling that time in her life she said, "The only thing I was sure of was that I was a very attractive woman and I had a good figure." So she tried to win attention with extreme styles of dress. The press photographed her wearing silver-sequined mini skirts, shiny black leather boots, and see-through blouses and labeled her "gauche." "If someone opened the door for me," Joan remembered, "I wrote a thank-you note." Her behavior was not the bravura of an assured woman. It was a cry for help.

She also tried romantic liaisons of her own, but they ended in failure and remorse. Traveling in Europe, she arranged a rendezvous with an old admirer. "He was supposed to meet me in my hotel room after a dinner party," she told me. "I gave him the key to my room and asked him to wait for me there. When I walked in smashed, he couldn't believe it. He had never seen me like that. This was to be a big night. And there I was, can you believe it, barely able to walk. I started crying my eyes out. He wanted to help me, but he didn't know how. Think of all the people we affected with our drinking who were helpless."

Her own family might have helped but her father had moved to New Orleans with his second wife, and her sister Candy was married and living in Texas. As for the Kennedys, they were not just any family. With their iron wills, they had survived tragedy without recourse to anything as frivolous as psychotherapy. And with their advisers, they may have been afraid—as was Joan herself—that a public admission of her "problem" would injure Ted's political future. In fact, very little was written about Joan or her problem, and among those close to the family who knew of it, sympathy was entirely on her side. A Harvard classmate of Ted's, a physician, was later quoted as saying, "The Senator came bounding in with his entourage, tanned and radiant and full of smiles. Behind him came Mrs. Kennedy with a vacant look in her eye, her hair awry, and food stains all over her blouse. It was impossible not to feel sorry for her. Her face was bloated. Your heart went out to her."

As is so often the case with alcoholism, Joan's disease was treated like a shameful secret. "I tried to talk about it," she said later, "but I was embarrassed by it and Ted was embarrassed by it. Everybody was embarrassed by it, but nobody would really talk about it." Everyone looked the other way, including Ted, who, according to one observer, "was not a confronter of reality." Joan was left to deal with her alcoholism virtually on her own. No expense was spared, however. Psychiatric help was sought, specialists were consulted, various programs and treatment centers were tried—all without success. "I was so unhappy I escaped for days at a time without telling anyone," Joan recalled. "Not even Rosalie, my secretary." Her pattern was to take an airplane somewhere, anywhere. And when she was discovered missing, a friend of the family would be dispatched to find out where she had gone and bring her back.

Then in November of 1973, while Joan was traveling in Europe, another tragedy struck. Ted called to tell her that their son Teddy, then twelve years old, had a rare form of cancer and would need surgery to save his life. Joan rushed home for the operation in which her son's right leg would be amputated. But even Teddy's illness failed to narrow the distance that had grown between her and Ted. Following the surgery Joan recalled, "We didn't even agree on how to cheer Teddy up. Ted slept in his hospital room at night and I went in to visit during the day. Ted brought in famous athletes to amuse Teddy in his room. We argued a lot about this. It was a circus all the time and I thought Teddy should be quiet."

Already tormented by what she believed to be her failure as a Kennedy and as Ted's wife, Joan was now tormented by her belief that she had also failed as a mother. Once again she managed to get through a crisis in her life without alcohol, but when she no longer felt needed she drank again. Other treatment programs were tried. In 1974 she went to exclusive Silver Hill, a luxurious facility set on rolling landscaped grounds in New Canaan, Connecticut, but returned again in a month. She was arrested and charged with drunk driving, and a further humiliation occurred when she was sent to an alcoholism rehabilitation unit connected to a New York City hospital. "It was awful," she told me. "I had three roommates, all women on welfare. They wouldn't let me leave for twenty-eight days. There were people there off the streets. One woman had gone from a hundred dollars a night to doing the same things for a bottle of wine. I was so upset that as soon as I got out of there and went home, I drank again."

Meanwhile, in Washington, it was politics as usual. In August of 1974, as the Watergate scandal shook the foundations of government, Richard Nixon became the first American President to resign, Gerald Ford succeeded to the presidency, and the leaders of the Democratic party began to urge Ted to enter the 1976 race, maintaining that only he could defeat Ford or Reagan. Ted, his family, his friends, and his advisers, pondered their decision.

Whatever positives there were in favor of his candidacy, they were far outweighed by the negatives: first and foremost, the fear of another assassination. When Joan was asked by a reporter if perhaps she exaggerated that fear, she replied breathlessly, "Exaggerate? Exaggerate? How can you say that? Let's get in my car and I'll drive you down the road just over a mile to Hickory Hill where Ethel lives. Let's go there and you can look at a house filled with eleven children without a father, and then tell me if I exaggerate the dangers of being a Senator Kennedy." Joan's father, Harry Bennett, commented, "Nobody wants him to run, nobody in the family on either side. They're all scared to death. Over and over, Joan keeps saying she hopes he does not run. Can you blame her? But they all know, and Joan knows it too and this is what terrifies her, that he's got to do what he feels he must. But they all pray he doesn't."

Chappaquiddick and Ted's "philandering," as it was sometimes called, were two familiar counts against his candidacy. His disintegrating marriage and Joan's "problem" were new. It was perhaps a relief to Ted that it was out in the open at last. In fact, he seems to have invited the disclosure when he asked a friendly journalist at

Hyannis Port if he would like to see Joan, then led him out the back door and pointed to a car where she had passed out in the backseat. Joan's alcoholism was unquestionably a heavy burden on Ted, but the presumption that he had "driven" his wife to drink would be difficult for any political candidate to overcome.

In addition to the eleven fatherless children at Hickory Hill, there were three more in McLean who merited consideration in Ted's decision. The operation to check Teddy, Jr.'s, cancer had been followed by a painful course of chemotherapy and he was still adjusting to the loss of his leg. Kara, anxious and insecure, was overweight, had experimented with drugs, and on several occasions had run away from home. Patrick was wracked by asthma. They, too, were terrified that their father would be shot like their uncles. They had been taunted by their classmates about Chappaquiddick. And to them, their mother's alcoholism was frightening, embarrassing, and incomprehensible. One reporter witnessed Joan's return to Washington from another treatment center "in a really awful condition." Her obviously distraught children met her at the airport without their father, and the journalist later commented that "if this guy takes this family through a presidential campaign, there is no pain in hell that is enough for him."

When Ted finally decided not to run, the same journalist remembered thinking: "This is the best thing this man has ever done in his life, as a human being: to take himself out of the race."

If 1976 ended Ted's presidential hopes, at least for the time being, it was a pivotal year in his marriage, and in the treatment of Joan's disease. According to one observer, many friends of the family resented Joan. No matter what Ted did, they thought, she had no right to behave like that. She was the greatest impediment to his political future, and if Ted didn't make it, they were out of business. As for Ted, although he resented the idea that people blamed him for Joan's alcoholism, he certainly felt responsible for her and for the outcome of her life. Their marriage was at a stalemate and divorce was out of the question, not only because they were Catholics, but also because it might look as if he had abandoned Joan. Still, something had to be done.

Some familiar with Kennedy methods believed that, as usual, intermediaries orchestrated the solution. "When things got tough," one remarked, "Ted looked to somebody else to clean up the mess and slid out the back." In his view, the well-oiled Kennedy machine was a myth. A lot fell between the cracks. And when the time came to make a decision about Joan—whether to help her or simply to get rid of her—someone probably said, "Just call McLean and put her in a cab." McLean Hospital, preeminent among treatment centers, was just outside Boston, Kennedy territory. An apartment on Beacon Street was purchased for Joan, and just after the Christmas holidays of that year she moved in.

Whoever else was involved, the ultimate decision to move was Joan's. She may have blamed herself for Ted's roving eye. She was aware that she was one of the reasons he had declined to enter the presidential race. Perhaps she thought it would be better for everyone—for Ted, for their children, for the Kennedy family—if she simply bowed out. Of one thing she was certain: she could no longer cope with her life as it was in Washington. "When I realized my drinking was becoming a real problem," she later told an interviewer, "I remember going to New York to see Jackie and talking about it. I'd been told that an alcoholic by nature starts to blame everything and everybody except himself. And that's when I knew that I had to get away from there and have some time for myself. So Jackie and I talked about all that. I felt close to Jackie, because both of us needed space to be alone. . . ."

When Joan left Washington, her home, her children, her husband, and all the reminders of her painful past, it was, in a way, an admission of defeat. Yet it was also her only hope. For Joan had come to another realization. "My mother died that year of alcoholism and I couldn't help her," she told me. "But I knew I had to do something for my own survival." It was a bold step for a woman with her conventional background, bold for the wife of a prominent political figure, bold for a woman who had never lived alone. But for Joan it was also a necessary first step that required both courage and a willingness to accept whatever consequences and controversy it might cause.

The seven-room condominium on Beacon Street was almost

empty of furniture when she moved in. To Joan it must have seemed like banishment. But it was also a new beginning in a different environment, an opportunity to seek new treatment, and a chance to find serenity in a place of her own away from the glare of publicity and the pressures of politics. She soon discovered, however, that Boston—for a Kennedy—was an even smaller town than Washington. She went to lunch at the Ritz with a friend, and only later learned that the woman had been one of Ted's paramours. "Everyone in this city knew about them but me!" she told me indignantly. "I was the last to know. And there I was, sitting in the Ritz with her."

Even away from the spotlight, off in the wings of her private niche in Boston, Joan still did not find the serenity she longed for. Although she enrolled in an independent study program at Lesley College and admitted herself to various treatment centers, she was alone, drifting without purpose, ambivalent about leaving her children, uncertain about her future with Ted, and unable to stop drinking. Her escape for survival may have given her hope, but it was unlikely to give her anything more than that. She remained dependent on the Kennedys, not only for protection, but for the privileges they provided. She depended entirely on Ted for financial support, and on his staffs in Boston and Washington for everything else she needed, including her treatment. And when that failed, counselors and family friends were there to see her through her anguished days and nights. Joan still lived as a Kennedy.

3

ONE DAY
AT A TIME

He is going to run! I don't think I can do it.

—JOAN

Perhaps the most significant difference between my life and Joan's was that mine did not become an object of public curiosity as a result of my marriage.

Born in Boston, I spent my childhood in Milton, a small, attractive town just south of the city. My three younger brothers and I walked to public elementary schools and came home for lunch. Early accomplishments, such as bringing home all A's and skipping a grade, received no special praise from my parents. Things like that were clearly expected but not discussed, and because we knew they cared about us, we wanted to please them. As the only daughter, I was, of course, overprotected. As the eldest I was also given many extra responsibilities, particularly setting "a good example" for my brothers. Like Joan, I was taught not to show emotion, and above all, to "behave like a lady."

My father, like Joan's, was an advertising executive, which meant some luxuries, new Buicks every few years, lovely homes near good schools, country club memberships. But it also meant moving to New York when I was thirteen and a year later moving again to Kenilworth, Illinois, a suburb of Chicago often compared to Bronxville. After graduation from New Trier High School in Winnetka, I went to Northwestern University's School of Speech where I earned degrees in creative dramatics and education. I had

53

always wanted to be a writer or editor, but I acquiesced to my mother's wish that I prepare to teach—"just in case" I had to support myself, at least until I married.

I decided not to marry, as Joan had, right out of college. Instead I accepted a job teaching in Milton. It would be a step toward independence, I thought, a chance to be myself before I became someone's wife. So with my black VW beetle loaded with hand-me-down pots and pans, lamps and linens, I drove across the country to Boston where I found an apartment in Cambridge with two former school friends. The three of us set off on the same adventure, starting our careers, acquiring more education, and learning to live on a careful budget.

That budget called for the purchase of one bottle of Scotch a week for us, our dates, and guests. Drinking was, after all, a symbol of our new independence and maturity. And so I drank, but as I had been taught to do everything else—"like a lady." Only later did I recognize the irony in the way that I, and so many other young people of my generation, became acquainted with alcohol: the carefully prepared drinks before dinner served on a silver tray; the cheerful conviviality of cocktail parties. One did not drink in secret or alone. One did not drink too much. But that was as far as the warnings went. If someone we knew had a "drinking problem," it was simply not discussed, much less acknowledged as alcoholism. I enjoyed drinking with my dates and friends. I handled alcohol well. I knew what alcoholism was, but I was unaware of its early warning signs. And I remember resolving I'd never have too much to drink.

The next three years in Cambridge and on Beacon Hill in Boston were wonderful. I loved my work, but as more and more of my friends married, I felt a subtle pressure to get married, too. It came from my parents, whom I still wanted to please, and from society as well, which still programmed women primarily to be wives and mothers. So at the dangerously ripe old age of twenty-four, I fell in love and became engaged to a handsome, well-educated young man from Boston. My parents were overjoyed that I had found the "right" man.

We were married in Boston and after a honeymoon in Spain and Portugal, we moved into a small townhouse on Beacon Hill.

We were very happy, and I found marriage so much fun I regretted
that I had been so cautious and waited so long. A little more than
a year later, when our daughter Dana was born, I felt my happiness
was complete.

But slowly, almost imperceptibly, clouds began to form. Both
my husband and I had unreal expectations for our marriage. Like so
many young couples of that time, we thought we would "live happily ever after." When I went back to work in educational television
for children as a writer and performer at Boston's WGBH-TV, I
was challenged and excited by my job, but I soon found myself in
the dilemma that would become all too familiar to women of the
next decade: the conflicts between the responsibilities of my job
and my responsibilities as a wife and mother. My solution to that
problem was to try to be everything to everyone.

Although I was as yet unaware of it, drinking was also becoming a problem. It started with the usual cocktail-before-dinner
ritual, and grew as a way to soften or blur the sharp edges that were
beginning to emerge in my marriage. My husband and I had discovered that we were two very different personalities. I was intense,
idealistic, and needed someone to share my thoughts and feelings.
He was a very relaxed man who took life as it came and kept his
feelings to himself. I had hoped our differences would be comple-
mentary but found instead that they created distance. And drinking
seemed to close that distance, to offer temporary escape, even though
it became apparent that I could no longer handle alcohol as well as
my husband did. I never connected my father's occasional heavy
drinking with my own developing problem and was unaware that,
like Joan, I carried a genetic predisposition toward alcoholism. Nor
did it occur to me that while my husband drank for relaxation, I
was drinking for refuge.

We had moved from Boston to a beautiful old house in the
country, and a year later our son Bradford was born. But the joy of
that event was immediately overshadowed when my husband became critically ill, then returned home to a long recuperation. The
following year, both my parents were stricken with cancer and died
only six months apart. Illness and death occur in every family, and
the events of my life cannot compare to the tragedies Joan endured

during those same years. Yet the effect on us was similar. We felt the same haunting loneliness and despair. And when we could not find the emotional support we so desperately needed from our husbands, we drank.

Eventually I became dependent on alcohol. And even if I did not yet know it, I could not conceal it from others. One night, feeling lonely but apparently in no pain, I left my home, two adorable sleeping children and a sleeping husband, and went for a walk. Dressed in my husband's jacket over a blue flannel nightgown, and wearing his big, black, rubber fishing boots, I carefully followed the yellow line down the middle of the road toward the village green and the police station. I must have reasoned that since the station was open all night, someone there would be up and might be willing to talk to me. If that thinking was wishful one thing was certain: they would not serve cocktails. I was prepared for that inevitability by arriving with a peanut butter jar half full of Scotch. When that was gone, so I'm sure was their patience, and I was ceremoniously returned home in a flashing cruiser.

I remember very little of that incident. Most of it was told to me later—with laughter but no real understanding—and I felt humiliated and completely baffled by my behavior. Confused by my inability to drink, especially after years of exemplary social drinking, I prayed daily for self-discipline, still unaware that I was a victim of alcoholism.

In order to compensate for my drinking, to make up for it to those around me and perhaps even to myself, I tried even harder to excel in everything else I did. From all outward appearances I functioned well (except perhaps to the night shift of the local police). I was a good mother, ran an efficient home, gardened, canned, cooked, played tennis, studied oil painting and the piano, attended seminars in Boston, did volunteer work in the community, and at the same time held creative jobs. My husband and friends knew I had a drinking problem, but they couldn't understand why it had happened to me. They didn't know how to help; I didn't know how to help myself.

Finally, in 1973, a doctor suggested that I might be an alcoholic and said, "Just stop drinking. Right now. Today." Although it seemed impossible, I did. At a cocktail party that evening when my husband asked what I wanted to drink I said, "A ginger ale, please." And for six weeks I did not drink. The feeling was exhilarating. But then the insidiousness of the disease returned. I fought against it but ultimately gave in to my elaborate rationalizations: my friends who drank as much as I did were still enjoying it; it was too soon to stop drinking; I didn't want to be "an alcoholic"; maybe it would be possible to drink if I were very careful. I tried. I changed from Scotch to white wine, I measured drinks, I spaced out drinks, and on certain occasions I did not drink at all. For two years I knew, but could not accept, that alcohol was a problem for me. Then on a beautiful day in May I had my moment of truth.

It was Mother's Day, sun-filled, warm, spring flowers in the garden bursting into bloom. The children had served me a delicious breakfast in bed—runny eggs, undercooked bacon, and very crunchy toast—and were happily whispering their secret plans for a picnic in the garden. Before lunch, my husband and I sat outside with them and had just one cocktail. Then after our picnic I felt a strange sensation—a craving for another drink—but there was no more liquor in the house and Massachusetts package stores were closed on Sundays. Something came over me. As if watching someone in a play, I saw myself go out to the barn, get in my car, and wave good-bye to my surprised and disappointed family, left to celebrate the rest of Mother's Day without their mother. I drove along Route 3A toward Cohasset to visit friends who always had open arms and a full liquor cabinet. I looked down at my hands on the wheel and my foot on the gas pedal and felt as if I did not know who was driving or what was pulling me along this ocean road. I considered turning back but some force outside myself propelled me forward. It was my first clear awareness of the overwhelming power of alcohol. I arrived at my friends' house and spent the afternoon in their garden drinking with them. But as I drove home later that night, I cried bitterly, deeply humbled by what I had at last been forced to accept. I was an alcoholic.

The next day I surrendered, acknowledged my powerlessness over alcohol and stopped drinking, the most significant decision I have ever made. It began what was to become a new way of life for

me—free, beautiful, gratifying, full of hope. And with clear eyes and
an unmuddled mind for the first time in years, I was at last able to
talk to my husband about the emotional stresses in our marriage
that had contributed, at least in part, to my drinking problem. Divorce was unknown in either of our families, and my husband was a
fine, gentle man and a wonderful father, but we both realized that
our marriage had failed to give us what we both needed and we
agreed to separate. I felt there was no other way for me to live without alcohol.

Still it was not easy. The children and I stayed in the country
and I returned to teaching. But while adjusting to the separation
and problems of single parenting, I reverted to an old pattern for
coping and drank again over the Christmas holiday. Fortunately, it
was a very brief episode, but it motivated me to want to learn more
about the disease and myself, and I enrolled in a well-known alcohol
education seminar given at a treatment center in New Hampshire.
At that time everyone was required to have a brief interview with
one of the staff psychiatrists, and when the doctor asked me why I
was there, I told him I wanted to take the seminar.

"But why do you want to take the seminar?" he asked curi-
ously.

"Because I'm an alcoholic," I told him.

This experienced, highly educated doctor, visiting from one of
the leading medical centers in the country, leaned forward across
his desk, looked at me for several seconds, smiled, shook his head,
and pounded his fist lightly on the desk, "But you couldn't be!"

When I told Joan about that interview, she said the same
thing had been said to her when she was seeking help in Washington. To me it illustrated one truth and one myth about the disease:
many fine doctors unfortunately have not been trained to recognize or treat alcoholism; and they and others expect alcoholics to
look like "shopping bag ladies" or their male counterparts who live
on the streets and convene on park benches to sip from bottles
wrapped in brown paper bags. There are, in fact, far more alcoholics
in the conference rooms of the Fortune Five Hundred and sitting
on prestigious community boards than on park benches. If a man
drinks too much, it is often overlooked, while a woman is almost

invariably condemned and suffers the additional burden of humiliation. But alcoholism knows no social or economic boundaries. And unless it is arrested, it is a progressively debilitating—and finally fatal—disease.

For most people, it is difficult to comprehend the development of a drinking problem. From the outside it looks so simple. If liquor is causing trouble, why not just stop drinking? Both Joan and I had been asked that question. We had asked it of ourselves. No one really understands what causes the mental obsession, or what triggers the physical compulsion to have another drink, and why the number of drinks is less important than their effect. Although it is a disease, usually hereditary, many still judge a drinking problem to be a sign of weakness or a lack of will power. Alcoholism makes its victims strangers to the world.

But those of us who have the disease and have been able to arrest it have an understanding among ourselves like none other—an empathy that comes from having been there. This unique bond Joan and I eventually came to share.

After we met in 1977, and on several occasions during the next two years, we went to concerts, the theater, and other events together. One memorable, snowy winter night, Joan invited me to go to Lowell House at Harvard to hear the late Marshall Dodge, of the famed "Bert and I" team, enchant his audience with "down Maine" stories and folklore. Afterward Marshall, Joan and I, and two of his friends trooped through the snow in boots and parkas across Harvard Square to Cronin's for more stories.

I saw Joan only at her best. But there were many days, and sometimes many weeks, when I didn't see her at all. Unable to stop drinking, she missed lunch engagements and classes, fell behind in her schoolwork, and neglected her music. Since her arrival in Boston, she had been in a treatment program at McLean but found only sporadic success. And when she returned to drinking, several old and new friends came to her apartment to help her. Hazel, a teacher of junior high sociology and the school's alcohol education counselor, spent hours and days talking to Joan. Sometimes during

Joan's agonizing times of withdrawal, Hazel walked the streets with her and took her to one movie after another to distract her until her desire to drink diminished. At one point, Hazel left her own home in the suburbs and moved into Joan's apartment. During the day she continued to teach and counsel young teenagers, then took care of Joan at night and on weekends. Nonetheless, Joan spent much of her time alone in her bedroom with a vodka bottle on the bedside table. Often she had to put on dark glasses and a scarf to walk unnoticed to nearby package stores to replenish her supply.

Another important person in Joan's life at this time was Kitty Gillooly, who had been hired by Ted to cook and oversee the Beacon Street apartment before Joan's move to Boston. During that fall of 1976 the Senator had used the apartment while campaigning for reelection, and Kitty had no idea that it was intended for Joan. When she was finally told that Joan was moving in, Kitty agreed to stay on. "She came quietly into Boston," she recalled. "No one made any fuss."

Joan stayed in her bedroom the first few times Kitty came to the apartment. Then one Sunday morning, when Kitty appeared unexpectedly to return a dress from the dry cleaners, they finally met. "Hello," Joan said, extending her hand. "I'm Joan Kennedy." "Her usual greeting to everyone," Kitty remembered. One of her first jobs was to collect sets of keys from Kennedy cousins, nieces, and nephews, who were using the apartment like "a regular flophouse." As far as Kitty was concerned, this was now Joan's apartment. And it was not long before Kitty became deeply involved with the family, with Ted's politics, and particularly with Joan's trials. "All Kennedy employees get emotionally involved. You can't avoid it," she told me. She talked often to Joan's doctors and counselors. "They said that Joan had to realize she had to help herself now," Kitty said. But like many close to Joan, she was afraid to leave her alone, afraid she would choke or fall or simply wander away.

Some days when Kitty came in to clean and take care of Joan's clothes, she did not see Joan, who rarely left her darkened bedroom. Compassionate and concerned, Kitty often stayed late to be with Joan as long as possible when Hazel couldn't be there. "She was never a nuisance," she told me, "but she was her own worst enemy. She would be walking around in her jammies and I'd try to get her into bed by saying, 'Mrs. Kennedy, I think you're coming down with the flu. Why don't we get you into bed?' We never referred to her drinking and besides the symptoms were almost the same." Finally Kitty would return to her husband and children but she couldn't stop worrying.

Recalling the years that Joan struggled to overcome her disease, Kitty told me, "The days all ran into each other. I'd go in, see if she was up or down, dead or alive. All the days were the same. I've always said that when she was good she was good, and when she was bad she was still good. She never took her illness out on me. She could be deathly sick, but her disposition never changed. She was very easy to get along with in those days. Never demanding. She was very appreciative of anything I would do for her. She probably didn't remember a lot of it afterward, but she certainly functioned when she had to. When she didn't have to, she slept."

One afternoon Joan woke up to find caterers in the apartment. "What's going on?" she asked Kitty. And Kitty replied, "The Senator is having a party."

"Oh," Joan said, then went to her room and Kitty thought, Oh my God, this is no time to make an appearance. But when Kitty let the Senator in the front door, Joan was standing in the living room, dressed completely in red, every hair in place. "She looked ravishing," Kitty said.

There were other times, however, when she did not function quite so well. One day, on her way to meet Eunice for lunch at the Ritz, she was walking "sort of lopsided," according to a Kennedy aide who was there in the apartment. "And she had on a transparent dress with no slip." As tactfully as possible the aide suggested that she put on a slip. But Joan said slips weren't in anymore and left the apartment.

Sometimes she was lucky. One night, driving back from the Cape, she passed her exit, and when she stopped to ask directions of two enlisted men, they realized she wasn't capable of driving. They brought her home, put her inside her apartment, and then called Ted's Boston office. As one friend said, "She led a charmed life."

But for the most part, it was a life led behind closed doors. Joan saw only a very few close friends and Kennedy staff. And when Ted came to Boston, he stayed in the apartment, "but he had the east and she had the west," one of the staff said, referring to their bedrooms, "and never the twain shall meet. We all knew the marriage hadn't been fine for a long time. It was in limbo."

Joan saw even less of her children. Ted, Jr., Kara, and Patrick were in school and living with their father in Washington. Among the other Kennedys, only Eunice appeared to care about her. Her welfare was largely in the impersonal hands of the Boston office. Once, afraid that Joan would hurt herself if she drove, a staff member took the keys to her car. Joan wanted them back, and when a young Kennedy aide was sent to pick them up, he was annoyed by the inconvenience.

But there were loyal friends whom Joan didn't even know she had. On one occasion, the superintendent of the building discovered her "absolutely legless" in the lobby, where she had dropped her mink coat, and took her upstairs to her apartment. Two days later, when she had not reappeared, he called Kitty's husband, who then called Kitty in Florida where she was visiting a friend. Kitty, in turn, called the Senator in Washington, begging him to send someone to the apartment to see if Joan was all right. Fortunately, she was.

Others also tried to help. The McLean staff kept in touch with her by phone; at critical times Joan's psychiatrist saw her every day; and longtime family friends Frank O'Connor and Sally Fitzgerald responded to emergency calls with support, patience, and love.

One evening after talking on the phone with Joan, Sally grew so alarmed about her condition that she left her four children and drove to Boston to see her. She knew of my friendship with Joan and before going to her apartment, she stopped unexpectedly at my door and introduced herself. "I'm so worried about Joan," she said. "She needs to go back to a hospital and I just know she won't go. Will you come upstairs with me and talk to her?"

I agreed although I had some misgivings. So far in our friendship Joan had talked of her dependence on alcohol but had spared me the details of her relapses. I had never seen her drinking. But Sally asked for my help and I knew I should go with her.

We went up in the elevator and knocked on Joan's door. Joan, dressed in wool pants and a sweater, did not look surprised to see us and invited us in. We walked together down the long dimly lit hallway. Then Joan went into the living room with Sally following her and turned on a light.

Still standing, Sally spoke lovingly, but firmly. "Joan, dear, let me put some things in a suitcase for you. Then I'll drive you any place you want to go tonight."

"Oh, Sally, I can't. I'm so embarrassed," Joan said, her voice soft. "I've been to them all so many times. I just can't go again." She pushed her hair away from her face and looked back at me.

I was still standing in the hall wondering what to do, how to help. Joan's fears about returning to the hospital concerned me. Even when her life was in danger, she felt ashamed and humiliated. If only people understood and accepted this disease as another health problem, I thought sadly, then women, even well-known women like Joan, would be less reluctant to ask for help.

After more soft refusals, Joan left Sally in the living room and came down the hall toward me. She stopped and stood in front of me, her eyes large and moist. Gently I tried to encourage her to go to a treatment center. Joan stood there looking at me, but I knew she wasn't listening. Then she said softly, "I love you." It was the only time in our years of knowing each other and working together that we shared a moment so vulnerable and tender.

Putting my arm around her, I guided her back to the living room. "I wish you would let Sally take you," I repeated. "Please, we really care about you."

Sally joined us and also put her arm around Joan. But she continued to refuse help, and Sally and I were reluctant to leave her alone. "Please don't drink anything else tonight," I said finally. "Go to bed now, and I'll call you tomorrow."

Joan nodded. "I'll go to bed."

Before Sally and I left, I wrote a note for Kitty, telling her of our visit and our apprehensions and left it in the kitchen. Then with great ambivalence and many silent prayers in our hearts, we said good-bye.

"Good night," Joan said softly. "Thank you for coming. I'll be all right."

We waited until she closed the door and then Sally and I returned to my apartment, where she picked up her coat.

"I'm so discouraged," Sally said, still reluctant to go. "A lot of us are almost ready to give up."

I put my arm around Sally. "No, we can't give up for Joan's sake. As soon as she realizes that no one can do it for her, she'll get well."

Joan did return to treatment and after a few months of steady progress, she felt self-confident enough to accept invitations from both *McCall's* and *People* to tell her story publicly. She excitedly told me about the interviews and her trip to New York to be photographed.

Both articles appeared as cover stories that summer. "For the first time Joan Kennedy talks about her drinking problem, her troubled marriage, her independent new life," proclaimed the August 1978 *McCall's* cover featuring both Joan and Ted. Joan's smile seemed frozen on her face and Ted looked slightly uncomfortable standing at an odd angle behind her. He had not been present for Joan's interview with writer Joan Braden in which she described how her drinking problem began. She talked of how she handled trips with Ted, her public performances, and their son Teddy's surgery without alcohol, but then always returned to drinking again. She compared the glamour and visibility of living in Washington to the privacy and reserve of Boston and recounted how the rumors of Ted's affairs had hurt her. It was a candid and sympathetic article, but Joan maintained that she had had a full year of sobriety, and she spoke about going to Alcoholics Anonymous meetings which, traditionally, is an affiliation not mentioned at a public level.

The August 7 issue of *People* featured Joan alone on the cover, and in this picture her expression seemed more relaxed, as if she were caught in midsentence. The caption beside her picture read "Joan Kennedy: She's proud of drying out and living alone, but if Ted ran for President she'd be at his side." Joan repeated to writer Gail Jennes that she attended AA meetings and had been sober for a year.

Although perceived by some readers as preparation for Ted's

candidacy, others, especially those who had experienced recovering from alcoholism or known someone who had, were touched by the articles and by Joan's personal revelations. Politicians, public figures, and men and women across the country wrote notes of praise and congratulation. Those letters had a profound effect on Joan—she was so proud and delighted when she told me about them. I hoped that she would be able to live up to the image of success portrayed in the articles. But as the weeks passed and the letters continued to arrive, the pressure of public acclaim for her alleged year of sobriety was too much to bear and she returned to drinking.

Once again Joan retreated behind closed doors, and by Christmas she was as unhappy and depressed as she had ever been. Because she was drinking she did not join her family for Christmas festivities in McLean, Virginia, and Aspen, Colorado, and stayed alone in her Boston apartment. I was busy with my schoolwork, my job, and my own family, and was not able to see her often. But when I did visit after Christmas, her sorrow showed in piles of unopened cards and no signs of holiday decorations.

"I cried for days and have never been so miserable in my whole life," she told me sadly.

It may have been this deep despair, intensified by drinking, that in the next several months led to liaisons with men whom she ordinarily would not have seen. A young graduate student, who did odd jobs for some of the people in the neighborhood, received calls at night from Joan and went to her apartment. But then one day he said to me, assuming I knew much more than I did, "I'm not going to do any more work in this building. I'm leaving right now before I get myself into any more trouble."

Other incidents followed. Several times at night when I was being dropped off in front of the building and still sitting in a car, I saw Joan rush in and go right up to her apartment, followed a few minutes later by a short, thin man in a trenchcoat. I did not recognize the man; I recognized only the secretiveness in which Joan's addiction was forcing her to live. But in spite of her continuing need for help, she tried to appear cheerful and in control of her life whenever we met for tea or a talk, and no mention was made of a relapse or a rendezvous.

All of Joan's friends, including myself, wanted to take care of her, afraid she might get hurt. Yet we knew that too much protection would get in the way of her helping herself and finding long-term recovery. Kitty continued to watch over Joan during the day, friends and professionals were there to help, and periodically Joan returned to institutions for care.

During the spring of 1979, she underwent the resident program at Appleton House, the alcohol treatment center at McLean. I tried to telephone her there, but I was told, "No. No one by that name is here. However, if you wish to leave a name and number and someone with that name checks in, she will receive the message and can call you."

I was impressed by the level of security provided for Joan. But of course she had to return all her calls, further isolating her from friends' support.

One night, Hazel and I drove out to visit her. We turned into the long hilly driveway, passed small brick buildings that dotted the landscaped grounds, and parked outside of Appleton House, a large, brick mansion. Inside, a formal entryway, fine architectural detail, soft lighting, and well-furnished living and sitting rooms created a serene ambiance. At the main desk, we asked for Joan.

"No. No one by that name is here," the receptionist said. Attractive, well-dressed people walked past us on their way to seminars or to pick up their medication in small white paper cups from the nursing station nearby while we tried to convince the receptionist that we were friends of Joan's and she was expecting us.

Eventually she was "able to locate somebody by that name," and Joan came down the long front stairway. Wearing plaid pants and a casual sweater, she seemed relaxed and glad to see us. But we thought she appeared tired so we did not stay long. Joan showed us the rooms on the first floor, pointed up the stairs to the bedroom floors where I was told a room was reserved for her at all times, even when she wasn't at the hospital. Then we chatted briefly in the dimly lit lounge and Joan described her seminars and discussion groups. Driving back to Boston, we felt very encouraged about her progress.

Soon Joan moved to a small halfway house on the grounds of

the hospital. Halfway houses are usually "the last resort"—although I don't think one has ever been named that. They provide shelter for those who have been in hospitals or treatment centers, have tried to live a normal life without drinking, failed, and still require supervision. Often, accommodations are simple and residents share the cooking and cleaning as part of the transition to an independent life. Curfews and other restrictions guide residents over a several-month commitment toward an adjustment to life without drinking. For most of these people, the consequences of drinking again would be having nowhere else to go for help. But if they finally realize, as many of them do, that continued drinking can lead to physical and mental illness, incarceration, or death, they work hard to complete the program and return home.

Fortunately, Joan was doing just that, and I saw her in June when she was permitted to return briefly to her Boston apartment. She looked well and we caught up on our news. I had graduated and started working again in television to develop a series on the arts for children at WGBH-TV. Joan's news was far more momentous. Ted was under increasing pressure to run for the Democratic nomination for President, and he would have to make a decision soon.

Although he had refused to run in '72 and '76, the time now seemed ripe for Ted. By the end of July, a New York Times-CBS poll showed that Democratic voters preferred Kennedy to Carter, 53 to 16, and at the same time, "Draft Teddy" organizations began to file with the Federal Election Commission. Another poll found that Kennedy had been forgiven for Chappaquiddick, and the Kopechnes said publicly that they would not oppose his candidacy. When Kennedy accepted a speaking engagement with Senator John Culver in Iowa, the first caucus state, supporters came out waving "We Need Ted" and "Kennedy in '80" signs. Rumors spread that Kennedy was increasing his staff, as Carter slipped even further in public opinion polls to about the same level as Richard Nixon in the last days of Watergate.

During the Senate recess in August, Ted met with his family and staff in Hyannis Port to consider the question of running, while Joan, who had recently completed her treatment program, drove back and forth between the Cape and Boston. She would be an important part of the decision, I knew, as advisers considered such issues as her drinking problem and her separation from Ted. One Kennedy aide conjectured that Joan could be "a loose cannon on a pitching deck." Ted's extramarital life, the fear of another assassination, and his mother's and Joan's long-standing opposition to his running also had to be taken into account.

In early August I met Joan unexpectedly in the lobby of our building. She had just driven to Boston from the Cape and her long, loose hair was windblown, her cheeks lightly tanned. She pulled me aside, anxious to talk.

"Ted's going to run!" she said breathlessly. "My God, what am I going to do?"

I felt such compassion for her. Only a few of us knew how very vulnerable Joan was at this moment in her life. Most treatment programs strongly advise that patients not make major changes in their lives for at least a year. And I wondered if Ted and his advisers intended to ask Joan once again to play the role of the dutiful and devoted wife, the pretty princess of America's royal family before she was ready.

The next time I saw Joan that summer she smiled and appeared much calmer. "He's decided *not* to run," she said, breathing a deep sigh. I, too, was relieved. She could stay in Boston now, have time to build a solid sobriety, go back to school, and lead a normal life.

But the suspense was not yet over. And I realized that Joan was on the same seesaw the public rode. It sank on a rumor that Ted's candidacy would divide the party; it rose on a rumor that he was jogging, dieting, and working out; it teetered when he admitted he "would not rule out the possibility."

In the middle of August, when Joan and I met again in the lobby, she looked pale and nervous. She was rushing in from a weekend with her family and another decision-making discussion at the Cape.

"He *is* going to run!" she exclaimed. "I don't think I can do it."

Not wanting her to know how frightened I was for her, I said softly, "I know you can, if you take it one day at a time."

4

THE
STRATEGY
MEETING

*I've heard a lot of talk around town. . . . I
guess the best thing about this is that I have
nowhere to go but up and Ted has nowhere to
go but down.*

—JOAN

I could only guess what voice, if any, Joan had had in Ted's decision. I suspected that Ted and his advisers had talked a great deal
about her, but seldom to her until, finally, that decision was made.
Ted was going to enter the race, but would she, or would she not,
campaign at his side? Some campaign strategists were against it—as
was Ted, according to one insider. Joan was, they thought, no longer
the pretty blond toy of the Senate races of the sixties. And she was
an alcoholic. Sober now perhaps, but what if she started drinking
again? As a potential First Lady, her every word and act would be
under the close scrutiny of the press. Memories of her appearance
and erratic behavior in the seventies were too fresh. Leave her out
of the campaign, they said.

There were, however, arguments on the other side. If Joan did
not campaign, all the ghosts of Ted's past might rise up to haunt
him: a failed marriage, an alcoholic wife, repeated infidelities, Chappaquiddick. But if she did, voters could assume that she and Ted
had reconciled and that if Joan could forgive him, so could they.
Joan herself took a stand on this side of the dispute. She felt she

could help Ted. He needed her. She knew well the pressure and
stress of a presidential race; she had been on and off the campaign
trail for twenty years. But she had a point to prove to Ted—and to
herself. She *wanted* to campaign.

But not without hesitation and doubt. I sensed that when she
told me of Ted's decision. And I had my own concerns. It was too
soon in her recovery, I thought. She had been sober only a few
months. If she started drinking again, it could be a disaster for the
campaign—and an even greater crisis for Joan. Were Ted and his
advisers aware of that risk? Although I admired Joan's courage, I did
not foresee the major changes the campaign would make in her life,
and as it turned out, in my life as well.

I knew, of course, that Joan would have the help, advice, and
support of the very talented and efficient Kennedy team. That's why
I was somewhat surprised, one weekend in early September as Joan
and I were sailing with Kendall on *The Curragh* to Martha's Vineyard, when she hinted that she would like me to assist her in the
campaign. Later, when we met for dinner at the Copley Plaza to
discuss it, she was more specific about what my duties might be.

"Campaign staff does everything and anything," Joan said. "If
there's a dog that needs to go out, you take out the dog." I knew
she was speaking metaphorically, but I was happy that no New-
foundlands or Rhodesian Ridgebacks waited at her apartment to
test my willingness and initiative.

"And the ultimate honor," she proclaimed with a broad smile,
"is packing my suitcases." Then she elaborated with an anecdote
from a previous campaign about several women in her hotel room
literally elbowing each other aside to pack her bags. Other stories
followed as she tried to convince me of just how exciting a political
campaign can be. She asked for my help, but beyond dogs and suitcases, she really couldn't predict my responsibilities. And when I
told her I knew nothing of campaigns or politics (even my parents
were Republican), she said that didn't matter at all.

I did have experience in public relations, education, writing, and
television which qualified me for the job. But I did not expect that
in the next year of my life I would have to call upon everything I
had ever learned in the previous thirty-nine. I thought then that

my chief qualification was knowing and caring about Joan. If I took the job, I could be there as a friend, a sounding board, someone who understood her alcoholism and who could help take care of the details of her personal and public life. Joan's welfare mattered much more to me than Ted's winning the nomination. So with the hope that wherever the campaign ended—in the White House, at the convention, or before—Joan would emerge healthy and happy, I agreed to become her assistant.

Before I started to work in mid-October, although it went unspoken, I had to pass several small tests. Could I figure out how to get Joan's gold ultra-suede outfit cleaned in one day in time to wear for the opening of the Kennedy Library? Could I schedule on short notice a hair color, a leg wax, and a clothes fitting in succession to save her time? Did I have ideas on women's educational issues? Did I pass the scrutiny of both Kennedy's Washington staff and the Boston advisers? I had heard stories about the "well-oiled Kennedy machine." And to me that meant my work had to be fast, bright, and right—the first time—a high mark to live up to. The thought of even the smallest detail slipping through the cracks made me uneasy, and I vowed to myself it would never happen. So with very little to go on, no office or staff but with a huge commitment in my heart and mind to Joan, I began.

In deciding to seek the nomination, Ted was doing the unthinkable—challenging an incumbent President of his own party. The rivalry between Kennedy and Carter was keen, and Carter was certainly aware that he would not only have to compete with the popular young Senator and his powerful adherents, but with the Kennedy legend as well. He paid court to that legend in October at the opening of the Kennedy Library in South Boston, and for his trouble was reprimanded by the press for his blatant "kissing of the Kennedy women and sitting with his hand in Joan Kennedy's lap." The press, and the public, were gearing up for a tough fight.

Political comparisons between Kennedy and Carter would largely determine the outcome, but inevitably, other comparisons would be made on the so-called "character issue." And there would be yet another dimension to this campaign—comparisons between

the candidates' wives: Rosalynn Carter—perhaps the most dedicated, hard-working, and devoted First Lady in recent history—and
Joan. Thus I realized that Joan's performance would be critical to
the success of the campaign, and as her aide and mainstay, I felt a
heavy responsibility. But the heaviest burden of responsibility would
fall on Joan.

She accepted the challenge eagerly. After midnight one Sunday
night late in October my bedside telephone rang. My anxiety rose
as I peered at the clock in the dark and then groped for the phone.
Could it be Joan? Was she all right? Late night calls can be a
sign of drinking. When I was still drinking, I remember trying to
decipher notes left by the phone about calls I had unknowingly
made the night before. Predictably illegible, their contents remained
a mystery until friends called back to repeat both sides of entire
conversations. With trepidation I put the receiver to my ear.

"Hi. I can't sleep," Joan said cheerfully.

"I can't either," I said, turning on the light and looking at the
clock again.

"I'm so excited," she went on. "I have so much homework.
I'm going to need a two-minute TV script for class in a week and a
half, November seventh. And Ted's announcing that day."

"In Boston?" I asked, settling back and turning off the light.

"Yes. And you and I are going to have a big powwow here next
Wednesday the thirty-first at noon about my making a statement at
Ted's announcement. It's never been done before, you know. No
other presidential candidate's wife has ever made a statement to
indicate her support."

It occurred to me that most candidates' wives would not have
to.

"Oh, yes, and I need a thirty-minute TV script on teaching
music to kids."

I turned on the light again and reached for a pencil and paper
to be sure I wouldn't forget anything.

Joan talked on. "We can write that Tuesday morning after you
go with me to meet my doctor. Sarah Milam is coming up from
Washington for our Wednesday meeting. She's the smartest woman
in Ted's office. And Ed will be here. He was Ted's press man in '62

and after that he worked for the old *Herald*. He has to be behind the scenes, but I wish he could be a front man. And Milty—he's so smart. Sally is coming, too. Anyway, they're all pros. I don't know whether I should make a statement or do a Q & A."

"What does Ted think?" I asked. I didn't know whether to try to write all this down or just lie back against the pillows and listen.

"He's so relieved that I'll handle the emotional subjects," Joan said. "Ted can answer any question on any issue, but when it comes to something personal, he just goes 'uh, er, ah.'"

"Let's wait to see what the Washington staff thinks," I said. "We'll figure out what to do at the meeting."

"I'm so excited," Joan said again.

And I was, too. Being there when she needed to talk I considered an important part of my job, and so I listened for a while longer as Joan grew sleepy and I more wide awake.

After we hung up I realized how little I knew about political strategy. In the past I had accepted at face value what I read about a candidate (or his wife) or heard them say in person or on television. I never considered what went on behind the scenes, how many people's ideas went into a statement or a speech, or the amount of orchestration required to produce just a single effect. Should Joan make a statement or do a Q & A? I didn't know. I turned off the light but didn't sleep again until 2 A.M.

The next morning, Joan and I set out to order new stationery for her campaign correspondence at Shreve, Crump and Low, where Brahmin Boston buys its expensive wares. We walked briskly along Beacon Street and then down the uneven brick sidewalks of Dartmouth Street. As we crossed Newbury Street toward Boylston, Joan talked of travel projections. As soon as Ted announced, she said, we would be off to New Hampshire and Maine on Wednesday, Chicago and Denver on Thursday, and Los Angeles and Miami on Friday. We started making plans for this first blitz trip. Joan talked of ordering designer clothes, and I thought about a quick trip to Filene's basement for luggage.

When we came to the New England Merchants' Bank, Joan went in and walked up to the teller's window while I waited in the lobby. She came back laughing, her hands full of envelopes. "They're always amazed," she said. "But they ought to know what I want by this time. It's always the same—a thousand dollars in fives. I have them put it in envelopes of a hundred dollars each." Kitty was no less surprised than I. One day a few weeks later, after she had been reorganizing sweater and lingerie drawers in Joan's bedroom, she came down to my apartment and said breathlessly, "Does Mrs. Kennedy realize she's got dozens of little envelopes with money in them? They're scattered in all her clothes." I assured Kitty that she did.

At Shreve's, customers and salespeople watched unobtrusively as we chose white campaign stationery with a red border and bold block letters for Joan's name and address and requested that dozens of boxes be engraved and delivered. On the way home we stopped at Ken's Deli in Copley Square to order sandwiches, pickles, and coleslaw to be picked up for our Wednesday meeting. They wouldn't accept Joan's Mastercard (which I thought could only happen to the rest of us) but finally charged the lunch anyway (which would *not* happen to the rest of us).

Tuesday morning, we left in Joan's 1976 blue Impala to meet with her doctor. I wasn't quite sure why I was being included, but I learned later that the Senator had already met with Joan and her doctor, presumably to discuss her ability to campaign, and when the two men raised the question of who would assist her, Joan had announced, "I've already found someone. She even lives in the building."

It was a decision that would ordinarily have been made by the Senator and his advisers, as they had made so many other decisions in Joan's life. This time she had spoken up for herself, an indication that she intended to have some say about her participation in the campaign. I don't know if any of my other qualifications were discussed, but this meeting had apparently been arranged so the doctor could make his own assessment of my ability to do the job.

As we walked into his office, he was just finishing a phone conversation with Rick Burke, the Senator's executive assistant and my counterpart in Washington. Introductions were made, and Joan and I sat down on either end of a brown sofa. The young doctor leaned back in his leather chair, his hands clasped in front of him. "Have you talked to Rick?" he asked.

"No," we said together.

"Well, your trip is off. I think it would be too hectic for Joan."
She and I looked at each other, our spirits plunging.

"Well, I guess I'm relieved," Joan said finally, accepting the
decision with grace. Perhaps, I thought, it was the kind of disappointment she had become accustomed to and had learned to ra-
tionalize. But I was impressed that the doctor, guarding Joan's interests, could say no to the Kennedy staff.

Then, as if it had been agreed on beforehand, they began to discuss the question of my salary. Joan and I had talked briefly about
the subject, but because she had little experience with money matters, it was referred to Washington for Rick to handle. He then
checked with Joan, who had apparently been surprised by my salary request. Now, to my embarrassment, the subject had suddenly
surfaced in the doctor's office.

"No one gets paid, you know," Joan said, looking from the
doctor to me. "People pay to work for the Kennedys."

I felt hurt because it seemed as if she were opposing my request, with the doctor there to support her. "Or to work for Harvard," I said, trying to make light of my feelings of intimidation. But
I was so stunned by what looked like a prepared confrontation, I
could not speak up about my own financial obligations. Nor the fact
that thus far I was all the staff Joan had, and I soon would be on
duty for a 168-hour week, doing the work of several people. My
commitment to Joan had already been made; it was too late to turn
back. But I knew that Rosalynn Carter had a staff of more than
twenty people. And except for some volunteers among the advance
team, the Senator's staff—mainly men—were adequately paid.

The salary question was left unresolved that day, but I began
to see the doctor in a new light. It seemed that he, too, although
chiefly Joan's advocate, was at least in part a functionary of this efficient Kennedy organization. It made me aware of how programmed
Joan had been and how it felt to be so powerless.

The doctor then turned to me and we discussed the priorities
for Joan's well-being in the months to come: sobriety, self-esteem,
campaign work, fun, and relaxation. Speaking as if Joan were not
there, he suggested that I "watch her for signs she may drink," and
offered to be available to me anytime. Finally, as we were leaving,

he said pleasantly to Joan, "Remember now, Marcia works only for a sober Mrs. Kennedy."

A few days later Rick called me to say, "You'll get fifteen thousand a year. Take it or leave it." Although it was not much more than I had earned ten years ago, there was no choice but to agree.

The next morning, bright and chilly, reminded me that Ted's November announcement was just one week away. After picking up the lunch in Copley Square for our strategy meeting, "the powwow" as Joan called it, I went up to her apartment. Through her huge plate glass windows, overlooking the Charles River, I could see small white sails darting across the navy-blue water as I set out a buffet lunch for our guest-experts. This would be my first, full-scale, Washington-staff-style meeting and I looked forward to learning how campaigns were created and what Joan's part would be.

When the guests arrived, I greeted them in Joan's silver and white entrance hall. Milton Gwirtzman, tall and serious, with a legal and writing background, came in first, followed by Ed Martin, who was known for his Irish charm and sense of humor. Both men had worked for the Senator in previous campaigns and were savvy about political strategy and handling the press. Sarah Milam, an intelligent and sensitive woman, had known Joan and Ted since the early days of their marriage and worked for the Senator in Washington. Sally Fitzgerald, a friendly and energetic woman, now terminally ill with cancer, had helped Joan when she was sick and had joined this campaign with gusto, knowing it would be her last. Each of them had come with special expertise and a loyalty to Ted. But beyond that they also wanted to help Joan.

Joan joined us in the living room, looking refreshed and enthusiastic. She exchanged warm hugs with her old friends and then offered sandwiches and coffee before we began to work. Balancing plates, we settled into upholstered black chairs and the black-and-white plaid sofa in the living room, and the meeting, quite informally, came to order. As I listened I took notes for Joan to review later.

The purpose of the meeting was to decide whether or not Joan should make a statement when Ted announced his candidacy on November 7. The men were against it, warning that if Joan spoke the press would focus on *her* rather than on Ted. Ed said he could just imagine a headline such as "Joan says she still loves him as Ted announces for President." With his brown eyes twinkling, he spelled out the words in the air to illustrate his point.

"You know, he's right," Sally said, shaking her blond head. "If a credible magazine like *Time* could—" She didn't finish her sentence, but we all knew she was referring to a recent article headlined "The Vulnerable Soul of Joansie," which concluded, "Public life has not been kind to Joan Kennedy. Its wounds can be seen in the puffy eyes, the exaggerated makeup, the tales of alcoholism. Today she is a sadly vulnerable soul and an unknown factor in her husband's electoral equation."

"Joan always wants to do what's best for everyone," Sally assured Ed.

Again, I noted with surprise that they spoke of Joan as if she were not present, something that seemed to happen most often when others were deciding her fate. Perhaps it struck her, too, because she sat up on the sofa and spoke out more forcefully than I'd ever heard her and would not again for several months.

"This is how I feel," Joan said, tossing back her long hair. "I want to do what's best for Ted, but I don't see if he sees what's best for him right now. I don't blame him for being skittish about me. He's very uncomfortable with what we call 'the personal questions.' But right now that's all that's on anybody's mind. 'Is Joan all right?' 'Will she be able to campaign?' 'Will she live in the White House?' Do you know, even my friends think we're divorced and just patching things up for the campaign?"

Then she spoke in whispered tones but with enough emphasis so that no one dared interrupt. "That's crummy stuff and I want to set the record straight. Ted said he'd be much more comfortable having me talk about it. It takes a lot off him. If I'm well rehearsed and feel confident, I can do a fantastic job. He said I can do something—a statement, or answer a few questions, or have a press conference to answer a lot of this personal stuff. I want to get into this sensitive, personal stuff at the beginning of the campaign and then in two months they'll forget about it and talk about the issues."

I was surprised to hear her speaking so directly. The men, too, seemed stunned by her unexpected candor and were probably wondering what had happened to the soft-spoken wife who usually acquiesced to every staff suggestion. Here was a tough lady. I suspected they had been sent to tell Joan she could not make a statement, and now they were going to have to talk her out of it.

Ed bravely entered the ring, waving diplomacy and charm. He agreed that we had to deal with the press as quickly as possible, but he wasn't sure which setting or time would be best. "My ideal sense would be that she sits up there on the platform and doesn't say anything. Just smiles and sits with the family. Ted makes the announcement; they go out the door and that's it."

I couldn't help thinking that that familiar scenario had contributed to some of Joan's past problems. But asking her to be just the ornamental wife seemed insufficient now; the public needed answers to questions about their marriage, and about Joan herself. And she was ready to give them, if not for Ted's benefit, for her own.

Although the group unanimously acknowledged that Ted would be asked questions, Ed wanted to know what would happen if someone said, "Senator, I want to ask Joan a question."

Milton, who had remained quiet until now, shook his head, brushing the suggestion away. "Nobody's ever asked a question of a wife. It's *his* day," he said firmly.

"But at other presidential announcements there were no rumors," Sally persisted. It was a crucial point.

"We aren't even living together!" Joan said, with a gesture of her hand at the living room as if to emphasize Ted's absence. The women nodded in agreement, sympathetic to Joan's need to end the rumors about her—or at least to explain them.

Milton put his plate down and set a crumpled green paper napkin on top of it with the look of a man about to play his trump card. "Do you understand that most people still don't think he's going to run?" he asked Joan directly. "Deep down, they don't really want him to run because they're afraid he'll be assassinated. People won't believe it until he says it."

"I see," Joan said. Her voice faded to a whisper and she sat back on the sofa. "Well, I didn't know that."

"So this is his chance to get up and say, 'I'm going to run,' and say why he feels he should be President instead of Carter or Reagan, or whomever. There are people in this country more concerned that he's going to be killed than are interested in . . ." he hesitated and his voice dropped, ". . . in, ah, your marriage."

"Well, I'm glad you told us that," Joan said, noticeably affected and possibly hurt by Milton's directness.

For a time, she withdrew from the conversation while the group discussed just when Joan should speak for public consumption. But then Sally said she was still worried about the questions reporters would ask on announcement day and suggested that Ted refer the personal ones to Joan.

Ed disagreed with energy and a little drama in his voice. "If they say, 'Senator, is Joan going to campaign with you?' or 'Is she going to live in the White House?' well, he can handle that." Then he sat back in his chair as if he had uttered the last word.

Joan, unwilling to give up, immediately turned to face him, "Oh, yes? What's he going to say? I'm not fooling—I would like to know that! Some of his answers are so asinine, so far from the truth."

"He should do all the question-answering," Milton told her calmly and gently, holding his ground.

Finally Sarah said, "It's your decision, Joan. The easy way out is not to make a statement. If you do, don't answer questions."

Discussion continued for a while longer, with the men still adamantly opposed to a statement. Then Sally said, "How about this?" She held up notes she had just written on a piece of paper on her lap. "I'm pleased and proud that Ted has chosen to seek the presidency. I share his aspirations and hopes. . . ."

Joan recoiled, folded her arms, and turned to face Sally, her longtime friend, "All right, sweetheart, that is bullshit. I don't share his aspirations. The only way I'm going to survive this is if I want it for me." She hesitated, glanced at each one of us, and held out her arms as if pleading for agreement. "I want you guys to write me a tough statement. Skip the sharing aspirations, because I don't. I'm not going to say anything about him or for him—I'm only good at talking about me."

Ed came to the rescue at this tense moment with a suggestion that brought about a compromise. "I'm inclined to be against your making a statement," he said to Joan. "So how do we get what you want to say across? It's against my own wishes, but to let you say something quick I'd go for 'a plant.' For example, the third question could be, 'Senator, is your wife going to campaign?' Ted smiles and looks around and says 'Joan.' Joan walks up very quickly and says, 'Of course, I'm going to campaign' and something else and sits down."

Joan clapped her hands together silently, then said, "I won't read anything. I'll have it in my head."

"We'll have the plant be the third question," Ed said, gradually becoming more comfortable with the idea.

With everyone in agreement, Joan had finally been successful in entering the campaign on her own terms. She would be permitted to make a brief statement covering three points: "I'm going to campaign. I'll be answering questions on the campaign trail. This is my husband's day." Even more important, it may have been the first time in her life she had presented herself to Kennedy staffers in a way that had to be taken seriously.

Next this experienced group discussed the idea of holding a press coffee for Joan sometime after Ted's announcement and her statement. Everyone agreed it would be a good idea, and Ed suggested having reporters with whom Joan would be comfortable, although he acknowledged that it would be unfair and subject to criticism. "The main thing is that . . ." he began.

"I'm talking!" Joan finished for him, looking around at Sarah and Sally who had been so supportive a few minutes ago.

"That she's talking," Ed agreed.

"Now, look," Joan continued, again using her hands for emphasis. "I know how I want to answer the questions, but that doesn't mean it's good for Ted. I want some points from all of you on what I should get across. No matter what they ask me, I'll have those." She paused, then said, "I've heard a lot of talk around town—I guess the best thing about this is that I have nowhere to go but up and Ted has nowhere to go but down. I mean in the polls. I'm seen as a really sick woman, who's vulnerable. But I think it's a nice thing to be able to admit you need help."

Once again she had the full attention of the group with her willingness to open her life to public scrutiny. And as if to underline the importance of the contribution she could make to the campaign, Milton pulled a news clipping from his briefcase that posed the question: Should candidates be judged by anything other than their public records? Milton said the columnist concluded that indeed they should be, noting the need to consider Senator Kennedy in terms of Chappaquiddick, his relationship with his wife, and other women. As he finished he nodded at Joan as if acknowledging that what she said about those subjects would be crucial.

"That's where I need help," Joan said slowly, almost pleading. "They're going to ask me the very first time how I feel about Chappaquiddick and other women." She hesitated for a moment, and I realized how difficult it must have been for her, even here with people she knew well, to talk about such personal things. "Those are the two hardest, because they don't have anything to do with me. I could say that was a long time ago—or the last reported affair was two years ago." She looked at Sarah, hoping for agreement.

Sarah gently shook her head. "I don't think you'll get away with that. The way you answered it a few years ago was good; you said it was difficult and very sad."

Joan's eyes widened. "Ted chewed me out like you wouldn't believe for saying that. If he doesn't want me to say *anything*, I wish he'd tell me."

Milton summed up what we all were thinking: that the past was certain to be dug up again. The problem would be how to handle it. "If you say that you both had problems," he suggested to Joan, "then you'll be like everybody else."

I wasn't sure Joan was willing to take responsibility for the breakdown of their marriage, but for political reasons she was ready to support her husband. I admired her resilience. "I just want to make it positive for him and say he's proud of me and give him some credit," she said. "I don't mind throwing all the kudos at him. I wouldn't have had a prayer of recovery if it hadn't been for him."

"That's fantastic," Milton exclaimed. There was silence in the room.

Sarah smiled at Joan. "That's good. And in most cases the truth works."

"Yes," Joan said softly.

After a discussion of how to handle the Kennedys' separation, the group finally agreed that Joan would say she left Washington because she had a problem with drinking. Everyone hoped that would allay the public's belief that the marriage was over.

"But the argument is that he drove her to drink," Ed said.

"We want to get rid of that one," Joan said clearly and with conviction. She had learned in treatment that alcoholism was not caused by people, places or things. It was a disease.

"You could say, 'My drinking goes back—it goes back to before he started chasing women,'" Ed offered, laughing good-naturedly.

"Oh, no, it doesn't, and I can prove it," Joan said, shaking her head emphatically. "I'll get help with some of the alcohol questions."

Finally the meeting drew to a close, and after taking Joan's guests to the door, I returned to the living room where she was still sitting curled up on the couch. We both agreed the meeting had gone well and began talking about all the things we had to do before Ted's announcement. Then Joan's voice grew hesitant, "Do you think I can do it, Marcia?" she asked, as if realizing for the first time what this campaign was going to demand of her.

"You already have," I told her, "you're on your way."

I meant what I said. Yet at the same time I felt a sense of what it must have been like for Joan to be a political wife for so many years. Our afternoon meeting seemed almost a microcosm of her life. How many times in the past had Ted's staff told her what she should or should not do—for Ted? How often had they asked her to share the blame for his foibles, and then to stand supportively by his side whenever he needed her? How often had her life been shaped to fit political purposes? How little opportunity there had seemed to be for choice or self-expression. But today had been different. She had shown courage in wanting to speak out for herself. It was a small victory, perhaps. But it proved to be an important turning point in her life.

By the end of the week, Ed and I had completed the arrangements on both sides for Joan's statement. He said he had found a friendly reporter and I had helped Joan work out exactly what she would say to the anticipated question.

A few days later, I received the mailgram invitation to the Senator's announcement:

> On Wednesday, November 7, I will announce my candidacy for President of the United States at Faneuil Hall in Boston, at 10:30 A.M. I would like to invite you to share this meaningful occasion with me, and hope you can attend. Please present this mailgram upon arrival at Faneuil Hall.
> R.S.V.P.
> Sincerely,
> Ted Kennedy

That day, Ted would officially enter the race. And Joan would announce her candidacy, too.

That Sunday night before Ted's announcement, Joan and I took a break from working to watch the CBS TV hour-long special report, "Teddy." Several weeks earlier Roger Mudd had enlisted Ted's cooperation in the project and asked for two interviews, one to take place at Kennedy's Cape home with his family, and the other in his Senate office. The Senator agreed and arrangements were made to send a crew of TV cameramen to cover a family weekend at Hyannis Port on September 29. The Senator's staff then called each of the children and Joan to ensure that every member of the family would be there. But Joan didn't feel up to the immense preparation required for a "casual" weekend in front of TV cameras. Kara and Teddy, Jr., had other plans and didn't appear either. The TV crews arrived, the Senator and his staff arrived, but with no touch football or family fun to capture on camera, Roger Mudd sat down with the Senator in captain's chairs on the lawn overlooking the ocean for what the Senator's staff later referred to as an impromptu interview.

When it was over, and the crew, equipment, and Mudd were on their way back to New York, Ted called Joan in Boston, a rare occurrence. She reported that he said he had never felt so down in his life, because the family had not come to the Cape and he didn't think the interview with Mudd had gone well. We understood the disappointment of not having his family around him when he needed them. But it wasn't until the night of November 4, as we watched the interview on the air, that we fully comprehended the reason for his concern.

That evening, Joan in a green terry robe and I in a red velour one sat down on the soft green carpeting in her living room close to the portable TV set so we wouldn't miss a word or facial expression of the interview. The reception was fuzzy and we strained to see and hear.

Mudd was a sympathetic interviewer, although he, too, seemed unprepared for the occasion. His questions were ones the press had asked the Senator before, which made it even more surprising that Ted's answers indicated no advance preparation. The Senator appeared uncomfortable, shifted in his chair, and did not look directly at Mudd or at the cameras. Even more devastating, his replies to Mudd's questions were both vague and inarticulate.

When Mudd asked, "What's the present state of your marriage?" Joan and I edged closer to the set to hear his answer. Ted became even more uneasy. He said that he and Joan had had "some difficult times" but had "been able to make some very good progress." Joan and I glanced at each other quickly and then watched Ted, anxiously wondering what he would say. Still trying to define their relationship, he continued, "It's—I would say that it's—it's—it's I'm delighted that we're able to share the time and the relationship that we—that we do share."

Mudd pressed further. "Are—are you separated, or are you just—what—how do you describe the—situation?"

I could hear Joan's sudden intake of breath beside me as Ted began, "Well, I don't know whether there's a single word that should—have a description for it. Joan's involved in a continuing program to deal with the problems of—of alcoholism, and—and she's doing magnificently well, and I'm immensely proud of the fact that she's faced up to it and made the progress that she's made. And I'm—but that progress continues, and that—it's the type of disease that one has to continue to—to work."

I breathed more easily with that answer. At least Ted's pride in Joan came through and he had been direct about her alcoholism.

Next Mudd recalled a remark Ted had made just after the accident at Chappaquiddick, when he said he felt "an awful curse hanging over the Kennedy family." Ted now responded that he felt his life had been more normal in the past ten years and he'd been able to put the tragic events of those years into perspective.

At this point in the telecast, the interview was interrupted in order to allow CBS cameras, with a voice-over by Mudd, to recreate the scene on Chappaquiddick Island. Mudd explained that he and a camera crew had gone to the island, and Mudd himself drove the car repeatedly over the route to relive as driver the actual road and light conditions Kennedy would have experienced. Finally, the camera crew had attached a camera to the car's left front fender, and with only the car's headlights to light the way, had retraced the route that Kennedy and Mary Jo Kopechne had taken the night of July 18, 1969.

As the camera car started its journey away from the cottage where the party had been held, I realized that Joan was probably seeing this road for the first time, too. Second by second the car moved forward almost smoothly down the paved road. Then suddenly it turned right, an abrupt right, onto a dirt road. The cameras seemed to dance, following the erratic movement of the headlights, as the car continued on its bumpy path. Finally it stopped, with the cameras focused on the narrow bridge over which Kennedy's car had plunged.

Neither Joan nor I could speak. It seemed that we could hardly breathe.

The interview continued, as Mudd suggested that Ted might want to "say something more to illuminate in people's minds what indeed went on that night, other than saying it's all in the record?"

The Senator continued to evade the subject, however, forcing Mudd to ask more specific questions: Why had Ted taken the right-hand turn? Why hadn't Ted noticed the bumpy road? Why had he referred to a clock in the car when the car had none? Did Ted think anyone believed his explanation?

The Senator answered, "Oh, there's—the problem is—from that night—I found the conduct, the er, ah, er the behavior almost beyond belief myself. I mean that's why it has been—but I think that's that's that's the way it was. That—that happens to be the way it was.

Now I find it as I have stated that I have that the conduct that—that evening in in this as a result of the impact of the accident of the— and the sense of loss, the sense of hope and the and the sense of tragedy and the whole set of—circumstances, that the er—ah—be- havior was inexplicable. . . ."

Joan and I waited silently through a commercial break before the special returned to the next interview held in Kennedy's Wash- ington office on October 12. Once again, as if no time had inter- vened, Ted was uneasy and inarticulate, even when asked why he wanted to be President. It was as if he had not thought about it, when in fact he had already made the decision to run.

For the few remaining minutes of the program Joan and I never took our eyes off the screen as we watched in disbelief Ted's answers disintegrate with each question. Then as the program ended and the credits started to run, Joan reached over and snapped off the TV. The picture disappeared and we just sat there with our heads in our hands. When we finally looked at each other, I could see de- spair in her eyes for the political ramifications of Ted's performance. But I also saw pain from having the past brought forward once again.

Still on the floor, Joan leaned back against the couch. In a voice barely above a whisper, her arms hugging her knees, she began to talk about Chappaquiddick, reliving every moment of its effect on her. She and the children had been at their Cape home when it happened.

"No one told me anything. Probably because I was pregnant, I was told to stay upstairs in my bedroom. Downstairs the house was full of people, aides, friends, lawyers. Ted called his girl friend Helga before he or anyone even told me what was going on. It was the worst experience of my life. I couldn't talk to anyone about it. No one told me anything. I had to stay upstairs and when I picked up the extension phone I could hear Ted talking to Helga." She shook her head and looked away. "Nothing ever seemed the same after that."

Several hours later we were still sitting on the floor talking. Just before midnight Joan said, "From my own experience I know what it's like to go through a personal ordeal and how painful it is. I know how Ted has suffered and grown because of it. Can I dare hope that from such a tragedy as Chappaquiddick there can actually come out of it some good? The good is the growth and the strengthening of a very human public person."

I quickly wrote what she said on a scrap of paper and later that night in my apartment typed it for her. We wouldn't need our experts to help Joan with answers to questions about Chappaquiddick. This one came from her heart.

5

TWO
ANNOUNCEMENTS

I look forward very, very enthusiastically to my husband's being a candidate and then as being the next President of the United States.

—JOAN

On the morning of Ted's announcement, before going up to Joan's apartment, I glanced out of my windows overlooking Beacon Street. It looked as if a circus had come to town. Directly below, crews of TV cameramen and reporters huddled under the black and white striped awning that covered our front entrance. Police cars with blue and white flashing lights were parked across the intersection at Dartmouth and Beacon streets to block and detour the usual morning traffic. Pedestrians with briefcases, students in jeans and jackets, and joggers in running clothes had gathered to wait for a glimpse of Joan and Ted and were being restrained by light-blue police sawhorses set across the sidewalk. On the other side of the street, three Secret Service agents, strategically spaced several yards apart, scrutinized the roof of our building and then looked up and down first one side and then the other of the carless street. On our side, a pack of well-groomed agents in dark three-piece suits paced back and forth along the sidewalk, whispering into walkie-talkies. This massive security had been ordered especially for Kennedy by President Carter, but it would soon become standard for all candidates in the 1980 race.

I rushed upstairs to be sure that Joan was ready to leave and had her 3 × 5 card with "the answer" in her purse. When the elevator doors opened on her floor, I was not permitted to step out; two expressionless agents held up their arms like wooden soldiers to stop me and would not let me go into Joan's apartment until Kitty confirmed my identity. In the front hall Joan was putting on her lavender jacket as Kitty, excited by the Senator's imminent arrival, helped her. Joan was quiet and a little nervous. I told her about the crowd gathered outside so she wouldn't be surprised by the flash-bulbs or the press of curious faces. I gave her a quick hug and then left to allow her a few minutes alone with Ted when he arrived to pick her up.

The normally serene and empty lobby bustled with more than a dozen Secret Service agents, while all of the phones recently in-stalled on top of the superintendent's office desk rang simulta-neously. Curious residents of our building had come out of their apartments and stood talking and watching for the Senator's arrival.

Suddenly an agent called out solemnly, "One minute."

Almost immediately, two police cars with flashing lights pulled up to the curb and stopped slightly past the building entrance. They were followed closely by one shiny black-paneled Secret Service sta-tion wagon, one long black and gray limousine, six matching blue Mercury sedans, five older sedans of various colors for staff, and finally one more police car with flashing lights. All doors on both sides of all cars in the motorcade opened at once. The Senator stepped out of the limousine and everyone else got out exactly at the same split second, swarming around the Senator and forming a flying wedge as he strode briskly into the building, up the marble steps through the crowd in the lobby to the elevator doors, which were being held open for him. With his arrival the noise in the lobby reached a crescendo.

A few minutes later Ted, accompanied by Joan, quickly walked back through the lobby, again surrounded by the Secret Service. Staff, including me, fell in behind. We ran out the front door past tracking TV cameras, questioning reporters, and speechless onlook-ers and ducked into the waiting cars. All doors slammed shut at once, the drivers maneuvered their cars into formation and the mo-torcade began its slow procession toward Faneuil Hall.

I had never ridden in a motorcade before and did not know

the rules familiar to the Senator's longtime staff: (1) Run. (2) Be on time (a motorcade waits for no one except the Kennedys, not even a split second). (3) Get in and out quickly. (4) Sit in the same seat in the same car. (5) Stay very close to the group (the entourage moves with lightning speed and the press swarms in around it). (6) Don't take a coat, no matter how cold (there's never any place to put it and it gets heavy in a hot hall after a while). There were other rules, too, but these were the ones I learned the hard way.

I didn't discover until later the reason TV camera crews always covered this huge group (which included a doctor and a specially trained nurse) as it entered and left buildings and filed in and out of motorcades: in case of an accident or assassination attempt the incident would be recorded on tape. As the campaign progressed, each of us on the staff was forced to face the too real prospect of possible violence, and each handled fear in his or her own way. In my case, however, not until the campaign was over did I learn how serious the danger might have been to those of us in close proximity to the candidate, and that fear of violence had been responsible in part for nervous breakdowns among several of the Senator's staff.

As the motorcade pulled into the historic Quincy Market area, twenty thousand people cheered and waved. Police on horseback restrained the crowd behind wooden barricades sectioned off with yellow nylon cord. Many had been waiting for hours to see the Senator and his famous family and willingly stood outside in the chill of that cloudy November day to hear his announcement over loud-speakers.

Joan and Ted, encircled by Secret Service agents, ran quickly from the limousine through a narrow passage in the crowd, made just for them, into Faneuil Hall. The doors closed behind them and no one else was allowed to enter. Milton and I, riding in one of the last cars of the motorcade, even though we ran, did not get to the doors before they closed. Ignoring restrictions, ducking under ropes, edging sideways between closely parked TV trucks, and stepping over cables, Milton led me to a side door. After a great deal of negotiating with three uniformed guards, we were let into the hall and then ushered to seats. I decided to stand along the side, however, where I would be more available to Joan if she wanted anything.

The Senator, Joan, and their children were already seated on the stage with white marble busts of John Adams, his son John Quincy Adams, Daniel Webster, and other famous historical Massachusetts leaders looking down upon them. In the rows of seats on the floor facing the platform, other Kennedys, invited politicians, and campaign staff waited. The Senator's mother, Rose, then eighty-nine, had been seated in the first row. His sisters Jean Smith and Eunice Shriver and their husbands, his sister Patricia Lawford, his sisters-in-law Ethel Kennedy and Jacqueline Onassis, and several nieces and nephews were also there. Other guests included national and state political figures, and the rest of the small hall was layered with rows and rows of stadium bleachers where six hundred reporters and photographers from around the world stood wedged together.

As I waited beside the press bleachers for the event to begin, a woman who was an acquaintance of both Joan's and mine glided over to where I was standing and said, "I heard you were working for Joan. Oh, it all makes me so sick. Look at them up there." She glanced fondly in Ted's direction, but her voice betrayed her anger. "Why do they have to pretend they're happily married?"

As I looked at her I remembered the photographs that decorated her bedroom—dozens of pictures in all sizes, of her with Ted framed and arranged on tables, shelves, and walls—and I realized her question was more than political. "Poor Joan," she said. "I feel so sorry for her. And I'm furious with Ted. I wrote him a letter telling him so. It just makes me sick." Then as an afterthought she added, "I suppose I shouldn't be here."

Uncomfortable with this apparent revelation, I focused my eyes on the stage and she finally moved away.

Seated behind the podium to the left of Ted, Joan smiled and tried hard to appear calm by making small talk with her children, whom she had not seen often in recent months. She was wearing a short lavender crepe dress with a pleated skirt and matching jacket, and her hair appeared a brilliant platinum under the harsh lights. She was holding a white card in her hand—the answer to the expected planted question with the words she wanted to stress underlined in blue by a ballpoint pen:

1. I am looking forward to campaigning
   with and for my
                 husband
2. <u>SOON</u> I will be talking with
   members of the <u>press</u>
3. <u>AND</u> I hope at that time to
   answer many of the questions
   you might like to
   ask me

The Senator looked energetic and forceful as he stepped to the podium to deliver the long-awaited announcement that he would run for President. He had replaced his Ben Franklin half-moon glasses with a square, horn-rimmed pair the public had not yet seen. He put his speech on the lectern and looked out at the faces of relatives, friends, and the press as the hall grew suddenly quiet.

"Today I speak to all the citizens of America," he began. "But I wanted to speak to you from home, here in Boston.

"For many months, we have been sinking into crisis. Yet, we hear no clear summons from the center of power. Aims are not set. The means of realizing them are neglected. Conflicts in directions confuse our purpose. Government falters. Fear spreads that our leaders have resigned themselves to retreat. . . ."

After formally announcing his candidacy, the Senator then went on to note that American pessimism was justified in terms of judging the effectiveness of the present government. And he concluded by saying, "Let us carry forward the golden promise that is America. And if we succeed at that, then someday we can look back and say that this hall was rightly chosen for this day by renewing the promise of our forebears. We will have earned our place on this platform."

As he finished, the audience inside and out cheered and clapped, and his family rose from their seats, their faces shining with love and pride. When the applause subsided, reporters began to call out questions, and the first one he answered concerned the crisis in Iran where sixty-two Americans had been held hostage at the U.S. embassy in Tehran since Sunday. I watched Joan. She seemed distant, as if reviewing the three points of her reply and listening for her cue to speak. The second question dealt with protecting the dollar from being held hostage by foreign nations, and the third covered differences the Senator had with the Carter administration that justified his challenge.

The third question had come and gone. Had "the plant" forgotten or changed his mind? I scanned the sea of reporters with their hands waving wildly, their voices demanding recognition, and wondered how Ted's nod could possibly indicate a particular person. I shared Joan's tension as she waited, hoping she would have a chance to speak.

The fourth question came from a reporter who asked how Kennedy felt about the Roger Mudd interview and whether he would continue to answer sensitive, personal questions.

The Senator cleared his throat before responding in a good-natured parody of the way he had answered Mudd's questions. "Well, the question well, how well did I do in my interview last Sunday and will I answer questions from the . . . uhh, the answer to the second is I will and the answer to the first is I could have done better."

The crowd roared at the Senator's honesty and ability to laugh at himself. But the next question broke the convivial mood.

"Senator, in order to give you an opportunity to answer one of the questions better than you were asked [sic] last Sunday: Your wife, Joan Kennedy, is living here in Boston and you are living in Washington. What role will Joan Kennedy play in your campaign?"

There it was. The crowd hissed and booed at the reporter's seeming lack of tact, but it was the question Ted—and Joan—had been waiting for.

The Senator looked silently out over the audience, as if wondering how to handle the question, then turned around slowly and nodded at Joan. "Joan, do you want to. . . ."

This moment had been planned, but it seemed completely spontaneous as Joan bounded from her seat to take Ted's place at the podium, touching his arm as he stepped away from center stage. He seemed uneasy as he watched her, even though he knew what she was supposed to say.

The hall grew hushed and still at this unexpected, unprece-

dented event. Joan grasped the edges of the podium on both sides
for support, looked up at the crowd and then down at friends and
family in front of her. Her lips began to move but almost no sounds
could be heard. She spoke louder and her voice quavered. "I believe
the question was directed at—will I campaign for my husband. I
look forward to campaigning for him. And not only that, I look
forward very, very enthusiastically to my husband's being a candidate and then as being the next President of the United States."

Her voice grew stronger as she concluded, "I will be talking
with members of the press and at that time I hope to answer all of
your questions that you might have on your minds today."

The crowd applauded in sympathy and support, Joan returned
to her seat and the press conference continued with questions on
the Senator's choice of a vice-presidential candidate and whether his
candidacy would divide the party. Finally it was over, ending in a
warm round of applause for both Ted and Joan. Family and friends
rushed forward to congratulate them and wish them well. Ted
politely praised Joan, gave his mother a loving hug and then greeted
his guests and fellow politicians.

Joan must have felt great pride at this moment: she had taken
her first shaky step on yet another campaign trail. But this time she
had come forward because she wanted to. And she had opened herself to questions and promised to answer them all.

Our primary task now was to find the right forum for Joan to
keep that promise. And the immediate task for me was to find a way
to handle the reporters who would be clamoring to interview her.
When I returned ahead of Joan to Beacon Street, where only a few
tumbled blue barricades remained from the morning's spectacle, my
phone was already ringing. I hurried in to answer the call in the
makeshift office I had set up in my front hallway.

"Hi. This is Tom Brokaw of the 'Today' show. I don't want to
put any pressure on you or on Mrs. Kennedy, but she can come here
and be on the show live or we will go there and tape at her convenience."

That was the beginning—Tom Brokaw at the top of a long,
prestigious list of requests. And the calls would continue day and

night for the next several weeks. But all were refused because we knew that Joan would have to be very carefully prepared. Meanwhile, reporters and feature writers, lacking new news, scrawled short pieces on Joan and editors ran letters about her. In the *Boston Herald American*, a columnist called Ted's announcement the latest episode in the "elongated soap opera tale of the Kennedys." But the writer praised Joan's openness about her alcoholism and went on to say that "her willingness to answer personal questions is refreshing in the light of her husband's hedging on Chappaquiddick. . . ."

Other writers turned to the question of how public a private life should be, or to speculation about what kind of a First Lady Joan might be. A letter to the editor of the *Washington Star* addressed her image:

> Historian Arthur Schlesinger Jr. recently described our age as "excessively preoccupied with the private lives of public figures." If he is right, I assume we shall be subjected during the forthcoming campaign to much gossip about Joan Kennedy. . . . "You know, she's back on the bottle." "Don't you think she looks heavy?" "Why doesn't she unbleach her hair . . ." Credit is due. She has made an enormous effort. . . . Would Joan Kennedy be the kind of First Lady of whom our country could be proud? Ask yourself whether you'd be proud of someone who has known loneliness, heartache, and despair and had fought them—and won.

Joan was encouraged and very gratified by the attention and interest of the press. Yet she was far from the self-confident heroine people wanted to believe she was. During the next few days, her long telephone calls to me and other friends seemed to signal a lingering loneliness. She missed her children. She did not know the future of her relationship with her husband. She could not be sure of continuing success in her fight against alcohol. And now these personal, very private and difficult struggles had become matters of public curiosity and concern.

In the next several weeks I would establish routines for handling the increasing demands on Joan. We met together regularly to go over requests for public appearances, interviews, and invitations to speak to recovering alcoholics. We talked over schedules for her school work, family gatherings, and campaign events, as well as personal and household matters, fan mail, and bills. Joan called our meetings "doing the mail" and I called them "work sessions." I brought all the necessary papers up from my apartment to Joan's, along with a glass of Tab and sometimes a tuna salad for each of us; there was usually so much to carry that it took two trips. I dressed casually in a sweater and slacks and Joan even more casually in a bathrobe and cold cream.

She was often talking on the phone when I arrived. I would let myself in and go to the oval glass dining room table where we worked. There I arranged various folders and papers at Joan's place and mine, and then waited. Joan usually came to the table with a soft drink or coffee and her calendar, and sometimes a piece of jewelry requiring repair or a suitcase with a broken zipper. Then she sat down and we began to work.

When we were finished, often several hours later, we could measure what we had accomplished by the depth of the papers that littered the green carpet under the table. I scrunched those I no longer needed; Joan tore hers into tiny pieces. But at the same time paper was accumulating around our feet, even more was being added to each of my work folders. Still we both enjoyed these sessions, and Joan was almost childlike in her enthusiasm about anything that had to do with the campaign.

Before I left, we gathered up the litter under the table, then I stacked the folders, added the items for repair, and finally balanced the empty plate and glass on top. I picked it all up, with the glass under my chin, but once loaded, and always precariously, Joan would invariably think of other things to give me to do or to show me, and it would be another half hour or more of following her around, accepting new projects at the bottom of the pile of papers or under my arms. It occurred to me that all these extra projects were less important than the additional companionship their discussion required. But that, too, was part of my job.

Press requests for the interviews Joan had promised at the announcement continued to pour in, and working together one Sunday, I read over the list, which now included Mike Wallace, Ellen

Goodman, London Television, and German newspapers, and explained what each would like her to do. Wearing no makeup and her face shiny with moisturizer, Joan leaned back in a black and white upholstered straight chair and listened for a few minutes. Then she said, sounding pleased, "I'm glad they're big time." But almost immediately she leaned forward and seemed to contradict herself. "But I'm not good enough to be interviewed."

There, in a phrase, was Joan's dilemma. She looked forward to the opportunity the campaign would give her personally, but still felt intimidated by the tasks in front of her. It was not a question of experience. It was a matter of finding the necessary self-confidence to answer the tough questions we all knew she would be asked, not only on the public issues but on her private life as well. I had already started to gather information on relevant public issues, along with suggested answers to the personal questions. At our request the Washington staff began to inundate us with additional briefing material. Notebooks, neatly indexed, were prepared especially for Joan on women and equal rights, education, the arts and humanities. But it was suggested that on such subjects as the economy, Salt II, national health insurance, Kennedy's positions in contrast to Carter's, the effect of the Senator's candidacy on the party or his liberalism, that Joan say, "I can't speak for my husband on this issue. You'll have to ask him for yourself."

She would have to speak for herself, however, on the personal issues, and big brown envelopes containing suggestions for questions and answers for her press conference, the date for which had yet to be set, arrived almost daily. Joan and I read them together, with me impersonating the reporter asking the question and Joan replying with the suggested answer or improvising one of her own. If campaign advisers had their way, her press conference would be as carefully controlled as the announcement. But both Joan and I knew that would be impossible and she had to be prepared for whatever might happen.

Washington staff also sent news clippings from all across the country, at Joan's request, so she would know what was being written about her. Some reporters were supportive, some were skeptical, some intended to "wait and see." But the letters Joan received from the public rarely expressed such reservations. One woman wrote, "You have my vote. I'm not sure about your Mr. yet. He's a little liberal for my taste." And another said, "When you went to the podium and answered the rude question put to you by that 'cad' of a reporter I literally rose from my chair and cheered."

Many people sent prayers, small cards with spiritual verses, and books for daily readings. Others sent advice on campaigning, some quite specific. One man wrote, "Campaign in your own sweet way . . . you don't have to be competitive to no one." Another fan advised, "Every day say to yourself by God I will make it! As an old hairdresser I would ask that you not part your hair in the middle, layer it up a little bit and add curl."

But perhaps the most affecting letters came from people with either a personal or a family drinking problem. One woman confided, "I have been in several treatment centers for alcoholism. I love music, have three kids, and a successful husband. I just want you to know that we all struggle every day. You are not alone." And a man wrote that if Ted was ever self-righteous about Joan's alcoholism, she should "remind him that there could be more of us than of them, and it's a tremendous vote you can deliver." Another woman pleaded with Joan to "hang in there. If I can't make it, you have to make it for both of us."

Joan and I were moved by these letters, and she wanted every one of them answered. Clearly, she had the sympathy and support of the public, and knowing that was certain to add to her self-confidence when she finally faced the press.

Another meeting of our panel of expert advisers was scheduled for a Monday soon after Ted's announcement, so that Sunday I walked over to Ken's in Copley Square to order a "gourmet" lunch of sandwiches, pickles, and potato salad. I picked up a paper at the newsstand and saw a picture of President Carter kissing Rosalynn good-bye as she left Washington for Thailand where millions of Cambodian refugees who had fled their homeland would die of starvation without assistance and U.S. aid.

The Cambodian refugee crisis had prompted Ted to call Joan and urge her to play the piano with Maestro Rostropovich at Boston's Symphony Hall in a benefit concert for Cambodia. But because she had not been playing the piano regularly, she would have had to practice for long hours. And that, in addition to the preparation necessary for her press conference, was more than she felt she could handle. I'm sure it was difficult for Joan to refuse Ted's request, particularly for such an important cause, but she was beginning to learn her limits and to take care of herself.

On Monday I piled up the deli boxes that had been delivered to my apartment along with all my folders and papers, with the usual soft drink on top, and staggered up to the meeting at Joan's apartment. Our guests began to arrive a few moments later, including the same people who had helped Joan with her "announcement" plus Mary Ellen Cabot, a college friend, and Lisa Gwirtzman, Milton's wife. Today we were going to brainstorm about which reporters to invite to the press conference, when to hold it, what questions Joan should expect, and how she could handle sensitive personal information.

Ed and Milton, Sally and Sarah and our new guests settled down in the living room, paper plates balanced on their laps, and they all agreed that Joan's statement had been well received. Joan's spirits were high as she acknowledged their compliments.

Talk began with which reporters to invite to the press conference. When Ed suggested a man from Newsweek, Joan said, "Great! Why not five men?" Everyone laughed, but the final consensus was to invite reporters sympathetic to women's issues who were between thirty and forty years old and "at least one attractive man." It was also decided to limit the press to Boston reporters, UPI, and AP. We would not permit television cameras; we would allow photographers only. The subject of the press conference would be limited to personal issues and the time to one hour.

Next on the agenda was choosing a date that would be advantageous to both Ted and Joan. We all agreed not to hold it during the last week of November when Ted would be campaigning, because he might be asked to comment on Joan's press conference rather than on more timely substantive issues. Among the most important of those issues was the continuing crisis in Iran where sixty-two Americans were still being held hostage in an attempt to force the U.S. into surrendering the deposed Shah whom President Carter had admitted to this country for medical treatment. We could not know at the time, of course, that the hostages would remain in captivity throughout the campaign and the election year, and the hostage crisis, perhaps more than any other single issue, would direct the course of the campaign, prevent Kennedy from getting the Democratic nomination, and ultimately lead to President Carter's defeat. Carter would announce his own candidacy on December 4, so we finally decided to hold Joan's press conference on the fifth, and by the time our meeting ended, plans, in theory and in some detail, seemed to be complete. Ed and Milton left, and while I was clearing away the lunch plates and bringing out soft drinks and tea, Joan and her friends continued to chat in the living room. Their conversation was both personal and practical. One friend thought Joan should ask her clothes designer for a discount in exchange for the publicity he would get. Another suggested that she bleach the roots of her hair. And they all seemed particularly interested in what she should do if Ted were affectionate when they shared their king-sized bed at the Cape for Thanksgiving. "Don't let him make a pass at you," was one woman's advice.

I decided not to join this conversation and returned to my own apartment. So it wasn't until several weeks later that I learned of another thing Joan's friends had influenced her to do.

ABOVE: Joan was a senior at Manhattanville College when Jean Kennedy Smith introduced her to "her little brother" Ted. This photograph, taken that same year, was submitted by Joan's father to a modeling agency, and she later posed for advertisements for Coca-Cola and Revlon.

BELOW: On November 29, 1958, Joan married Ted in the wedding of the year, with brother Jack as best man. The ceremony, performed under floodlights and recorded on film, marked the beginning of Joan's life as a Kennedy. "I had no idea what I was getting into," she recalled.

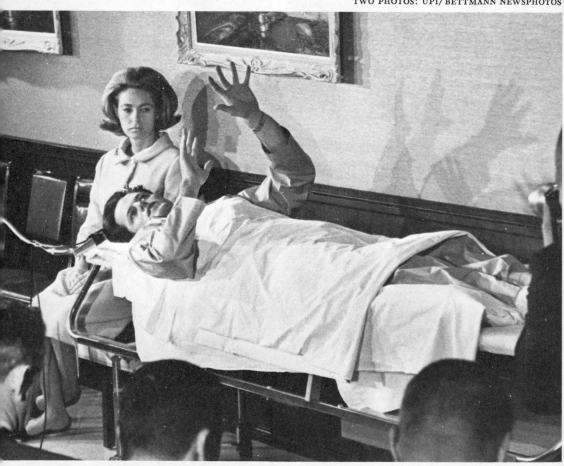

BRUCE DAVIDSON/MAGNUM

OPPOSITE TOP: Joan and Ted watch Inaugural Ball festivities in January 1960 with the President and his wife, Jackie. Two years later, Ted was elected to the Senate and the young couple joined the glittering but tragically short-lived court of Camelot.

OPPOSITE BOTTOM: Less than a year after Jack's assassination, Ted narrowly escaped death in a plane crash. Joan, shown here at his bedside press conference, campaigned for her husband in the Massachusetts senatorial race—probably her finest hour as a Kennedy.

ABOVE: Joan, with Teddy, Jr., and Kara, getting ready for a party in 1965. Beneath the glamour and excitement of her life, Joan was already beginning to feel the pressures of being a Kennedy. "Everything was done and taken care of and I didn't do it," she remembered. "I was nobody, nothing, not needed."

ABOVE: The Kennedys—Pat Lawford, Stephen and Jean Smith, Ted, Rose, and Joan—attend a fund-raiser in 1969 to help defray the late Bobby Kennedy's campaign expenses. Joan's grief after this second assassination was so great that she fled from Bobby's funeral service at Arlington.

OPPOSITE TOP: Another tragedy struck when Ted's car plunged over the bridge at Chappaquiddick and Mary Jo Kopechne was drowned. Joan, pregnant at the time, is shown here returning from the funeral with Ted. "It was a terrible experience, one of the worst in my life," she said. "And it was the beginning of the end for Ted and me." She miscarried soon afterward.

OPPOSITE BOTTOM: In the early 1970s, reporters commented acidly on Joan's extreme styles of dress, even hinting she sometimes drank too much. "I drank socially at first," she said later, "and then I began to drink alcoholically. But at the time I didn't know it. No one really ever does know."

UPI/BETTMANN NEWS PHOTOS

WIDE WORLD PHOTOS

ABOVE: When her son Teddy, Jr., lost his leg to cancer in 1973, Joan managed to get through this latest crisis in her life without alcohol. But when she no longer felt needed, she started drinking again.

LEFT: Her problem with alcohol could no longer be kept secret after Joan was arrested for drunken driving near her Virginia home in October 1974.

ABOVE: Jimmy Carter, soon to become her husband's bitter rival in the 1980 race for the Democratic presidential nomination, holds Joan's hand at the dedication ceremony of the Kennedy Library in Boston.

BELOW LEFT: Ted announced his candidacy for the nomination in November 1979. Joan, who had left her family and moved to Boston where she finally conquered her alcoholism, came forward, in response to a "planted" question from a reporter, to say she would campaign at her husband's side.

BELOW RIGHT: The indomitable Rose Kennedy campaigned for her son in Illinois in the opening round of the race. Joan, always in awe of her mother-in-law, thought Rose was "a saint."

THREE PHOTOS: UPI/BETTMANN NEWSPHOTOS

ABOVE: Ted and Joan sailing with their youngest son Patrick at Hyannis Port. Would they live together as President and First Lady if Ted won the election? No one knew.

OPPOSITE, TOP: A radiant Joan meets reporters for the first time in her Boston apartment after Ted's announcement. Predictably, their questions focused on her marital problems and her alcoholism.

OPPOSITE, RIGHT: Joan and Ted looking for votes in Iowa. Although they seldom appeared together, Joan proved to be an effective campaigner for her husband.

OPPOSITE, BOTTOM: Jackie Onassis, with Joan and Ted at a campaign event. Jackie and Joan, dubbed the two "outlaw in-laws" of the Kennedy family, were particularly close. Joan considered Jackie "the most sophisticated woman in the world."

ABOVE: After withdrawing from the race at the Democratic National Convention in New York, Ted receives a thunderous ovation from the crowd and a kiss from Joan. It was the closest the public had seen them during the entire campaign.

OPPOSITE, TOP AND BOTTOM: The campaign over, Joan hoped for a reconciliation with Ted. But an intimate lunch date in New York turned out to be, Joan recalled, nothing but a well-timed media event. A few days later, a photograph taken at an unguarded moment in the living room of their Virginia home seems to reveal the futility of her hopes.

TWO PHOTOS: UPI/BETTMANN NEWSPHOTOS

DAVID HUME KENNERLY/GAMMA LIAISON

UPI/BETTMANN NEWSPHOTOS

WIDE WORLD PHOTOS

ABOVE: A flamboyant farewell to the Secret Service agents who had guarded Joan and Ted during the campaign. On a flight to the Cape together later that night, Ted abruptly left the plane at Montauk and Joan flew on alone. "It's all over," Joan remarked. "I know that now."

LEFT: Joan listening to Ted describe his future political plans in an October 1980 speech in Boston. She now knew she would no longer be his wife. Their decision to divorce would lead to a bitter two-year wrangle over the terms of property and financial settlements—Joan's final ordeal as a Kennedy.

LILLIAN KEMP

Joan, shown here with the author aboard Ted's yacht *Curraugh*, was ambivalent about asking for a divorce. "How many women in the world would give their eyeteeth to be married to Ted Kennedy?" she said. "And here I am planning to give him up."

ABOVE: Joan with Ted and their children at her graduation ceremony from Lesley College in May 1981. It was a proud moment, and the first step in Joan's path to an independent new life.

BELOW: Turning to her own family for security, Joan invited her father, Harry Bennett, to Hyannis Port in August 1981. There he suffered a heart attack and died soon afterward, leaving Joan truly alone.

JOHN TCUMACKI/GAMMA LIAISON

With the divorce still pending, Joan's romance with Boston doctor Gerry Aronoff made headlines. They were trailed by reporters and photographers wherever they went, and on occasion Aronoff was forced to hire protection.

TWO PHOTOS: UPI/BETTMANN NEWSPHOTOS

Today, with years of unhappy memories behind her, Joan can face the future not only as a Kennedy but as a person in her own right.

6

OFFICIAL
MADNESS

If you don't arrange an interview with me,
you'll regret it. Some of us might get the wrong
idea about Mrs. Kennedy.

—An Irate Editor

I began hearing bells—all of them for Joan—day and night no matter where I was in my apartment. The telephone company had installed three new business phones, one next to each of my three existing telephones, making a grand total, including the extension for my children's sitter, of seven. The business phones had a call-holding device which meant I almost always had two callers at once on those lines, sending the next clever caller to ring the family phones. Talking on both phones was one way to stop the bells, but not the voices—voices of celebrities, schedulers, Joan's friends, doctors, the advance team, Kennedy's staffs in Boston and Washington, family members, service people, the public, and of course campaign staff.

But in the days following Ted's announcement, the preponderance of voices were those of the press asking to interview Joan. Reporters called over and over, growing more insistent with each call. They, of course, had no way of knowing that Joan was not yet ready to talk to them, and that we were devising a format to make her first press exposure as protected as possible. Naturally they all expected to have their questions answered immediately. And with no press experience or staff, I relied on intuition and prayer to keep them happy while holding them off.

As yet I had no real office either, so I ran from room to room, feeling phones for vibrations because side by side they sounded the same. As the messages accumulated, my officeless plight became even more desperate. And notes, file folders, newspaper clippings, schedules, and fan mail rose higher and higher on my desk in the front hall, overflowing into neat piles along the hall rug.

When Joan and I talked originally, I assumed my office would be in one of her small back rooms. Our apartments were identical, but while Joan lived alone, all my rooms were occupied by my daughter, my son, their sitter, and me. But to spare herself the stress and chaos of ringing telephones, piles of paper, and the comings and goings of campaign helpers, Joan preferred that I work in my own apartment. As soon as that decision had been made and I began to set up an office in my front hall, I realized there would no longer be any separation between my business and my personal life. I had turned over myself and even my home to Joan. By creating an extension of the protective cocoon that had always enveloped her, I had inadvertently become a part of it, treating Joan like a fragile butterfly, continuing her dependence.

Kennedy staff, however, expressed relief that I would be near Joan day and night. And when the Boston campaign staff, in the process of setting up its new headquarters at 53 State Street, heard that I had no equipment or supplies, they invited me to their sparsely furnished offices to look for anything they could give me to help set up an office. There I ordered a huge gray metal desk and two large gray metal filing cabinets from an office supply catalogue for delivery to my apartment. And with the help of a young, blond campaign volunteer, I returned home with an armload of office supplies and an IBM Selectric typewriter on a rickety gray metal typing stand. In the next few days, as desk and filing cabinets arrived, pieces of my own furniture were removed until the front hall bulged with gray metal. My long hall table remained but soon was lost to view under stacks of folders, supplies, and Joan's stationery, stockings, cosmetics, and drugstore items waiting to be delivered upstairs.

My phones continued to ring, as most of Joan's calls went through me or Powers Answering Service, which often came to my rescue. Of all this Joan was blissfully oblivious, living in solitude a few floors above. In fact, during one of our work sessions, she remarked rather wistfully, "You know, I never get any calls anymore."

Right after Ted's announcement, I began work on several projects for Joan. One was a mailing to some of her friends and relatives who might be interviewed, briefing them on how to handle questions on such subjects as alcoholism, the Kennedys' separation, and Chappaquiddick. We suggested they not refuse to talk to the press, which would only intensify curiosity, but rather answer questions as circumspectly as possible.

The ringing phones were a constant interruption, but by contrast, outgoing calls over the next few months would be relatively easy. A simple "This is Joan Kennedy's office calling" got me anyone and anything I asked for: an appointment for a manicure when none was available, a visit from Joan's hairstylist to her apartment on a Sunday, a clothes fitting promptly, the windows washed without the customary six-week wait, orchestra seats on the day of a performance, an invitation backstage to meet a visiting celebrity, a taxi in record time. I realized that since becoming a Kennedy, in matters such as these Joan had never had to wait in line, take second best, compromise, adjust, see a play from behind a pillar. She had become accustomed to having her desires met immediately. Surprised by the number of people who were always willing to accommodate her, I wondered if that, in part, had not contributed to the creation of a kind of privileged status or a sense of entitlement that all the Kennedys seemed to enjoy. But I soon learned that the magic of the Kennedy name would make my tasks much easier.

Meanwhile, preparations for the press continued and among the top priorities was briefing Joan on how to answer questions about alcoholism. Her doctor called to say he had prepared a cassette. In fact, he announced, it was already on its way to me in a taxi. Could I transcribe it right away? Determined, I called the Boston campaign office for volunteers who soon arrived to answer phones while I retreated to my bedroom with a small recorder and a dozen pencils to transcribe the tape.

Once again, as in other areas, every conceivable question that Joan might be asked about her alcoholism was posed and then answered for her, including whether or not she was cured of alcoholism, when she had had her last drink, and how to respond to reports that she had been seen intoxicated in Boston.

Answers were also provided for why she had moved to Boston, if she had lived in a halfway house, and whether Ted's career and behavior had caused her alcoholism or whether it was caused by her "not being up to being a Kennedy." To the last question she was to answer, "Doctors don't really know what causes it, but they do know that someone can't give you a case of alcoholism." When asked whether or not she and Ted were separated, Joan was to answer no, that it had been recommended she leave Washington for treatment. To an inquiry about her husband's involvement with other women, she was to label it gossip. To a question about why she had not been attending classes or doing her homework, she was to explain that her first priority was recovery from alcoholism.

I was still coping with the mechanics of transcribing this tape when my thirteen-year-old daughter Dana came home from school and cheerfully joined the volunteers stuffing and stamping envelopes in the front hall. Then a new friend, Gail, stopped by to ask for advice and taking in the situation at a glance offered to help me instead. A former legal secretary, she sat down at the typewriter in the front hall, deftly typed my handwritten transcript, went to Copley Square to make copies, and stayed on as my secretary for three years, mostly as a volunteer.

Joan's doctor was also concerned about her appearance. A few days after I had delivered the transcript to him, he called again to suggest that I do something about her exaggerated makeup. Friends had made similar requests, but I could not comply. I did not want to do or say anything that would upset her or diminish her already fragile self-confidence. I was probably being too protective of Joan, but I felt that her makeup was the least of our worries at this point. I nevertheless promised the doctor that I would try to make a few tactful suggestions at the right time. And over the next few months a number of Joan's women advisers would do the same.

The doctor thought Joan's clothes were a problem, too. "She likes your tailored classic style," he said, and asked me to help her achieve the same look. I was puzzled by that request. My style—whatever it may have been—was definitely not Joan's. She liked bright colors and bold plaids. But I did tell the doctor I would try to guide her choices for each occasion from the clothes she already had. And since she was reluctant to throw anything away, there were closets to choose from. In the months ahead, we would not have time to shop, so a Boston designer made Joan's new clothes, and he and Joan selected the styles, fabrics, and colors. I continued to wear my old clothes, most of which were beige. In fact, it grew to be a joke between us. "What are you going to wear?" Joan would ask with a laugh before we went anywhere together. "Something beige?"

The list of reporters requesting interviews grew longer with every passing day. Barbara Walters called from California offering five minutes on "World News" and promising "not to hurt Joan." Ellen Spencer from Philadelphia said she would use a "soft approach" to tape five or six minutes on "Joan Kennedy, the Woman" and offered to come to Boston. A local radio show host asked for an hour on air to interview Joan. Barbara Harrison writing for *The New York Times Magazine* said she was delighted the Senator was running and wanted to spend several days with Mrs. Kennedy "to do a profile, not an interview." Glenn Collins of *The New York Times* said his staff was sympathetic, "not out to get anyone." Gary Clifford of *People* called reminding me he had millions of readers. Jessica Savitch from NBC said that hers would not be a news piece, but a "profile piece, very friendly and pleasant." "Good Morning America" wanted Joan to talk with David Hartman about what she would do as First Lady and offered to send a crew to Boston.

It was difficult to turn them all down. In most cases, they were honest, sensitive to Joan's fragility, and willing to promise just about anything to interview a woman who had been cloaked in controversy for years. But one well-known editor took a different tack. After calling several times, she finally threatened, "If you don't arrange an interview with me, you'll regret it. Some of us might get the wrong idea about Mrs. Kennedy."

I knew she was right. If Joan didn't appear publicly soon, people would suspect she was drinking again. But paradoxically, if she appeared before she was mentally and emotionally ready, the public might draw the same conclusion. So we made only one concession to the press during this period. Gary Clifford of *People* offered once again to include Joan among the top twenty-five prominent people of 1980, along with the Pope and President Carter. It was an opportunity Joan could not refuse, and since it did not require talking about her personal problems, she accepted, delighted by the honor. She spoke briefly on the phone from her apartment to a handpicked reporter, sympathetic both to women's issues and her alcoholism.

That, without doubt, was the single most important question in the minds of the press and public. Would Joan stay sober? No matter what else she said or did during the campaign, everything depended on that. And rightly or wrongly, it shaded the opinions and decisions of all of Joan's friends and advisers. I myself felt an enormous responsibility to help her maintain her sobriety. So in addition to holding off persistent reporters, helping prepare her for her press conference and for the campaign, I had the even more important job of being ever watchful for signs of stress and offering Joan the support she needed. The Kennedy power structure was generous in its confidence in me, but that made it all the more imperative that I not fail where Joan's sobriety was concerned.

Although I was closer physically to Joan—just a few floors away—others were just as vigilant as I. I was grateful for the help of Hazel, the friend who had stayed with Joan through the dark days after her move to Boston, and who was always quick to call me when she was worried. Overwork, not making sobriety her top priority, and grandiose or compulsive behavior alerted her to potential danger for Joan.

Just a few days after Ted's announcement I received the first of many warning calls from Hazel, "Joan's going to drink, I can tell. I know the signs—she needs a meeting."

That evening Joan and I cancelled a work session so we could attend an informal gathering of women at Trinity Church in Copley Square. We met the group in the huge book-lined library of the church, and in the dimly lit room that night the focus of the discussion was the importance of sharing our self-assessments with some-one else. One by one each woman in the group reflected on what had happened to her while she was drinking and what harm she had caused herself and others.

Joan listened, although she seemed preoccupied, and when it was her turn to speak, she said how glad she was not to be drinking and how happy she was to be there. As several women leaned forward to catch her whispered words, I could sense they were far more concerned about Joan's sobriety than about who she was. Because I knew Joan as a friend with whom I shared a common problem, and because we both recognized the importance of fellowship and vigilance, it did not occur to me then how extraordinary it was for a potential First Lady to have the humility and courage to attend a meeting like this and speak out in discussion. But unlike the stir her presence often caused elsewhere, in this group of compassionate and understanding women Joan received no special treatment or attention. And that alone made it much easier for her to be there and benefit from their support.

In the months ahead, in response to other warnings from Hazel, or because Joan herself requested it, she attended a variety of programs and workshops for recovering alcoholics, no matter how busy her schedule was. In addition to Women for Sobriety, Alcoholics Anonymous, and other large organizations, there were seminars in hospitals, clinics, and rehabilitation centers, as well as meetings of individual groups formed by friends to choose from. As often as possible we would go together.

Although most of my time was spent getting Joan ready for her press conference, now only three weeks away, other more mundane matters continually intruded. The Boston office called to remind me to get an inspection sticker for her Chevrolet. The car had been in the jurisdiction of that office but now it seemed to be in mine, and I was to receive several calls about it during the next few months, most of them reports that it had been stolen. Rick made frequent calls to discuss the family's plans for Thanksgiving dinner at their Cape home, such as arrival times, menus, and mealtimes. And after decisions were made, he or I called the appropriate people to make arrangements. It struck me as odd at first, and a little sad, that even family holidays were handled by staff, but perhaps that was the way it had always been done.

Joan's doctor also called to urge Joan to get a physical exam. I made an appointment for her at Massachusetts General Hospital. But I was reluctant to see my doctor. Within a day of Ted's announcement I had started smoking again.

Plans were underway for Joan's participation in the campaign, and the Senator's advance team, which preceded him on the campaign trail, made all arrangements, and mustered a welcoming crowd, called no less than every twenty or thirty minutes with ideas for Joan's schedule—how she could help Ted, where she could travel, what she could say. Even though the public's eagerness to see Joan was growing, her schedule was prepared very carefully. While the Senator would travel from San Francisco to Reno to Fargo to Memphis to Des Moines to Orlando to Denver to St. Louis to Cedar Rapids to Concord, New Hampshire, in December Joan was scheduled only to campaign in Florida with Ted and see his mother, to attend two fundraisers, to join the family for Christmas, and then to campaign in Iowa in early January.

As Joan's daily life took on more and more order, mine fell into disarray. The laundry was rarely done and my cupboard looked like Old Mother Hubbard's. No time to shop for food, cook, get gas, or even keep ahead of the meter maid. Despite the demands of my job, I had hoped to keep one time—dinner at six—for my children and me, but inevitably I was on the phone in the kitchen even then. And after dinner I was at my desk or upstairs with Joan, sometimes until midnight. No longer was I available to talk with my kids or hear their daily stories. They could see me and I hoped my visibility was some consolation—but usually on the phone I could only manage a wave when they came home from school and communicated with notes I wrote with my free hand. "Hi! How was your day?" and lots of nods and pantomiming. If they wanted to tell me something or were going out after school, they slipped a note in big print under my nose or onto my desk. Dana studied and made decisions by herself, turned to friends and her music for companionship, and helped as much as she could with the housework.

Brad, on the other hand, was three years younger, highly energetic, and less resourceful. He fought hard to keep his mother his mother. I anguished over the situation and often felt as if I were giving up my most important role to work for Joan. But if I hadn't had this job, I thought, I would have had another—although it might have left me more time for my children.

Joan did not eat regular meals. She never cooked, and ate only when she was hungry—something from a can or the freezer. Sometimes my children carried dinner on a plate in the elevator up to her, but one evening when Joan had no special plans we invited her to join us. It would ensure that she had dinner and also put some focus on the fragmented life my children endured because of Joan's and my crazy existence. They knew Joan as my friend, but now they realized from the news that she was also a celebrity and they were thrilled. Brad, who was ten, offered to go to the Star Market. Dana set the table and made a personalized placecard for each of us. Joan's had TVs, airplanes, a motorcade, and lots of limousines. I poked and stirred boeuf Bourguignonne between phone calls.

At six the children were too excited to do homework so we lit the candles in the dining room and waited. At seven we blew out the candles, but continued the vigil. At eight the three of us finally sat down to eat. Joan arrived about 8:30 apologizing profusely. She graciously admired the namecard Dana had made for her and asked Brad about school. But I knew it was such a disappointment for my children, which was all I was providing these days, that we did not try it again. Instead, every now and then, we continued to take up hot meals for her—without candlelight and silver.

Norma Nathan, or "The Eye," a gossip columnist for the *Boston Herald*, was one of the most adroit reporters who called about Joan. She wanted a scoop, and beginning in an innocent fashion, full of friendliness and fun, she knew just how to wheedle herself into my confidence. Sometimes she began with a question about my health, sometimes with "how sorry she was to bother me." She even lamented how hard it was to have a job like hers. At other times she would ask innocuous questions just to keep me talking, and then topple my guard with surprise snippets of accurate inside information. I soon learned that she was as skillful at digging out a story as the pros from the *National Enquirer*.

One evening Norma was bent on running a story involving Joan and me and she began cheerfully, like a skilled prosecutor, with simple questions: "Are you a friend of Joan's? Do you live in Boston? Then you are neighbors? Do you live on Beacon Street?"

Soon it began to feel like an interview. I scheduled or refused to schedule Joan's interviews, but tried never to give one. While I was searching for a way to extricate myself, Norma asked, "Can I have Joan's campaign schedule?"

I told her it was still being decided.

"Is she going to campaign?"

"Yes," I said, hoping to dispel any notion that Joan was ill or had returned to drinking. To explain her present absence on the campaign trail, I added, "Depending, of course, on her school schedule."

I was taking notes of our conversation with one hand when I realized from the rhythm of a typewriter in the background that Norma was also taking notes. This conversation, regardless of its substance, would have ample documentation.

"Is she going to Lesley full-time?"

"She's spreading the work over more than a year," I said evasively, hoping to make Joan's one-year program, which was taking several years, sound intentional. Joan was proud of going back to school, but she had not always been able to do the required work. During the campaign it would be even more difficult.

"Is her Boston University media course a full year?" Norma asked.

"No, just fall semester," I answered, surprised by the question and wondering naively how "The Eye" knew about the course at all.

Finally, in desperation, I told Norma I had a cold and work to do and couldn't talk any longer. I worked until eleven, went to bed at three and woke up with a cold.

My first call of the morning was "The Eye" again on the family phone. In an endearing motherly manner she began, "How are you? How's your cold?"

I explained it wasn't much better.

Then after a few more questions Norma asked, "Do you live with Joan?"

I suddenly realized that was what she really wanted to know. "I live in the same building," I said, "but in my own apartment."

"I thought you lived with Joan," Norma said. "Does she have anyone living with her?"

"No, she doesn't." Even though the Senator's office had offered to send a bodyguard and chauffeur, someone to take care of her car, carry luggage, fix things, do miscellaneous errands, someone who could have lived in one of Joan's empty back bedrooms, she refused. She wanted privacy and independence.

"I heard two women were living with her."

"No, that's not true," I said, relieved that I had stayed with this conversation long enough to correct that piece of misinformation. If Norma had intended to print it, I hoped it wasn't too late to pull the copy. And then I added, "Please feel free to check out any other rumors with me."

"Thank you, I'd like that," Norma said. And she did. She checked with me often and didn't print anything I labeled untrue. But she unearthed enough in the next few months on Ted, Joan, their friends and lovers, and even on "Zealous Chellis" to keep her readers bewitched with blurbs and barbs.

Thankfully, a few days later, Milton Gwirtzman's wife, Lisa, a former reporter for the *Berkshire Eagle*, was hired as Joan's press aide and a phone was installed in her home office in Newton. I hoped that would silence my phone, but Lisa was a team player and conscientiously ran everything through me. She called to tell me every time someone called her. And the reporters who were accustomed to calling me continued to call. I referred them to Lisa, who then called me to tell me they had called. So both phones kept on ringing day and night.

I was grateful for many things that year—most of all for Thanksgiving itself. All of us needed a few days away from the incessant demands of the campaign. Even though important calls followed me to Manhattan and Locust Valley, my children and I enjoyed being with my family for Thanksgiving dinner and a weekend of walks in the woods with aunts, uncles, and cousins. Joan met Ted and their children at Hyannis Port for a weekend of sailing, walking the beach, and playing charades at night. When she returned she told me that a family of skunks had moved into their garage. "The Secret Service didn't know they were in there," she said with delighted laughter, "but they soon found out." She made no mention of how cordial her reunion with Ted had been—and I didn't ask.

On the Tuesday after Thanksgiving, Eunice Shriver's secretary called to announce that Mrs. Shriver was on her way to spend the night at Joan's apartment. We were working there when she arrived, and Joan received her sister-in-law with a mixture of pleasure and timidity. Eunice was an attractive woman with fine features, a smart simple hairstyle, and the unmistakable Kennedy look. By far the most energetic and forceful of the Kennedy sisters, she was devoted to her brother, her family, and their causes, and it seemed quite apparent to me, and perhaps to Joan, that she was here to make her own personal assessment of Joan's condition and her campaign capabilities. The press conference was uppermost in her mind, and munching saltines because of her ulcers, she talked earnestly to Joan until late that night.

Eunice was uneasy about how Joan would handle the personal questions, and while she was careful not to undermine Joan's self-confidence, she was articulate in her expression of the points Joan should convey. She wanted Joan to emphasize the positive characteristics of her brother, to describe their marriage as supportive, to handle carefully the issue of abortion, and to avoid the subject of alcoholism. She urged Joan to consider ways to handle Chappaquiddick and to speak with examples of substance about her future role as First Lady. Of particular interest to her, however, were Ted's fine qualities and their marriage.

I admired Eunice and I knew she cared about Joan. But I suspected she had always set standards that Joan had found impossible to measure up to. And that night, for Ted's benefit and for the family, she seemed to be encouraging Joan to shade or evade some unpleasant truths. Her advice may have been sound strategy—all part of the political game—but if Joan followed it, I realized that for her this campaign would merely be a continuation of another

game she had been forced to play all her married life—the tug-of-war
between being a Kennedy and being herself.

A day or so after Eunice's visit, I called Rick in Washington.
It was Joan and Ted's anniversary and she had several questions for
the Senator. She wanted to know which day the family would be
opening Christmas presents in Virginia, when they were going to
New Hampshire, when Ted was leaving to work on his proposed debate with Carter in Iowa, and what was the date and time of the
debate. Finally, Joan wanted to know when she could call Ted to
wish him a happy twenty-first anniversary.

Rick efficiently answered all of Joan's questions, including the
phone number she could use to call the Senator that night and another number for the next afternoon between 1:20 and 2:00. I hung
up the phone, still wondering how many other arrangements had
been made between Joan and Ted by impersonal staff members,
how many other anniversaries had been spent apart.

My phone rang again almost immediately. It was Lisa calling,
"A screaming woman with a knife just ran into the Senator's office," she said.

I gasped.

"That's just how you're *not* supposed to react," Lisa said. "Anyway they caught her, but a security guard was nicked. I don't know
who's supposed to call Joan. Stand by in case you have to go up and
answer her phone."

I realized that all this must have happened just after I called
Rick, whose desk was right outside the Senator's office. The phone
rang again. "Sorry to bother you," Norma Nathan began, "but I just
heard on the wire that there's been an assassination attempt on Ted
Kennedy's life."

"I understand that it wasn't that serious," I said with new-
found sophistication.

"Well, has Mrs. Kennedy been told?" Norma demanded.
"Who's going to tell her?"

"I'm sorry, Norma," I said. "We don't know yet." And I hung
up the phone.

The other phone rang. "Rick has already told Joan," Lisa said.

I hurried up to Joan's apartment anyway and found her with a photographer's assistant looking at slides that had been taken of her at the Cape over the Thanksgiving weekend. They were projecting them on the white wall of Ted's blue and white bedroom.

"Rick just called," she said with surprising calm. "I try not to think about the awful possibilities."

I was relieved that she was not more upset. Or perhaps she had learned out of necessity to control her reactions.

Joan invited me to look at the slides, some of which she wanted to use for the campaign. She had been photographed walking barefoot on the beach and she looked lovely—a perfect image to project in the months ahead. It was time to replace old memories with new pictures, and I gladly sat down to help her choose some.

7

CROISSANTS
AND
COMPLIMENTS

INTERVIEW QUESTIONS

TO JOAN:
When did you have your last drink?
How do you feel being number two to politics
in your marriage?
How will the pressure of the campaign affect
you, given your situation?

TO ME:
What did you have for breakfast?
Can Joan be in a picture?
Where did you get your cat?
Can Joan be in a picture?

Throw them all out. They can't find her here with dead plants!"

That was the opinion of the plant lady who had been called in for a consultation on the Sunday morning before Joan's press conference. To emphasize her point, she swung her arms in enormous arcs to include all the big plants standing around the edges of the bright green carpeting like trees bordering a manicured golf course.

"It bothers Ted to see them, too," Joan said, shaking her head.

This was the first time Joan had to think of how her apartment would appear to others, especially reporters with notebooks and cameras. Three years ago when she moved in, she had hired Boston decorator Robert Luddington, who had worked for nearly all the other Kennedy women, to advise her on furnishings and color schemes. They had created an apartment that looked like a show-room with a glass-enclosed fireplace, mirrors, shiny silver wallpaper and several different bright shades of carpeting. In the living room beneath plate glass windows with a dramatic view of the Charles River was an oversized L-shaped black and white plaid sofa, a modern black love seat, and a low glass and chrome coffee table. An oval glass and chrome table and a black baby grand filled the dining room. Both rooms and the long entrance halls were covered with thick Kelly green carpeting. There was little, I thought, that reflected Joan's own femininity, little feeling of family history or heritage. And when she was ill, in and out of treatment centers or confining herself to her darkened bedroom for days at a time, it had been merely a place to be, not really her home.

But as her recovery progressed, Joan had added warmth with plants, and personal touches with family mementos and pictures from her Virginia home. There were photographs of the Kennedys, pictures of the children, a drawing by Patrick, and large framed portraits of Joan on the piano and on the walls. A delightful picture of Ted showed him on his boat with his children, nieces, and nephews, all laughing as the gunwales sank to water level. Still, she seldom entertained here, and fastidious herself, she insisted that Kitty keep the apartment in perfect order.

The plant lady exaggerated. All the plants were not dead, but Joan wanted most of them discarded, and new ones added. After the plant lady left, promising to return with replacements, Joan and I sat down at her dining room table to focus once again on the more important concerns of the upcoming press conference.

During the next several days, Joan's study of the Q and A sheets provided by Kennedy staffers and other advisers would be intense. Dressed in a nightgown or bathrobe, she often sat up in bed to go over them again and again, a white mug of coffee or a soft drink on the beige wicker cupboard next to her, notebooks and papers spread out on the beige satin quilt. Sometimes she sat on the edge of her bed with white United States Senate memorandum pads and yellow lined legal pads on her lap and wrote out her own questions and answers, making notes of points she wanted to emphasize, particularly about drinking—which no one in Washington could prepare as well as she could.

Then we would meet, and as she read from her notes and discussed her feelings, I was glad that Joan had come to consider her alcoholism "an asset, not a liability," and that she believed she was "so much stronger for having suffered and come through it." She saw things differently now after enduring that kind of physical and mental pain, and she wanted to talk about what she had gained from feeling "guilt, humiliation, the ache of being honest, the hard work of recovery, and the absolute miracle of having survived." She also wanted to remember "to be positive, not defensive," and "to keep it short—keep it factual."

As this reviewing process continued, Joan became quieter and more introspective, aware of just how important her first press conference would be. But she never stopped moving forward, and as a sign of her growing self-confidence, she did not always accept what others prepared for her. She drew circles and stars around the answers she liked, but for those she did not like, she wrote "need another answer." I sometimes thought it rather sad that she was forced to spend so much time and effort on questions such as: "Do you still love your husband?" "Looking back, do you think you made the right choice of a husband?" "Did you ever consider divorcing your husband?" "Do you think your husband is a 'philanderer?' " "Do you believe the stories you read about his relations with other women?" "Do you think his reputation as a philanderer should be publicly discussed during his campaign?" "Have you and Ted ever discussed his relationships with other women?" "How did Ted break the news to you about the death of Mary Jo Kopechne?" "What were your own feelings about Chappaquiddick?" "Is your husband continuing to have affairs?" "Do you have 'an arrangement' in your marriage?" "Have you ever had any extramarital affairs?"

Joan herself realized, of course, that the wives of other candidates were able to study answers to quite different questions. But we had promised ourselves that she would never appear in public, whatever the campaign event, without complete preparation. And Joan had promised herself, contrary to her sister-in-law Eunice's advice, that she would deal directly with every personal question so that alcoholism and living apart from Ted would not become her Chappaquiddick.

Joan came down to my apartment that Sunday evening to discuss what she should wear for the news conference. She wondered what I thought about a white wool dress, pearl earrings, and the string of pearls Ted had just sent her for their anniversary. I suggested that a casual outfit would be more appropriate, and we agreed on a gray wool herringbone blazer and gray pants with her hair pulled back simply. She wanted to wear a black sweater and I offered mine.

The plant lady reappeared the next morning as scheduled, and I escorted her up in an elevator full of huge plants wrapped in brown paper, which were unveiled, arranged, and rearranged in Joan's apartment. I was pressed into service, watering and misting and trimming dead leaves off the plants already there that would be allowed to remain, and the final effect, I thought, was somewhat overabundant. As did the plant lady. After proclaiming that there were now far too many plants, she left us to deal with the rest of the conference stage ourselves.

Joan looked pale and drawn that morning. Dressed in her blue bathrobe, she sat down at the dining room table with a steaming cup of coffee and I joined her. The tough personal assessments of the past few days seemed to have sent her into a downward spiral, and I knew she was also troubled about Sally, our tireless and energetic scheduler, who hadn't long to live. Sally was driving Joan as hard as she drove herself, urging her to travel and make campaign appearances before Joan felt she was ready. She could not refuse Sally and agreed to all of her plans. But then she would call me, her doctor, or Ted's staff to extricate herself from her promises.

"Ted Kennedy forgets how exhausting it is," she said, molding her hands around her coffee cup for warmth, "because he's been in politics since he was an infant. It's so tiring to always have to be alert and say something. If I get too strung out, I can't do it." If she and Ted had been closer, I thought, they could have planned her emergence into the public eye with the intimate support a husband

and wife can give each other. Joan had the help of his competent
staff and of friends, but it was not quite the same.

When Gail arrived at my apartment on Tuesday morning, we
immediately went upstairs to borrow a blue and white Royal Copen-
hagen tea set offered to us by a neighbor for the press conference.
We appeared at Joan's apartment cradling a tea pot, coffee pot,
plates, cups, and saucers in our arms. Kitty opened the door and
looked wide-eyed at us, balancing this beautiful china. "I wouldn't
touch that!" she exclaimed, and I laughed to think that Kitty drew
the line at china when she had done almost everything else for Joan
over the last few years.

Gail and I put the tea set down carefully on the dining room
table, and I asked her what she thought of the apartment.

"It's transformed!" she said, touching the leaves of one of the
new plants. And it was. The plants, the rearranged furniture, a new
selection of books, the lovely china—everything was ready. But was
Joan? It was a question that would be answered that afternoon
when our panel of advisers arrived for a full-scale dress rehearsal.

Just before three I went back to Joan's apartment to let them
in. That day, author and longtime Kennedy supporter Doris Kearns,
joined Milton and Lisa, and all were cheerful and optimistic as we
set up a row of straight-backed chairs to face the sofa. Joan came out
of her bedroom, quietly greeted her friends, and then tucked herself
into the corner of the sofa where she would sit for the news conference. Her reserve made me wonder if she was up to this practice
session. We sat down stiffly in chairs across from her, looking rather
stern. In fact, we were probably a far more ferocious group than the
press would ever be.

I began the rehearsal with the one question we all expected
would be asked. Clearing my throat first, and with no twinkle in my
eye, I said gruffly, "Mrs. Kennedy, when did you have your last
drink?"

Joan answered in a whisper. "In the treatment program what's
important is not the past days, but today and future days."

Although it was a rather vague reply, I understood Joan's hesitation to be more explicit. Her preference was to put the emphasis

on each day as a new beginning, but I wondered how reporters unfamiliar with alcoholism would respond to that.

When asked what sort of things she would do as First Lady, Joan again answered without much conviction, saying she would like to teach music to children and music appreciation to their parents. A hostile reporter would be critical.

Then Milton asked, "Mrs. Kennedy, when or how did you get alcoholism? Did pressure cause it?"

Joan hesitated, lowering her head, her back sinking into the sofa. "It isn't contagious. Ted Kennedy or politics couldn't have given me this disease."

I knew what she meant: that alcoholism is an inherited disease. The real issue is not how or why the problem develops; it is doing something about it. But to many listeners her reply might have sounded sadly defensive. In spite of hours of preparation, was she really ready to answer questions about her alcoholism?

After only a dozen questions we stopped because Joan seemed tired and not nearly as effective as we had hoped she would be. Silently wondering if she needed more time, more preparation, or more encouragement, the group praised Joan for her efforts, but whispered to me as they were leaving that the press conference might have to be postponed.

That evening, just before Joan and I were to leave for a fundraiser in Cambridge, Hazel called me again to say she was worried about Joan. "She's skipping meetings because of all these other activities," she said. "But she won't be able to do any of them if she isn't sober."

I agreed and promised Hazel that we would try to go to a meeting after the fund-raiser. Hazel's concern, on top of Joan's performance that afternoon, left little doubt in my mind that Joan was not yet ready to face the press.

The fund-raiser, held in the beautiful home of Boston architect Graham Gund, was for a cultural rather than a political cause: to keep Gilbert Stuart's portraits of the Washingtons, now at the Museum of Fine Arts in Boston, from being moved to Washington, D.C. An elegantly dressed crowd circulated through the exquisitely

decorated federal rooms admiring Gund's collection of contemporary paintings and sculpture. Against a background of muted sounds
from a brass quintet, conversation was lively, but Joan seemed very
subdued.

Finally, leaving behind the prominent guests and talk of the
arts, the maids and bartenders and clinking glasses, Joan and I took
a taxi to a church on Marlborough Street in Boston, where we
picked our way down narrow steps into a dark smoky basement. The
contrast between where we had just been and this dingy room was
dramatic. Metal and wooden folding chairs faced a stark podium.
But the blue and gold banners that adorned the walls—"One Day at
a Time," "First Things First"—reminded both Joan and me of what
really mattered. And as we waited for the meeting to begin, I
thought how appropriate it was that Joan should be here. For it
was precisely in a simple setting like this, among people like those
gathered around us now, that she might find the strength to meet
the ordeals that lay ahead.

The next morning Lisa and I met to decide whether or not to
hold the press conference. We were reminded of the Senator's interview with Roger Mudd by a critical reference to it in the papers
that morning. Richard Cohen, in the *Washington Post*, told about
campaigning with Kennedy, describing him as "no happy warrior,"
and noting that his speeches were cold and lifeless. Cohen wrote,
"It is hard to battle a President who has become, thanks to Iran, a
sudden Commander-in-Chief. But there is something else going
on—something. You could see whatever it is in that Roger Mudd
interview on CBS. This inability to answer the question, this awful
fumbling on Chappaquiddick, this inability to say why he was running, and this feeling you have that he is holding back, talking
about himself in the third person, somehow not letting you in."
We did not want to risk Joan's giving a performance reminiscent of
Ted's.

Another consideration was the possibility of uninvited and unfriendly reporters arriving for the press conference. Frank O'Connor, who had frequently offered to do anything for us, agreed to
stand guard at the entrance to our building. Everything proceeded

as if we were going ahead as planned, but we still had not made the decision to hold the conference.

Before Lisa and I talked again, I went upstairs to make sure Joan's tape recorder was in working order for the next day and to take her my black cowl-necked sweater. Kitty said Joan was in the bathtub. In Joan's modern bathroom, a dramatic blend of black and beige, dressing-room lights surrounded a wall mirror reflecting soft shadows. Beside the black marble sink, black glass tiered shelves held rows of lipsticks, bottles of all sizes and shapes, and containers of eye shadow, rouge, and brushes. Baskets of hair curlers, bottles of bubble bath, shower caps, and electric roller sets filled the shelves behind the tub.

"Hello," Joan called as I walked past the open bathroom door into her bedroom to leave the sweater and look over her clothes for the next day. I replied in a deep mock-male voice, "Mrs. Kennedy, when did you have your last drink?" She laughed delightedly and seemed in wonderful spirits, completely unaware of a possible postponement. I returned to my office, feeling much more positive about going forward.

When Lisa called again, we once more weighed the risks and benefits. In the two preceding days Kennedy had opposed the granting of permanent asylum to the deposed Shah. He had also suggested that after the American hostages were released there should be a forum for Iran to air its grievances against its former ruler. "Support for the hostages does not mean support for the Shah," he had stated. Since the Senator was receiving a barrage of criticism for these statements from both the press and other candidates, it seemed even more imperative that Joan perform well and get positive press for the campaign. We decided to hold her first press conference, as scheduled, the next morning.

Gail and I arrived at Joan's apartment at about ten o'clock to set everything up for the conference, which was due to begin at eleven. When we walked in carrying croissants, white narcissi for the tables, and four of my kitchen chairs, we were dismayed to see Joan in the hallway, still in her bathrobe, her hair undone, and a frantic look in her eyes. Behind her stood a harried building superintendent holding a wrench. As Gail and I made coffee, arranged croissants and flowers, and set up the chairs for reporters, Joan dressed and told us what had happened.

A pipe under the kitchen sink had burst at four in the morning, and water had soaked the kitchen carpeting, seeping into the dining room, on into the living room, and finally pouring down into the living room on the floor below. The sounds had wakened the family who lived there, the superintendent had been routed from his sleep and sent to Joan's apartment to stop the leak. They had all been up since early morning.

We had prepared Joan, I thought ruefully, for almost every eventuality—except a flood. But she took it in stride, and when she emerged from her bedroom, she had dressed, done her makeup and hair, and acted as if a plumbing disaster was an everyday occurrence in her life.

Just as Gail left to return to my office, Lisa arrived, and Joan asked us to stay but to keep out of sight so she would appear independent to reporters. She used the Senator's term, "T.M.B.S." (too many blue suits), to explain. Lisa and I went into the flooded kitchen with the enthusiasm of dogs going to the vet, and Joan closed the mirrored pass-through shutters and swinging door behind us.

Trying to keep our feet dry, Lisa and I spaced piles of newspapers across the soaked kitchen carpeting, but every step we took made an audible as well as a visible squish around our already wet shoes and stockings. Our laughter brought Joan out to the kitchen once more. Smiling and shaking her head, she closed us in again as the doorbell rang.

Joan opened the door herself, and in a charming and relaxed fashion, told the reporters about last night's flood. She offered them coffee and croissants, but I could hear them decline refreshments— they wanted only the coveted conversation with Joan. They sat down in the living room, facing Joan on the sofa, and immediately began to ask questions.

Even standing right behind the kitchen door, Lisa and I could barely hear. The squish of the wet newspapers under our feet, the drone of traffic from Storrow Drive, and a piano concerto from

Joan's stereo nearly drowned out the voices. I pressed my ear against the swinging door and it sounded as if Joan was talking about . . . skunks. Lisa moved closer until we were stuck together like spoons. I listened and Lisa took notes with pencil and paper on the back of the kitchen door. Images flashed through my mind of us tumbling into the dining room like the Marx Brothers. Not surprisingly we had missed the first questions. Then we heard, "When did you have your last drink?" "How do you feel being number two to politics in your marriage?" "How will the pressure of the campaign affect you, given your situation?" "What will your role in the campaign be?" In all, thirty-one questions.

When I could hear Joan's soft answers, she sounded cheerful, strong when she had to be, and amusing. We, on the other hand, felt none of those things, just wet and worried as we watched the minute hand on Lisa's watch creep around to 11:50, the scheduled time for pictures. Materializing from the kitchen and ignoring her dripping shoes, Lisa went to the front door to let in the waiting photographers. Then Joan sat down at the piano, and played a few bars of "Smoke Gets in Your Eyes" while the photographers clicked and flashed their cameras. Exactly at noon I appeared from the kitchen to let in one of Joan's friends, who had been asked to appear to signal the next "appointment" and the end of the press conference. The reporters, to their credit and our immense relief, left promptly.

Even though I hadn't heard everything Joan said, I gave her a big hug and told her she had been terrific. She danced around the living room, pleased that it had apparently gone so well. I hoped she was right. But I was in no mood for dancing. My feet were so wet I returned immediately to my apartment for dry shoes. Predictably every phone was ringing. "How'd it go?" Ed asked. "What's the lead story going to be?"

Joan's doctor was on the other line. "Was it timed? Was my name mentioned or the name of the treatment center?"

Next, Rick called from Ted's office. "How was it? What happened?" Then on to, "How many of the Senator's books does Joan want for Christmas and when will she be arriving in Palm Beach?"

A *Newsweek* correspondent was next: "Are you Joan Kennedy's assistant? I heard you've done work in children's television.

Aren't your interests very, very similar to Mrs. Kennedy's? What do you do? Is it a paid position?"

I wondered why she had asked about me and not Joan. That made me uncomfortable but not as uncomfortable as the next call. Joe Gargan, a Kennedy mainstay, angrily announced, "The editor of *Time* is having a shit fit. Why didn't you let their editors know about the press conference? Here's their number so you can let them know next time!"

And then Hazel called. "How's Joan and how are you?"

I told her I thought the conference had gone very well. We had the questions and the tape, but not the reporters' reactions and impressions. Just like a Broadway opening, there was nothing to do but wait for the morning papers to find out how Joan had done.

Now that Joan's press conference was behind us, whatever the outcome, I had to face the prospect of encountering yet another reporter—this time to answer questions about myself. When I was outside Faneuil Hall after Ted's announcement a month before, an attractive woman with bright red lipstick had approached me, introduced herself as Vera Vida, the feature and fashions editor for the *Patriot Ledger* in Quincy, and requested an interview with Joan. She had called me regularly ever since, and when she finally realized that a private interview with Joan would be impossible, she lowered her sights and asked if she could talk to me.

"To me?" I asked. "No, I couldn't do that."

"This wouldn't be about Joan," she said persuasively. "I want a story on you. You used to live on the South Shore and we're a South Shore paper. I promise not to ask you one question about Joan."

She was so insistent that I checked with Joan and Lisa and it was agreed that I would talk to Vera right after Joan's press conference. As the time grew near, I made out some Q and A's for myself, certain the one thing she would ask was why I was working for Joan instead of continuing my own career in arts and children's television. Friendship would of course be included in my answer, but I also wanted to say that I believed Joan's example could make a difference to thousands of women. It then occurred to me that Vera might ask why I felt so strongly about help for women alcoholics, and I tried to decide whether I was ready to be as open about my own alcoholism as Joan was. I didn't know the answer then (and the subject never came up), but it made me even more aware of Joan's courage in speaking out.

Fashionable, and as blond as Joan, Vera came to my apartment as scheduled with a photographer in tow. Sitting on the sofa while I sat across from her on the loveseat, she lavished praise on me, asked what I had for breakfast, where I got my cat, and if Joan could be in a picture. When I explained that she had a full schedule of appointments, Vera cheerfully continued to ask questions far less probing than any that had been asked of Joan: what was my typical day like, what kind of arrangements did I make for Joan, what did I think of the Senator? Then she asked my children who were sitting quietly nearby, "Do you want to live in the White House?" In tandem, they answered, "No."

After thirty minutes Vera called in her photographer, and as he was setting up pictures at my grand piano in the dining room, always of someone holding the cat, the doorbell rang. Seven women from a musical fraternity had arrived to present Joan an award for "Distinguished Woman of the Year." I excused myself, left Vera and the photographer, and took the women upstairs.

When Kitty opened the door, Joan, caught by surprise, dashed into the bathroom to get ready to have the presentation photographed, and I waited outside in the hall with the ladies until they were invited in. Then I returned to my apartment to finish the session with Vera, who once more, with a reporter's persistence, asked for a picture with Joan.

The doorbell rang. Joan's next appointment: two Cambridge women had arrived for a "think session"—Joan's term for brainstorming ideas and strategy. Leaving Vera again, I took them up to Joan's apartment, already quite full of guests.

Lisa answered the door and after I introduced the women, I mentioned Vera's request for Joan to be in a picture. It seemed exactly the wrong moment to me, but Joan overheard from the living room and said she would. Impulsively abandoning her other guests, she rushed past Lisa out the door and into the hall.

"Oh, my God," she whispered. "There's someone in there

who's a recovering alcoholic. I used to see her on Tuesday nights. Isn't it terrific? There are so many of us!" she said, clapping her hands and stepping into the elevator.

When we both walked into my apartment, a surprised Vera leaped to her feet and extended her hand to Joan. "I'll only ask you one question," she said. "What do you think of Marcia?"

Joan put her arm around my shoulder, pulled me toward her and said, "I love her. She's my right arm."

Breaking her promise, Vera continued to ask Joan questions while the photographer took pictures.

Then Joan returned to her guests, and when Vera left a few minutes later, I realized, with bemused admiration, that she got what she came for: an exclusive interview, including pictures, with Joan.

By that afternoon, the reviews had already started to come in, and for the next few days nearly every paper in the country ran a feature or a news story on Joan. Headlines such as "Joan Meets the Press and the Pressures," "The New Joan Kennedy—Poised and Articulate," "Joan Strides out of Her Dark Age," indicated that the press conference had been a success. Most articles spoke of her poise and openness, her quiet manner punctuated with genuine and easy laughter, and her promising future as an asset to Ted Kennedy's campaign. There were comments about her lack of a wedding ring, but everyone seemed convinced that her marriage was in a new and mutually supportive stage.

Joan had triumphed. She had succeeded in answering the tough personal questions and sending the message that she was getting well. From the news coverage of the press conference and the sympathetic letters that began to pour in, we knew that people were listening. And we welcomed their applause.

My interview with Vera appeared a few days later as a news story on the first page of the *Patriot Ledger*. Since there was a picture including Joan to accompany the piece, my work made headlines. I was pleased by what Vera wrote about me. And she was especially complimentary about my cat.

8

JANUARY IN IOWA

I need a man in my life . . . Ted asks, "Are you having fun, lunch with the girls?" If he only knew.

—JOAN

Just before leaving on her trip with Ted to Florida, Joan wanted to shop for matching luggage for the family to use during the campaign, and because the luggage would be her Christmas gift to Ted and the children, she wanted it delivered to their Virginia home in time for Christmas dinner and present-opening, December 22. When I knocked on her door at eleven on Saturday morning for the shopping trip to Jordan Marsh, Joan didn't answer. When I let myself in, the apartment was dark and the door to her bedroom was closed. I made coffee and took a cup into her bedroom, and as soon as she got up, she insisted I follow her into the bathroom.

"Look at that!" she said, standing on the scales and pointing down to the numbers swaying between her feet. "Can you believe it? All I do is eat. Last night after midnight I had three bowls of cereal, each with half an inch of sugar, and six pieces of toast. I have to go on a diet." Unspoken was her knowledge that her response to stress often was to overeat.

The campaign was never very far from our minds and while Joan dressed, she began talking about what she would do in the White House as First Lady, a subject we knew would always come up. She said she could teach music, but I hoped she would also do more. In addition to teaching, I suggested she use her position to focus attention on all the arts, especially for children. We discussed putting together a team of arts education advisers to provide ideas and write articles for national publication under her name. "Ted never writes his own articles—all the sophisticated people know that," she called out from the bathroom where she was doing her hair. "And it would be much easier than doing interviews!"

We settled into a cab a few minutes later and I read her an editorial from the *Boston Globe* titled "The Greening of Joan Kennedy," which commented favorably on her and speculated about what the campaign might do for her personally. We compared the friendly coverage she was getting to Ted's press, which had become painfully negative because of the criticisms he had leveled at Carter for the way he was handling the hostage crisis in Iran. That, according to Democrats and Republicans alike, was not a legitimate campaign issue.

When our conversation changed to men, I put my finger to my lips. I sometimes felt mother-henish when Joan and I rode in taxis because she often talked about intimate matters within earshot of the drivers. I could imagine the dispatcher calling for a cab for Joan Kennedy, and drivers all over Boston screeching around corners racing toward Beacon Street for the chance to listen in on the next installment of her life. During today's ride Joan talked of planning a secret trip to the Midwest to see her friend Gordon, who had recently left Boston banking for a corporate consulting job in Ohio. He had been an occasional visitor to Joan's apartment, usually bringing a bag of groceries and cooking dinner for her. Low key, undemanding, and kind, he had offered her companionship and warmth at a time when her relationship with Ted had been the most distant.

"Gordon's so good for me," Joan said. "I need a man in my life and I don't just mean 'safe' men." A "safe" man, in Joan's terminology, meant that he was a friend, not a lover. "Safe men are OK; they're good for talking and that's fine. But I need more than that," she continued. "Ted Kennedy is being nice but he doesn't even talk to me. He calls and says you've got to come or I'll lose the election, but when I get there, he doesn't notice me or say I look nice, or thank me, or ask my opinion on anything."

I understood, but when Joan said she wanted to meet more men, I said I thought that might be difficult, and even a little risky, during the campaign. She nodded, but said her friends would help.

Joan had several friends in Boston, New York, and Washington who supported her without reservation, offered unconditional love, and would willingly do anything for her, including introducing her to interesting and available men. I often thought about the qualities in her that inspired such devotion. Perhaps it was her apparent helplessness or the innocence that enabled her to talk about her most intimate thoughts. She shared nearly everything about herself. Often she phoned friends late at night because she was lonely or couldn't sleep, and each of us got up and good-naturedly turned on the light to listen because we felt special and needed. We all treasured her candor, but I for one thought she should draw the line at taxi drivers.

As we sped up Beacon Street, past the Boston Common, already decorated with Christmas lights, and rumbled down the hill toward the financial district, Joan continued talking about men. My finger flew to my lips again, but Joan laughed at my caution, nudging me with her elbow. "Ted asks, 'Are you having fun? Lunch with the girls?' If he only knew." When we finally stepped out of the cab the driver smiled and said, "It's been a pleasure." I was sure it had been.

Joan's presence caused the customary stir in Jordan's first-floor luggage department. Looking over every kind of luggage on display, we carried pieces up and down the aisles, compared prices, colors, and weights, and asked questions of a befuddled young salesman. Joan finally chose tan canvas luggage with brown vinyl trim. But Jordan's didn't have all the suitcases she wanted in stock, so we left an order for ten twenty-six-inch Pullmans, two carry-ons, five roll-totes, and an additional tote for Joan. Everything was charged to the Senator's account.

On our way out of the store Joan stopped at a hat tree and donned a cowboy hat, fluffing her hair under the stiff brim. Twirling in front of a mirror she said, "Wouldn't *Women's Wear Daily* love this?" Her behavior in public, I thought, was sometimes as delightfully uninhibited as her conversation with friends. But later, seated across from each other in Dini's Seafood Restaurant, she grew more serious as she talked about her friend Sally.

"I think I know a small part of what she's feeling," Joan said in low tones. "It's like drinking. When I was sick I didn't know it and I couldn't accept it."

"Do you mean you knew it but couldn't really accept it?" I asked. It was something we both understood.

"Yes," Joan said. "Like Sally about dying. I don't know how to be her friend. She doesn't talk about herself, and so we all ignore what's happening to her because it seems she wants us to."

Just then our waitress came over. Plump, middle-aged, she glanced at Joan several times, and when she was sure it was Joan, she leaned down and whispered, "I love you, you're beautiful. You'll be the best First Lady ever. Even better than Jackie." Then she straightened up, once more a waitress, handed us menus and said she would return.

Her words seemed to echo our own deep feelings for Sally. Joan and I looked at each other as tears came to our eyes and for a few moments neither of us could talk.

A day or so later, Jordan Marsh informed me that they would be unable to get all eighteen pieces of luggage by Christmas. I called Joan, hoping she would consider another kind, but she preferred what she had chosen. So the rest was up to me. Assuming that nothing was impossible if you worked for the Kennedys, I never questioned whether I could do something, only how. First I called Gertrude Ball in the Kennedy family office on Park Avenue in New York. She wrote down the list of luggage sizes and agreed to make some calls. An hour later she reported her lack of success, but said to call Kathy at the Kennedy-owned Merchandise Mart in Chicago. Gertrude had been told that Joan had an appointment at the Mart that day and suggested that she pick out another kind of luggage while she was there. I explained that Mrs. Kennedy was en route to Florida, not Chicago.

Kathy called a few minutes later with the same information. Again, I explained that Mrs. Kennedy was not going to be in Chicago and wanted the luggage she originally selected. The next call was also from the Mart. "Marcia, this is Sylvia Gold. We're going bananas here. What do you mean Mrs. Kennedy's not keeping her appointment? I'm having a heart attack. My buyer is coming in on her day off to help her pick out a fur." In the middle of my explanations, the other phone rang. It was Marv Leibman in luggage from the Mart. "Look, that luggage is all wrong for her. It was made overseas and the handles will fall off."

Returning to Sylvia I told her the appointment must be with another Mrs. Kennedy. Then I spoke into the other phone and pleaded with Mr. Leibman to get the luggage anyway. "I don't carry it," he said. "There's another new line, not even in the catalogue yet, black with a snappy green and red stripe."

So much for the "well-oiled Kennedy machine," I thought, as I opened the Boston Yellow Pages to "Luggage" and started to dial. By 6:30 that night I had arranged for all eighteen pieces to arrive in McLean from various parts of the country in time for Christmas.

Joan's trip to Florida with Ted was her first foray onto the campaign trail. But the pace of the campaign was beginning to accelerate, shattering the normal peace and quiet of Beacon Street and our building. The night of her return from Florida, Joan was scheduled to appear with Ted at a fund-raiser at the Copley Plaza, and although the Senator was not due until later in the day, all signs indicated his arrival would be imminent. Secret Service agents began to appear in various parts of the building—on Joan's floor, on the first floor, in the back halls—and a truck was towing cars away from in front of the building to make room for the motorcade.

During the campaign, our neighbors would often be inconvenienced by having their cars towed and by the Secret Service agents who prowled the building. For the most part, they seemed to take it all with good grace. But that morning, at 5:15, the President of the Board of Managers, Elizabeth Hunter, had been roused from sleep by a call from Mrs. Parker, the oldest resident in the building, who had looked out her windows and noticed Secret Service agents on the rooftops of the buildings across the street. She was worried because her window washers were due that morning at nine, and she wondered if they would be mistaken for assassins and shot. Mrs. Hunter got up and went downstairs in her bathrobe to consult with the agents on duty. Explaining the window-washing situation, she asked when the Senator would arrive and when he would depart. The agents, of course, were not at liberty to reveal the details of his schedule for security reasons. Thus, a dilemma was posed, and to be on the safe side, Mrs. Parker had to forgo clean windows until a time when the Senator was nowhere near the building.

Later in the day I spoke to the same agents when they asked me to come to the first floor to check the identity of two tailors sent over from Louis to fit new suits for the Senator. Not knowing what else to do, I brought the tailors up to my apartment and settled them in the hallway on red metal folding chairs from my kitchen, and there they sat for over an hour waiting for their summons. Meanwhile, I went up and down between floors with Joan's clothes for that night, folders of schedules, last-minute arrangements for her unexpected trip to New York the next day, and finally, after the Senator arrived, the tailors. On my next visit to Joan's apartment to repack her suitcases, the tailors had finished their fitting and the Senator was still walking around the living room in boxer shorts.

He left as abruptly as he had arrived, and at midnight that night, after the fund-raiser, with Ted and his staff already en route to the West Coast, Joan and I returned to her apartment. Sliding into chairs around her kitchen table, we talked and Joan decided to cancel her trip to New York the next day for a fund-raiser with Jackie. "I felt tired midway through the receiving line tonight," she said. "I don't want pictures taken of my eyes drooping or the press will suspect the worst." But there was another reason. "I've been the queen the last couple of days," she said, admitting candidly that she was afraid Jackie would upstage her. Again I saw Joan's lack of self-confidence and her reluctance to invite comparisons, and I tried to reassure her. But she had made up her mind. She would go to Washington for the weekend to see Patrick.

Soon after Joan's return to Boston and before she left again for the Christmas holidays in Palm Beach and McLean, she asked me to hostess and order sandwiches for a meeting of Ted's Harvard advisers to be held in her apartment. At dusk on the night of the meeting, I went up to her apartment to turn on the lights and was surprised to find they were already on. A purse and a camera had been put down in the front hall, and a woman's luggage sat in the doorway to Joan's bedroom. Rock music from the stereo, instead of Joan's usual classical music, filled the apartment and a light shone under the closed bathroom door.

"Hello?" I called tentatively to whomever might be in the bathroom and introduced myself. "Is there anything you need?"

"Hello," a woman's voice called back, and then she said who she was. Although we had never met, I recognized her name from conversations I had had with campaign staff.

"I came up to turn on the lights and I'll come back to say hi to Rick," I said to the closed door. Then I found some paper on Joan's dining room desk, left a note with my phone numbers and an offer to order dinner for the meeting, and went back down to my own apartment. Slightly shaken and thinking of Joan, I dressed for a cocktail party a few blocks away. And on my way out, I left my host's phone number with agents on the first floor, asking them to notify me when the Senator's motorcade arrived. Half an hour later they called. "The Senator's in."

Walking briskly home along Beacon Street on a chilly but clear night, I could see a lone figure standing on the sidewalk outside our building. Rick was waiting for me and greeted me warmly. "Hi, I got your note," he said.

"What shall I order for dinner?" I asked, glad to see him.

"Gee, he doesn't need anything. He's gone to bed and is going to sleep late in the morning."

"You don't want sandwiches for the meeting?"

"No, it was cancelled and all the aides have left," Rick said, hunching his shoulders against the cold. "So we're all set and don't need a thing."

We said good night and I unlocked the big front door to the building as he went off in the direction of Copley Square.

Opening my apartment door, I could hear a phone ringing in my office. I rushed in and picked it up.

"Hi," said a low, well-modulated voice. "This is Ted Kennedy. I got your note and thanks very much, but we, uh, don't need anything here. I appreciate your offer to help—we'll just have some meetings and so we're all set here."

"All right," I said.

"And thank you for what you're doing for Joan, Marcia. Please feel free to call me anytime. If there's a problem, Rick or his assistant Connie can always get hold of me and I'll call you. I depend on you to keep things going well and you are. I appreciate your help. You've got a good sense of things."

He was right, although I wished at that moment that I didn't. As I hung up the phone, I wondered how many other Kennedy staffers accepted his praise in return for their silence. And how many others were a party to these arrangements. I knew I couldn't tell Joan, not out of loyalty to Ted, but because I wanted to spare her feelings.

Ironically, just a week earlier after the Boston fund-raiser, Joan and I had talked about her relationship with Ted. Sitting at her kitchen table, she had worried about misleading the press. "All those pictures of Ted and me in a haystack and I'm smiling up at him so adoringly," she said. "I don't feel that way at all. And Myra MacPherson, the best woman reporter from the Washington Post, saying my new radiance is really showing through—that's starting to bother me."

It bothered me, too, for it seemed that Joan was caught in a completely untenable situation. She was realistic enough to know that things were not going well between her and Ted, and it made her feel uncomfortable to pretend otherwise. Yet she genuinely wanted the campaign to be a success, hoping that might make a reconciliation possible. She had been trapped, it appeared, into deceiving the press and public, and perhaps even herself. And that kind of dishonesty, and the inner conflict it caused, could endanger her sobriety.

But for one segment of the press, at least, it was Ted's behavior, not Joan's, that was the point at issue. In an article published in the Washington Monthly in December and titled "Kennedy's Woman Problem: Women's Kennedy Problem," Suzannah Lessard wrote:

> The type of womanizing that Kennedy is associated with is a series of short involvements—if they can be called that—after which he drops the lady. Sometimes he hasn't even met the woman previously. She has been picked out by one of his cohorts as the type of woman who appeals to him, and asked if

she would like to have a "date" with the senator. . . . The
picture does not exclude longer relationships, but the short-term
pattern evidently is a deep part of Kennedy's nature, as well as
an image that Kennedy seems in some way to enjoy. . . .

But if a man of middle age acts in this way, and over a
long period of time, over decades, then the behavior becomes
quite unsettling. What it suggests is a case of arrested development, a kind of narcissistic intemperance, a huge, babyish ego
that must constantly be fed. . . . Certainly it suggests an old-
fashioned, male-chauvinist, exploitive view of women as primarily objects of pleasure. . . .

It was this aspect of his behavior, the author argued, that led many
women to suspect that Kennedy's interest in women's issues was no
more than political expediency and to doubt his ability to be President.

To the surprise of neither Kennedy nor Carter campaign strategists, the so-called "character issue" was beginning to emerge. And
that, in addition to the forceful, if futile, measures Carter initiated
to resolve the hostage crisis in Iran, sent Kennedy plummeting in
the polls. It seemed all the more important now that Joan begin to
campaign in earnest for and with Ted. Plans were already well underway for a debate between Kennedy and Carter on January 7 in
Iowa, prior to their first political contest—the Iowa caucus—but at
the end of December, the Russians invaded Afghanistan and Carter
cancelled the debate, claiming he could not leave Washington merely
for political reasons. It was the opening round of his "Rose Garden"
strategy that would permit him to remain aloof and almost indiffer-
ent to Kennedy's challenge for the nomination. Nevertheless, Kennedy campaign forces in Washington continued preparations for a
full-scale, Kennedy-style assault on Iowa—with Joan conscripted for
duty on the front line.

Meanwhile, Joan had spent a few days before Christmas with
Ted and their children in Palm Beach visiting her mother-in-law.
She and Rose, "Gramma" as Joan called her, had, I knew, a polite
but somewhat distant relationship. When they talked on the phone
or had dinner together, it was usually during the summer months
when they were both on the Cape. I can only imagine what was

going through Rose's mind as her last surviving son embarked on his quest for the presidency; I do not know what she thought of Joan's alcoholism, her marital troubles with Ted, or of Joan herself. But Joan held her in awe and was always eager to please her. They went to early mass together in Palm Beach, and I thought that if Joan were not intimidated by her mother-in-law's legendary strength of character, or did not feel, as she had in the past, that she suffered by comparison, she could do no better than follow Rose's example in the months ahead.

I spent Christmas in Boston with my children. Joan celebrated the holidays, complete with eighteen pieces of matched luggage, with her family in McLean. Then she returned to Boston briefly to prepare for our Iowa trip. It would be her first major campaign effort, and she was determined to take on more substantive issues, such as abortion, the ERA, arts education, and economic justice for women, in order to move beyond the familiar personal questions that reporters usually asked.

A week and a half after Christmas, we were on our way to Iowa, via Washington, with advice from Frank O'Connor as he drove us to the airport. "Carry Hershey bars in your purses. You'll never get fed." The East Coast was in the middle of a blizzard, so my brother John, a lawyer in Washington, met us at National Airport in his yellow four-wheel-drive truck and drove us to the McLean house, where Ted was holding a meeting on Afghanistan with his advisers. Joan stood in the large front hall and threw up her hands in dismay. "There's not a room in the house." So I went home with my brother, with instructions to return by 8:45 the next morning to ride in the motorcade to National Airport.

Snow was still falling when my brother drove me back to the McLean house. The motorcade filled the circular driveway, luggage filled the front hall, and tension filled the air. Everyone was ready to leave except a frantic Joan. She had set her hair that morning on electric rollers and one roller had become so entangled that the cook finally had to cut it out. Her beautiful hair, which had been all one medium length, now had a very short section on the left side.

Joan was still upset as we rushed out of the house, the last to leave. Our boots slipping on the ice and our heads tilted against the snow, we started toward a staff car at the distant end of the motorcade. But just then Ted opened the door of his limousine, jumped out, and beckoned to us to ride with him. All three of us were tucked into the backseat, each in boots, gloves, and a heavy winter coat. Ted's sister Jean Smith stood outside the house in the falling snowflakes, waving good-bye as our caravan began to creep carefully forward on the icy driveway. Ted rolled down the window on his side and called back to her, "This is the Greeaat Amerrrican Dreammmm."

By the time we got to the airport, the campaign plane—a 727—was already full with nearly a hundred members of the national press corps seated in the tourist section. The first-class section had been redesigned as a lounge with sofas, end tables, a sound system playing soft rock, and an area for staff filled with electric typewriters, telephones, duplicating equipment, and a video machine. Staff sat in assigned seats. First row: Bob Shrum (speech writer), Tom Southwick (press), and Carey Parker (speech writer); second row: Paul Kirk (strategist), me, and Teddy, Jr.; third row: Ed Martin (New England coordinator) and Dick Drayne (press). On the other side of the aisle, Ted, Sally, and Joan sat on sofas with a huge platter of fruit and cheese on the low table in front of them.

Our stops that day were in Quincy, Illinois, and Keokuk and Burlington, Iowa. The pace was hectic. The timing, in most cases, split-second. I marveled at the planning that must have been involved. And this was only the first day of the swing through Iowa. Late that night we finally arrived in Des Moines, where our exhausted group descended on the Howard Johnson's Motor Lodge. Sally, Joan, and I were assigned to one suite, Ted and Rick to another. But about midnight, a hurried staff decision was made to regroup to suppress reporters' suspicions that the Kennedys were occupying separate suites. Quickly we gathered up Joan's clothes from the closet and her makeup from the bathroom and clandestinely moved her to Ted's rooms. For our efforts, Sally and I got shaving cream, men's suits, and Rick in exchange.

We were on the road again by 8:30 the next morning. With Ted and Joan riding together in a limousine, our motorcade traveled to Perry for an organization meeting at City Hall, to Boone for a reception and coffee at the Colonial House Restaurant, and then on to Ames where the Senator spoke to students at Iowa State University, while Joan gave an interview to the *Ames Daily Tribune.*

For the next leg of our journey, we all piled into small planes at the Ames airport and twenty minutes later, landed in Carroll to greet Kennedy supporters. But as Joan and Ted shook hands in a reception line, outside the weather began to change. It became dark and a heavy wet snow started to fall. Minutes later one of Kennedy's aides rushed up to me and shouted, "Leave for the airport right now and go to the next stop—if they let the planes go!"

In the next half hour aides tried to get as many of us into the air as possible. Most of us headed for Des Moines for an important fund-raiser and where we would again spend the night. But Ted went on to Marshalltown to meet with the fifteen hundred people waiting there for him. The family was separated intentionally into different small planes because the thick snow made flying conditions extremely dangerous. Kara and I flew together with several reporters, and just as our plane taxied toward the runway, I saw Joan rushing toward another small plane, the snow dusting her plaid suit and hair.

Kara had just arrived in Iowa to campaign for her father, and she and I were ashen as our pilot, behind a wet snow-covered windshield, got out a book and started flipping through the pages as if reading storm instructions or looking for directions to Des Moines. Finally we were airborne, swaying and bumping through the dark night, nothing but blackness outside the windows. "This is it," we thought. No amount of advance planning could have prepared us for this. There seemed little chance that any of the planes would arrive at their destinations.

Miraculously we made it to Des Moines and volunteer drivers took us to a beautiful English Tudor home filled with a crowd of people who had contributed heavily to Ted's campaign and were waiting to meet him. Although he had gone to Marshalltown, Joan soon arrived, and then Teddy, Jr., came rushing in, his hair windblown and his tie askew. With immense charm and no outward signs of fatigue after such a long day and tense flight, he filled in for his father and spoke to the crowd. It was, I thought, a perfect example of the familiar Kennedy campaign style. It had always been a family affair, and if one Kennedy was not available, there was always another to take his place.

Our weary group was reunited at another Howard Johnson's after midnight, the luggage tagging along an hour later. I could see that Joan was getting tired, and she and Ted spoke very little to each other, both staying close to their aides. But she again spent the night in Ted's room to quell the suspicions of the press.

At 7:45 the next morning, we left in two-degree weather for a motorcade trip to Indianola to visit the Ellis farm. Joan wanted to look fashionable, even tramping around a hog farm, but it was so cold that she continued to wear her heavy wool red, white, and black plaid suit under a matching plaid coat to almost every event. At one point during our trip, the comedians of the press corps passed a hat to buy her another outfit.

Our tour of the Ellis farm was a carefully orchestrated campaign event. All of us, press included, hiked around the farm, hung over fences, and talked to the hogs, while photographers recorded our every move. Then Joan and Ted, along with a few members of their staffs, were invited into the cozy living room of the house, where Ted listened to a group of farmers tell him their problems, as Mrs. Ellis served coffee and passed platters of warm lemon bars.

The scene was quite different at Knoxville, our next stop. Hundreds of people had been waiting behind barricades nearly three hours for a glimpse of Joan and Ted, and as our motorcade sped through the town on the way to the courthouse, I could tell from the startled expressions on their faces that they had never seen anything like this before—the long line of shiny cars behind a police escort with wailing sirens, Joan and Ted jumping out of a limousine surrounded by Secret Service agents, staff, reporters, and photographers. As a matter of fact, I had never seen anything quite like this myself.

After Joan gave a short speech and answered a few questions at the local bingo parlor at Knoxville Four Corners and again in Oskaloosa, she and I rested that afternoon during "private time" at the Friendship Inn. We had just shed our coats and boots and were beginning to relax when Rick knocked on the door to ask if Ted could take his bath in our bathroom. Frequent baths were necessary as therapy for his old back injury. Rick ran the tub and then came back to turn it off. The next time he knocked, he came in shielding the Senator saying, "Don't look." Wrapped in a towel Ted padded through the room mumbling greetings, and disappeared into Joan's bathroom. The blur of Ted in a towel or in his undershorts was becoming a campaign ritual.

Another event had been cancelled earlier that day. The campaign plane was to have been christened *The Joansie*, a nickname Ted had given Joan when they were first married, but in view of the possibility that it would have to be given up for financial reasons, the christening had been called off.

It was an omen. The polls showed that Ted's campaign was floundering, either because the Kennedy magic was no longer as powerful as it used to be, or because Ted himself had failed to live up to Iowans' expectations. Time was running out and the mood was grim among Kennedy staffers, as they left with Ted on a brief foray into Minnesota on a campaign that might be over before it had barely begun. Joan and I were left to fend for ourselves. We flew back to Boston, without security and carrying our own suitcases for the first time since we had left home. And when we arrived at Beacon Street, there were no agents, no reporters, no photographers—just the residents' cars parked in their regular places in front of the building.

Whatever the outcome of the campaign, the Iowa trip had been a success for Joan. She had proved that she could keep up with the grueling pace; she had charmed reporters and voters alike. Although the press had commented frequently on her obvious estrangement from Ted, she was back on the Kennedy team. Now the question was not whether she was up to the campaign, but what—if anything—she would be asked to do next.

9

DECLARATIONS OF INDEPENDENCE

Well, I was an unknown factor. Now I'm not.
They'll have to listen to me now.

—JOAN

"I'm so tired I'm scared," Joan told me after our trip to Iowa. I knew it was her way of saying she was afraid she might drink again. So when she announced a few days later that she was going skiing for a week with friends in Vermont, I was relieved. She was putting her sobriety first.

On Friday afternoon of that week, Lisa stopped by my office while I was writing thank you notes to Iowans and outlining an NEA report for Joan. We were just beginning our work session when a telephone call caught me off guard.

It was the Eye in my ear once again. "Where's Joan?" she asked. She was friendly, but there was an urgency in her voice.

"I really can't tell you that, Norma, because this is 'private time' for Joan."

"Well, I've got a report that she's been in a hospital under a fictitious name having a face-lift. The name she gave was Virginia Joan Stead."

"There must be some mistake," I said without hesitation. But I was alarmed because I knew it was Joan's mother's maiden name. "She's away with friends," I said, volunteering more information than usual because I knew Norma would persist.

I turned over the rest of the calls from Norma that day to Lisa and, under pressure, she finally said that Joan had gone skiing in Vermont. To warn Joan, I immediately called the number where she told me she would be staying in Stratton. No answer. I called nearly every half hour for the next twenty-four hours and through the weekend. When there was still no answer, I became uneasy, recalling how fatigued and afraid she had been only the week before. I thought of calling her doctor or friends who might know where she was. But then I remembered that she was due back on Monday. I didn't want to sound an alarm unnecessarily.

That Monday a small item appeared in the *Boston Herald* on "The Page." Although not about a face-lift, it was the kind of story that I knew would not please Joan. "While Ted Kennedy is pounding the pavements preparing for Iowa's January 21 Democratic primary, wife Joan has quietly defected pro tem from the campaign. Over the weekend and through yesterday, Joan was schussing the slopes of Stratton, Vermont, with old friends, said her press secretary, Lisa Gwirtzman. . . ." I prayed that it was true.

At six that evening, Joan arrived unexpectedly at my door, dressed in "the Iowa suit" and carrying a suitcase. I was so surprised to see her that there were lots of exclamatory greetings. She looked lovely and rested and I told her so. My children, whom I'd left at the dinner table, were now crowding around and Dana nodded her agreement.

Joan beamed and said, "I washed my own hair, used my hot rollers, and packed in an hour. I'm on my way back to Iowa. Sally's meeting me at the airport. I'll be home tomorrow night."

"Are you all set?" I asked, stepping out into the hallway.

"Yes," Joan said and picked up her suitcase. "He really needs me out there. Things aren't going too well."

"I know," I said, as I helped her into the elevator and waved good-bye. There wasn't time to tell her about the face-lift rumor and my denial. She did not tell me where she had been, nor did I ask. I was just glad she was all right.

Kennedy lost the Iowa caucus to Carter and a huge Republican turnout gave George Bush a victory over Ronald Reagan. Two days

after the defeat, Martin Nolan reported in the *Boston Globe* the
Senator's staff's analysis of what was going wrong in the campaign.
They acknowledged the impact of events in Iran and Afghanistan,
but knew these did not entirely account for a thirty-point drop in
the polls. That left as the major problem Kennedy's failure to face
the issue of Chappaquiddick directly. His stand that there was "no
new information" fed doubts in voters' minds, particularly women's.

Further analysis of poll results indicated that it was women
who had defeated him in Iowa, and it was suggested that they were
antagonistic toward the Senator when they saw Joan campaigning
for him: the more often she appeared, the lower he fell in the polls.
This dynamic became known as the "Joan Factor." Kennedy staffers were well aware of the possibility that Joan's presence and image
as "the wronged wife" were turning voters against Ted. Joan herself
couldn't believe it. "But I'm terrific, I'm an asset," she said. "Women
love me."

Women did love Joan. Many wrote to say how closely they
identified with her. "I have known your heartaches, but continue to
help him through this mud-slinging campaign." "I appreciate the
way you are helping him in this campaign." "I am so glad you are
standing by the Senator, and I pray for you." But there were others
who saw her as Ted's victim, "a loyal helper who was being trotted
out." Many wrote that "he may be the best candidate, but I can't
vote for him."

The women's vote, recognized as a powerful political force for
the first time since the women's movement began in the sixties, was
both an opportunity and a necessity for Kennedy. So the Washington staff, to counter the decline in the number of women supporting Kennedy, began to put more emphasis in his speeches on day
care, health care, and economic justice for women, and pointed
proudly to his voting record on women's issues.

Meanwhile, rumors of a face-lift continued to persist which, if
they were true, might further alienate many women voters. Joan
and I still had not discussed the subject, and when the Eye called
again and said, "I have a confirmation that Joan did have a face-
lift," I listened to her account in silence, refusing to confirm or
deny.

Then Ed called. "Say listen, Marcia, there was a small piece on Joan having a face-lift with scrub nurses secretly flown in from New York to keep it quiet." Then his tone changed, not quite accusatory, but rather perturbed, "Is that true?"

I didn't know how to answer Ed. He was a longtime friend of the Kennedys who had given his advice and help on many campaigns. To help us with this problem he needed to know the truth. When I told him Joan had been skiing, he didn't sound convinced. Then I asked if there were something we could do to dispel the rumor.

An experienced newspaperman, he chided me good-naturedly for my naivete. "Well, we can't run a story saying she *didn't* have one," he said. We both laughed—but it was to be the last time we would laugh about this subject.

Although the term had the melodramatic ring of a spy thriller, the "Joan Factor" in Ted's campaign could no longer be ignored, and to talk over the situation, Joanne Howe, the women's issues expert from Ted's Washington staff, came to Boston to meet with us in Joan's living room. Doris Kearns joined us, and sitting across from Joan, who was curled up on the sofa, they began to analyze the problem.

"Where Ted stands on the issues is fine, but people aren't listening. They're mad at Ted because they think he's hurt you," Joanne explained carefully. "They think you're being propped up. And it looks like that. You have to convince people to think differently by your presence with him."

I knew Joan didn't like hearing herself described as a puppet. She sat in silence with her arms folded in front of her.

Suggesting how she might counter the "Joan Factor," her advisers proposed that she give a women's issues speech, do radio spots talking about Ted, and tape TV interviews to show how her life was similar to other women's. In short, they wanted to keep Joan's visibility high, but they also wanted her to campaign alone and appear side by side with Ted only when necessary.

Talk then turned to Joan's role in the "character issue." Our advisers seemed to agree that it came down to this scenario: women identified with Joan; women for the most part remembered Chappaquiddick; women were influencing their husbands' votes; the women's vote was crucial for Ted to win the nomination; if Joan supported Ted, women would vote for him. It was exactly what she had done in Iowa, and women had *not* voted for him.

Joan had another suggestion. "Can I say lots of good men have made mistakes, that Ted's admitted this and feels bad?" she asked.

"You can say," Joanne remarked cautiously, "that he's been an exemplary Senator, father, and public figure."

Joan sat forward abruptly, her hands on her knees. "We can't be careful now," she said. "There's no place to go but up. We have to be gutsy." She suddenly seemed inspired, exhibiting the same energy and enthusiasm of her powwow.

To my surprise, Joanne agreed with her. "Yes, and you'll have to take the offensive on Chappaquiddick," she said. "You'll have to meet it head on." She also suggested that Joan retain her honest approach in talking about her relationship with Ted, advising that she not make it appear happier than it was, because many people could relate to a troubled marriage.

It seemed like solid advice, for the estrangement between Joan and Ted had become more evident. Although Ted's staff often encouraged him to show affection toward Joan in public, too many times, with the cameras rolling, he had walked away without speaking to her. More than one friend had asked me why he seemed incapable of talking to Joan or being cordial to her in public. His charm disappeared in her presence, and with no apparent rapport between them, voters concluded that Joan was indeed being "propped up." Today's discussion alerted Joan to her public image. If she had to campaign for her husband, but not *with* him, it was because of the impression he gave when they were together and through no fault of her own. But supporting Ted was not enough; Joan would also have to speak out for herself.

"Well, I was an unknown factor. Now I'm not," she said as the meeting ended. "They'll have to listen to me now."

Two days later Joan was still feeling strong and positive. She didn't mind this time when Sally booked her for four fund-raisers on the West Coast while Ted concentrated on New Hampshire. As we reviewed plans I told her that Betty Friedan wanted to meet her. Recognition from a leader of the women's movement added to Joan's high spirits, and she made several rapid-fire announcements, as if I were more than just an audience of one sitting at her dining room table among the notes, papers, and pencils.

"I'm going to plan my own campaign because Washington overbooks me—I know what's best for Ted and me. I'm not going to stand around shaking hands. I don't want to do coffees in New Hampshire." She turned around to face me, her hands flat on the table. "From now on, I'll campaign mostly by myself or with Kara and Teddy. I'll have a complete media campaign. I'll speak out and give my own impressions on the ERA. Lisa will write out the issues for me on colored cards. You'll help with a speech on arts education. I'll set my own guidelines and if they don't want me on my terms then that's their problem." She straightened up and tossed her hair back, determination in her eyes. Then we dispensed with the day's business with an efficiency we hadn't achieved before.

At about the same time, the Senator and his staff were also re-arranging priorities at a meeting in his McLean, Virginia, home. It was decided that he should cancel a campaign trip to New England in order to focus on a major policy address to be given January 25 at Georgetown University.

His speech called for immediate and drastic measures to curb inflation, the institution of price and wage controls, and the adoption of gasoline rationing. He introduced his opposition to a peacetime draft; he criticized Carter for his response to the Soviet invasion of Afghanistan and his handling of the hostage crisis in Iran. Once again he defended his conduct at Chappaquiddick, and finally, reaffirmed his candidacy. The speech was a success and infused new life into his faltering campaign.

The next important event on Joan's schedule was a TV special with Natalie Jacobsen, the highly respected anchorwoman for Boston's Channel 5. It was to be taped in several segments, and at Joan's request, Ted was to appear in one of them and would stay at the apartment for a few days while he campaigned in New England.

Just before his arrival, I was amused to see that Joan had taped a note for Ted to her refrigerator door.

> No meals here!
> Not even toast!

It was another sign of independence, which Ted took in stride. Possibly because he and his staff knew the standard fare in Joan's refrigerator—frozen lobster newburgh, creamed chicken, diet root beer, Tab, and Dr. Pepper—they gladly had food sent in. They also accommodated Joan cheerfully, stayed out of her way, and Ted slept in his own bedroom. Even the Secret Service tried to be less intrusive than usual.

While Ted and his staff busied themselves campaigning, Joan and I held the first of several meetings with Val Crane and Joanne Linowes about public speaking, dress, and how to project the image Joan wanted the public to perceive, particularly for her upcoming TV special. They were attractive, bright, professional women who worked effectively as a team, often speaking every other sentence in turn, as in a well-rehearsed duet.

Val began by asking Joan, "What do you want to change about your image?"

Sitting in her accustomed place on the sofa, Joan said she wanted to get rid of what lingered of her girlishness and defensiveness. She told us about an incident at the White House when she was wearing a mini skirt and noticed a photographer on the floor taking pictures of her. At that time she said she had blamed "the dumb photographer" for his distorted angle and told people that if they checked with the White House Social Secretary, they would find out that her skirt length was appropriate. Now she thought she could say she was wearing what she wanted to wear.

"Maybe I was revolting then, but now I've changed," she added. "What they're writing about me is sickening. Everyone thinks I'm so sweet to be at Ted's side looking wifely, that I love him and that I'm doing it for him. Well, I'm not."

Tucking one leg under her, Joan continued, "I'm seen as pathetic, sad, taken over by the Kennedys with no say of my own. If I look stronger, it's good for me and it's good for him too. I'm seen as warm and honest, but what I want is to be brilliant. And I know I'm not. But whatever I say, I want to be believed. I want people to take me seriously."

Joan not only wanted to be taken seriously, she also wanted to be considered important to the campaign. "This is the first time I've been the special one—I say this in all modesty. I don't want to do the things the sisters can do well; I want to do only those things the candidate's wife can do. I should put myself where I'll be listened to, and once I get an audience I want to be believable, personal, anecdotal. People just want to know about me, what my days are like."

When Joanne asked what kind of audience she preferred, Joan explained that she did not like to appear before a small group because it seemed too intimate. She liked large anonymous crowds where she couldn't see particular faces. She felt threatened in front of a group of "social equals" and preferred what she called a "typical group of Democrats." "I like to speak to women, but not to a group that's too smart," she added.

Joan also said that since many supporters would never see her husband, she wanted to be more articulate when she substituted for him. "Most people will never clap eyes on Ted. I'd like help with saying, 'I'm sorry my husband can't be here, but I'm here instead.' I'm sincere, but I would like a better way of saying this."

After so many years on the campaign trail, it was surprising that Joan still seemed so inexperienced and unsure of herself. But at the same time, she was able to make a candid assessment of her own strengths and weaknesses. In the past, she had been presented to the public by the Kennedy image-makers, or caught by the press in unguarded moments. Now she was concerned with correcting and creating her own image.

After further discussion about the importance of "packaging" and the psychological impact of colors and the choice of clothes that Joan wore, our image advisers left, and Joan and I reviewed how she could use some of their techniques for her TV special. The first segment was scheduled to be taped the next afternoon at Lesley College in Cambridge, followed by a televised walk along the Charles River with Ted. Joan had chosen Lesley College as a backdrop that would give her an opportunity to talk about women's issues. The walk with Ted would be taped without sound.

When I went up to her apartment that day at 12:15 to take her to Lesley, she was nervous, excited, and not dressed. She said she hadn't figured out what to wear and had been up all night thinking of things for Kitty and me to do. I believed her—I could see the evidence in a trail of white notes for me and a trail of yellow ones for Kitty, all lying along the green carpeting in the front hall, across the living room and into the dining room. I leaned down and gathered up my messages.

"I haven't even thought about what I'm going to say," Joan called to me from the bedroom.

I joined her and sat near the window as she held up a white leather cape and plaid pants suit to show me what she planned to wear for her late afternoon walk by the river with Ted.

"I went to sleep at six last night and set my alarm for midnight. Then I got up and washed my hair and slept from two to eight. You've got to do something about the Service. They were looking around in here this morning at eight. I could have been standing in the hall nude, you know, when they walked in."

We both laughed and then she said, "I need just a little more time."

I looked at my watch. We were nearly due in Cambridge. The taxi was waiting, but I suggested she sit in a chair, close her eyes, and think for a few minutes about what she wanted to say, and I would go into the kitchen and make some calls for her.

Finally she was ready to go and we were almost out the door when Joan said, "What coat should I wear?" She stood in front of the hall closet taking out every coat and holding it up in the light. "I can't wear fur—Teddy doesn't want me to wear fur in an election year." She decided on a long black wool cape, which I carried to the waiting taxi.

In the cab we reviewed and practiced the four types of questions: yes/no, opinion, loaded, and multicomplex. Then I suggested that Joan rehearse. From note cards scattered on her lap, she read, "I'd like to talk about Abigail Adams. She was really terrific. She had five kids and was way ahead of her time. She wrote letters to her husband who was always away at constitutional conventions. Back then, men owned women and she told her husband to 'remember the ladies.' "

When we arrived at Lesley, the taping began immediately. As the cameras followed, Joan walked with Natalie Jacobsen past the brick buildings on campus, her black cape and yellow hair flying in the cold winter wind. Then they strolled through the school's current exhibition, and later went inside a classroom where students gathered to watch and listen. Joan was uncomfortable when she noticed them and came over to me. "Can you have all the students leave?" she whispered. "I don't want anyone to hear what I'm saying to Natalie, because it's so personal."

I reminded her in a whisper that her conversation was being taped for television.

Ted was waiting for us when we returned to Joan's apartment with the television crew in a caravan behind our cab. They stayed downstairs in the lobby while Joan changed to the white cape and returned with Ted. They crossed Storrow Drive separately and then, with cameras rolling, walked side by side along a bicycle path by the river, Joan's white leather cape billowing like a full sail, the red round sun setting behind them. From a distance Ted appeared to listen and nod as Joan appeared to be talking in a friendly, intimate way. It was a polished performance—and this time Joan did not have to worry about being overheard.

Late that evening, in bathrobe and slippers, I gathered together some papers for Joan and messages for Rick and went upstairs. I knew that Ted and Rick were there, and I intended to hand the material quickly to the agent standing guard at Joan's door and return to my apartment. But Joan came to the door in her bathrobe and asked me to come in. I hesitated because of the way I was dressed, and because the work could wait, but Joan insisted. Ted and Rick were working together in our usual place in the dining room, so Joan and I sat at the kitchen table and pored over our notes. The two twosomes could see and hear each other through the pass-through, but words were rarely spoken except when necessary between Rick and me. The tension and apathy were chilling, and I thought of Joan's earlier description of her husband: "Ted is the last of the Irishmen who revere their mothers and put their wives on a pedestal, but don't talk to them."

I realized that night how perceptive the press had been and how powerful the truth was. For no matter how many words were written or spoken, no matter how many photos or video frames were taken and published to create the picture of a happy couple, the press was not deceived and the public suspected instinctively that it was not true.

Still, on important occasions, it was mandatory that Joan and Ted appear together. The day before Joan was scheduled to tape the next segment of her TV special, Ted asked her to campaign with him in the few remaining hours before the Maine caucus. His request was a last-minute one, and Joan invited Gail and me to accompany her. Thalia Schlesinger, the sister of Massachusetts Senator Paul Tsongas, drove us to Logan Airport where a bright blue and white, twin-engine plane and two pilots stood waiting. As we flew north along the jagged New England coastline, the three of us settled back in the comfortable seats and clicked the tops off our Tab cans. The sounds reminded Joan of a recent experience. Before attending a fund-raiser on the tour of the West Coast she had just completed, she had stayed alone in a guest cottage on the grounds of a lovely private home. The cottage was exquisitely furnished, Joan said, including a full bar of expensive liquor, and as Gail and I held our breath, she told of opening the cabinet and touching the bottles. "I took down a bottle of Russian vodka. Then I actually opened it and sniffed it."

Joan put the cold can of Tab against her cheek as if to cool off the unpleasant memory, then continued, "I considered drinking. No one would know. I could have covered the evidence with makeup the next morning. And it would have made giving the fund-raiser speech so much easier." She shook her head as she remembered this delusion. Then she said she thought about the possible consequences of drinking and remembered Reinhold Niebuhr's prayer: "God grant me the serenity to accept the things I cannot change, the courage to change the things I can and the wisdom to know the difference."

"That helped me put the cap back on the bottle and the bottle back on the shelf," Joan said. "I'm so proud of myself."

I was proud of her, too. I knew from my own experience what a strenuous personal test she'd been through and how good that made her feel.

When we landed, drivers took us to the Stable Inn in Brewer where Joan met Ted along with Maine's Governor Joe Brennan and Senator Bill Hathaway. Minutes after our arrival I noticed that she and Ted were having a tense, uncomfortable conversation alone in the corner of the room. Their stern looks had vanished, however, by the time they appeared together on the stage of Brewer High School. Joan smiled as she was presented with pink carnations and Ted with the key to the city of Brewer. Then he gave a speech, greeted supporters, and that was it. He flew back to Washington in a Lear jet without speaking to Joan again.

At the airport, Joan, Gail, and I met Wayne Cashman and John Bucyk of the Boston Bruins, who had come to the Brewer event to support Ted and planned to fly back to Boston in our chartered plane. They invited us to join them for dinner before we returned, and for two hours, while the pilots waited patiently, we shared stories about fishing, children, horses, and hockey. As a result, it was early morning before we arrived home, and Joan's second taping session for her TV special was only hours away.

That same morning, February 6, a splashy front-page story broke in the *Herald American*, comparing two large closeup pictures of Joan—one taken on August 8, 1979, and the other taken on January 30, 1980. Norma Nathan wrote:

> Her chin firm, her forehead unfurrowed, her face unlined, Joan Kennedy looks terrific at 43.
>
> So terrific she could pass for 30. So terrific she might have had a face lift, say, 27 days ago on January 11, the day a tipster called the *Herald American* to say Joan had checked into Hahnemann Hospital in Brighton.
>
> While there was no Kennedy on the hospital's register that day, a woman named Virginia Stead was admitted privately for an "operative procedure" by plastic surgeon Steven Sohn of Boston.
>
> Virginia Joan Stead was Mrs. Kennedy's deceased mother's maiden name. Joan Kennedy was christened Virginia Joan Bennett when she was born September 5, 1936.

Neither Joan Kennedy nor her staff is talking about Virginia Stead's surgery. . . .

Dr. Sohn admits he operated on Virginia Stead on January 11 at Hahnemann Hospital. . . . "I'm not going to comment on that," said Sohn. . . . Pausing he added, "How do you find out these things? No, I won't ask you that. . . ."

Worried about Joan's reaction I tried to call her, but the phone was continuously busy and I finally went up to her apartment. She met me at the door, the *Herald* lying open to the story on the hall floor behind her.

"At first I laughed," she said. " 'This is a scream,' I said to myself. Then everyone called and said, 'What are we going to say?' Isn't it funny? If they were out to get me, they could have said I'd had my tubes tied or a mastectomy and then it would have been 'poor Joan' again."

As I stepped inside, she slammed the door shut, ruffling the papers in our path. "By the way, I didn't have one," she said.

I said nothing except to ask how I should handle it.

"Just deny the whole thing," she replied. "I'm going back to bed."

As I refolded the *Herald*, I remembered the conversation of several weeks ago when some of Joan's friends had encouraged her to have a face-lift. Apparently, she had acted upon their advice, but it surprised me that they—and Joan—thought they could keep the operation a secret during such an intensely personal political campaign. Most women who undergo plastic surgery do not have to contend with "before and after" pictures blazoned on the front pages of newspapers.

A few hours later Natalie and her TV crew arrived. While the cameramen crisscrossed Joan's living room with a web of thick black cables and set up two cameras and several lights on tripods, Joan and I talked through possible interview answers in her bedroom. Minutes earlier Natalie had asked me how she should handle the face-lift question, so much on everyone's mind, and I mentioned it to Joan, hoping she would decide to tell me so we could plan a strategy.

But she continued to deny it. "Can you believe it?" she said, pulling a gold sweater over her shining hair. "It's really funny, isn't it? How could they write such a story?"

I left it at that. Yet Joan's response confused me. I recalled a lighthearted conversation we'd had at the Cape about plastic surgery. Using her hands to demonstrate and describe various procedures, she had said, "Jackie and her friends think the way you do it is first the eyes, second the face, and third the boobs. Then there's thighs or a fanny tuck." She had seemed amused and comfortable with the subject then, and I wondered why she was so apprehensive now.

We both came from a generation of women who generally preferred to keep beauty treatments private. But since we had shared nearly everything else about ourselves, I was hurt that Joan had not confided in me. Perhaps it was her way of trying to make it easier for me to handle reporters' questions the way she wished. But it put us both in a difficult situation. In continuing to evade questions about a face-lift, in the light of evidence to the contrary, we risked our credibility with the press. And anything less than complete honesty with herself could be a risk to Joan's sobriety.

The face-lift question did not come up during the taping. "It will be the kind of piece where people will come away liking Joan," Natalie had said to me earlier, "not feeling sorry for her." She and Joan sat on the sofa, talking like two close friends, and at the end of the interview, Joan went to the piano and played "Smoke Gets in Your Eyes." The special would end with a tape of Joan campaigning in New Hampshire the following Saturday and then it would be ready for airing.

The TV special was an attempt to change the way the public perceived Joan, but when she invited Ted to watch it with her, it occurred to me that for Joan the way he perceived her might be even more important. The evening of the show, a suite was reserved at a Boston hotel where Ted was attending a fund-raiser, and Joan asked me to join them.

Joan and I arrived first to find the living room of the suite softly lit and the furniture arranged around two large TV's. Then Ted and Rick came in and conversation was strained as we waited for the program to begin. One unspoken question hung in the air: how would the special affect Ted and his campaign?

The screen lit up with a series of full head shots of Joan, very close and revealing, zooming in on her features and facial expressions as she talked in a whispery, soft voice. The dialogue with Natalie focused chiefly on alcoholism. A shot of Patrick introducing Joan at a campaign breakfast in New Hampshire brought visible emotion to her face and the camera closed in on her tears.

No one spoke as Joan and I watched the double screens and each other for reactions. I could read none on the Senator's impassive face. This must be hard for him, I thought. No other candidate's wife was making TV specials which had the potential for diminishing her husband's constituency. But as Natalie had promised, the portrait of Joan was entirely favorable, and after a few minutes, Ted and Rick, nodding at each other, stepped out of the room briefly to talk and then quietly returned to watch the rest of the show.

When it was over, Ted stood up immediately, politely congratulated Joan, and still with no visible show of emotion, left the room. They might have been mere acquaintances for all the warmth that passed between them.

Although she must have been hurt and deeply disappointed, Joan did not comment on Ted's perfunctory reaction. Instead, she talked about how pleased she was with the show, and then we returned to the fund-raiser still in progress in the ballroom. I, too, was pleased with the show, but felt sad that Joan's attempt to create a stronger image for herself had aroused little or no response from Ted. Perhaps he was confused by her independent course, unusual for a Kennedy wife, unusual for a candidate's wife. But their brief and almost wordless encounter seemed to follow the pattern of their marriage—neither was able to articulate intentions and reactions, or to share in common objectives.

Before the tapings for the TV special were completed, Joan and I had started work on another project: her women's issues speech, its purpose again to strengthen her image and to convince women voters that she was sympathetic to their concerns and problems. Joan was enthusiastic about this new avenue, and although several writers were contributing to the speech, she wanted it to reflect her own personal experiences and ideas as well. Before going back to school, she admitted that she had thought of herself as a wife and mother with no interest in the ERA. "I just could not relate to it then," she told me. "I really thought it was for other women. Now I know it's for me, too."

On February 15, the day of the speech, there was the usual last minute panic and confusion. The new plaid suit Joan intended to wear was late arriving from the dressmaker, and minutes before we were scheduled to leave for the Parker House, with the driver waiting for us downstairs, Joan insisted that Lisa and I and Linda Jamison, one of our favorite advance women, sit down in the living room and listen to her rehearse the speech. She seemed nervous and unsure of herself as she read the words typed on new yellow cards. But at the Parker House, after an articulate and upbeat introduction by Barbara Mikulski, Joan went to the podium, smiled, looked up, and spoke easily and confidently to the huge crowd standing in the reception hall. She eloquently aligned herself with all women's concerns, and citing statistics, she talked of the plight of the working mother and called for an end to economic and social injustices. She concluded, "I know that one of my husband's top priorities is to see that the Equal Rights Amendment becomes at last the 27th Amendment to the Constitution. And I know that if Ted is elected President, I will commit myself to the ongoing struggle for women's equality with everything I have and everything I am."

The crowd responded enthusiastically, as did the press that covered the event. Joan was well on her way to diffusing the personal issues and winning the women's vote, both critical to the success of Ted's candidacy. Yet they continued to campaign independently. A few days earlier Ted had delivered an important address at Harvard without telling Joan. We learned about it on the news, and about his impending arrival at Joan's apartment from the agents who preceded him. Once there he walked around the living room in his shorts, talking informally to aides, seemingly unaware of Joan's and my presence.

For her part Joan refused to go to New Hampshire to campaign, and now newly aware of the plight of working mothers, namely me, she made several calls to Ted's staff insisting that I be put on the payroll, which had not yet been done. Stung by Ted's continuing indifference, she also began to think about other men and made plans to travel incognito to see her friend Gordon.

"I'm so confused," she told me. "You can help me think. Everything's going so well for me now, especially in the campaign, but I want to go out. We have to do something nice for ourselves, you know. I thought this campaign was going to be over soon, but I have the funny feeling it's going to lumber on. I feel guilty if I ask for one more thing."

Then she mentioned three other men she would like to see: a well-known tenor, a man in the arts, and a young tennis player. "But I have to think it out, about the men I mean," she said. "I'm not embarrassed about it anymore. But I can't be seen in public with a man, so it always has to be his place or mine."

Although Joan was obviously showing more independence and self-confidence, there were still many moments of anxiety and vulnerability. One night, by herself, she took a taxi to a city halfway house she had heard about. Sitting among derelicts and drunks hauled in off the streets, she thought about where she had come from and where she would be if she continued to drink. She remembered the woman who was the focus of the nation's attention, in the spotlight on TV and in the news, and then thought about the one who was sitting there in a halfway house. The next day she said to me, "I just wondered to myself, which one is me?"

10 TOWARD NEW IMAGES

I have to talk to Ted. . . . He might be mad that I went off on my own. Ted thinks I'm getting out of hand, making decisions without asking his aides.

—JOAN

Although many reporters commended Joan's efforts to overcome the image of loyal helpmate, propped up for the campaign, not everyone was convinced. Ellen Goodman perceptively wrote in the *Boston Globe*: "The story of the alcoholic and absent wife has become the saga of the Independent Woman. The tale of the philandering and separated husband has become the evolution of the Full-Time Father. The rockiest years of their marriage have been re-marketed as a Growth Experience, and they are now reconstituted as a Semi-Liberated Couple."

Other references to "the remaking of Joan Kennedy" attributed changes in Joan to staff efforts, campaign rhetoric, and image makers—a part of the political process. But I knew it was far deeper than that: Joan's recovery from alcoholism had provided the foundation for her "remaking." It was finally being able to acknowledge a dependence on alcohol that had given her freedom from the illness and freedom of choice. She had to surrender to win. Freedom from alcohol was also helping Joan develop self-confidence, a healthy assertiveness, and the ability to do many things on her own. She no longer saw herself as a victim, nor as a Kennedy pawn. She was getting well and growing up. And the campaign, which had been the

159

motivating force for her recovery, now became the vehicle for creating and expanding her choices.

For the first time in years, Joan began to know what she wanted and to let others know. She initially refused several staff pleas to attend the Massachusetts Probation Association dinner to receive an award for Ted, and she turned down requests to campaign in New Hampshire. Still accustomed to pleasing others, however, she later agreed to both appearances.

She chose to campaign alone in New Hampshire and occasionally selected her own topics, such as talking about her ancestors buried in the Wiggin plot in Pine Hill Cemetery in Dover. "I was shaking like a leaf," Joan said, "when I told everyone that Abraham Bennett had been born in 1672 in Old Durham, that my great-grandfather Harry Wiggin Bennett had been born in 1866 in Dover, and that returning to New Hampshire was like finding my roots." Campaigning vigorously throughout the state, struggling to attract last-minute votes before the primary, Ted found himself competing for news coverage with his wife.

"Ted Kennedy never thought about my background. He thought I was from Bronxville and that was it," Joan told me. "He was annoyed that the press followed me instead of him. And his staff looked like they wanted to call out, 'Hey, we're here too.'"

There was good news and bad news from Joan's doctor. He phoned me to say I would go on the payroll "soon." But he also said that the Washington staff wanted me to stay on with Joan after the Senator withdrew from the race. Both Joan and I were startled. The New Hampshire primary was a critical test we knew, but neither of us realized that Ted was thinking of dropping out. "I'm the one this is going to hurt," Joan sighed.

Yet, in view of the possibility of Ted's withdrawal, Joan waged her own campaign with even more determination and boldly accepted an invitation to be interviewed on "60 Minutes." "Only the big time from now on," she said. "And '60 Minutes' is the big time, baby. It'll get me ready for anything. I'd rather be on with a man who's tough. They have to make it tough to be interesting, but they know they have nothing to gain by wrecking me."

Without Ted's knowledge, Joan asked me to have our advisers put together information for her to use on "60 Minutes." She wanted them to help her prove she could do things now she never could have done before. "My enthusiasm from within will show," she said. "That's the number one thing I feel I can contribute." There was no guarantee that the correspondent on "60 Minutes" would be as kind to her as some other reporters had been, but she was to be admired for her willingness to take that risk.

In the same spirit she requested that one of the Senator's speech writers prepare "a funny toast" for her to give at Ted's forty-eighth birthday party at the Harvard Club. Rose Kennedy flew up from Florida for the occasion and sat regally at Ted's side in an elegant red dress, large diamond and pearl drop earrings, three strands of pearls, and a large brooch—once again the bejeweled matriarch of a royal family. Even at eighty-nine her shoulders and spine were as straight as if she were sitting in a church pew. Ted gave a short speech, then finally it was time for Joan to make her toast and cut the enormous birthday cake shaped and decorated like the White House. But before she said a word, she dropped her speech cards into the thick gooey white frosting. Charming everyone in the room, she carefully retrieved the cards and delicately licked her fingers as a preface to her remarks.

"I always look forward to celebrating this day with Ted. I feel that if either of us has to have a birthday, I'm glad he's the one . . . I remember in February of 1958, not too long after we first met, Ted took me skiing in New Hampshire. I think he has fond memories of that time, too, because he keeps asking me to go back to New Hampshire. . . ." The crowd laughed and applauded and Joan seemed so happy to be with her family and friends. There was a dreamy look on her face when she danced briefly with Ted.

On the morning of February 26, the day of the critical New Hampshire primary, Ted asked to use Joan's apartment for an emergency strategy meeting with his staff and family but she refused. She wanted to rest and be refreshed before returning to New Hampshire that night for what we all hoped would be a victory celebration. So at about two that afternoon, I received an urgent request to hold the meeting in my apartment in an hour. I agreed, hung up, and turned to Gail who was sitting at the typewriter. Without a word we both moved at once: I vacuumed, she dusted, and we collided on our hands and knees under the grand piano in the dining room, where we scooped up my son's model trains.

At three, Ted, his sisters Pat Lawford, Eunice Shriver, and Jean Smith, campaign manager Steve Smith, and Paul Kirk walked in. Within seconds coats landed on chairs in the front hall, all phones went into use, and the meeting began in the living room.

I went upstairs to work with Joan, who had put on a robe and was resting in her bedroom with the draperies drawn. Then at four I returned to my own apartment just as the meeting concluded. I learned that four plans of action had been drawn up, ranging from full speed ahead to a withdrawal from the race. The choice depended on the results of the New Hampshire primary.

As the Senator walked out the door, he thanked me, handed me a teacup and saucer and asked if they could return at six. Once again I was galvanized into action. In between answering calls for Joan and from people trying to reach the Senator, I emptied ashtrays filled with cigar butts and loaded glasses into the dishwasher. When the sitter volunteered to take Brad, my disenfranchised train engineer, out for dinner, I quickly agreed. Then I put a very small ham into the oven for a fast supper for Dana and me before the Kennedys arrived for their next meeting.

Jean Smith returned early. Petite, pleasant, and attractive, she asked for white wine and sat down in the kitchen to watch the six o'clock news. When strategists Carl Wagner and Paul Kirk arrived, each picked up a phone on my desk and started to dial. Then Eunice Shriver came in wearing a thick wool purple coat that was missing a button, which she handed to me. I found a needle and thread and as I was sewing the button back on—Eunice was still wearing the coat—we talked of arts education, and Eunice and Jean looked with interest at a book on TV arts programming for children for which I had coauthored the first chapter with a friend, David Rockefeller, Jr., Chairman of the Arts, Education and Americans Committee. "Do you know him?" Eunice asked with apparent amazement.

More Kennedys soon appeared. Steve Smith came to the

kitchen looking for wine, followed by Joe Kennedy, Robert's son, who professed his attraction to the smell of cooking ham. I handed him a plate and took another out to the living room for Patrick. Next Rick came into the kitchen and asked, "Can you get the Senator something to eat?" I handed him the plate I had just prepared for Dana, but Ted graciously refused it and said, "Cover it and take it up to Joan." I did and returned to slicing more of the tiny ham for the others. Like the loaves and the fishes, miraculously, there was enough to go around.

As predictions for the outcome of the New Hampshire primary started to come in, someone moved the television from the kitchen to an end table in the living room. By now the group had multiplied, with Kennedy children, more aides, and speech writers who nervously sipped, ate, paced, and talked over the monotone of the news.

I was overcome by the power and energy in the room, the sheer force of the Kennedys in action. Without time to hesitate or question, I was swept into a subservient role, filling demands as fast as they were issued. To the Kennedys, I supposed, that kind of imperious behavior came naturally, and they were undoubtedly unaware of its effect on others. But I felt briefly what it must have been like for Joan swirling around in that powerful maelstrom for so many years.

Suddenly the aides announced it was time to go. I hadn't eaten; Dana hadn't eaten. I dashed into my bedroom for a coat and briefcase and found tall blond Pat Lawford talking on the phone. Outside the motorcade was waiting. Joan got into the Senator's limousine, and I was assigned with speech writers Carey Parker and Bob Shrum to the car known as "the Struggler," without significance, we hoped. Then the long unwieldy motorcade began traveling rapidly north over snowy interstate highways. All of us, drivers and passengers alike, felt the danger, hurtling through the cold night, listening to primary results on the car radios.

Finally we slowed to a stop outside Kennedy headquarters in Manchester. Tonight was also to be a twentieth birthday celebration for Kara. Joan adored her daughter, and as we walked upstairs together, she lamented, "When I cut the cake I want to say something, but I can't think of a thing." All I could suggest was a flimsy parallel of beginnings—"Of adulthood and great things to come for Kara, of the primaries and great things to come for Ted." I was glad it sounded better at the party where family and friends sang "Happy Birthday" and Joan and Kara hugged each other.

But great things were not in store for Ted. He lost the New Hampshire primary by one delegate vote—ten delegates for Carter and nine for Kennedy. And news pundits reminded the nation that no candidate in American history had become President without first winning the New Hampshire primary. It was a discouraging night for all of us, and I wondered which of the four strategies the campaign staff would adopt now.

With the Senator behind in the delegate count two to one after the first primaries and caucuses, Joan became nervous about the effect her new independence might be having on him both politically and personally. "In New Hampshire my genealogy brought down the house, but Ted didn't like it," she said to me. "And he didn't like his birthday toast either. He can't handle the new me."

Joan knew that her sobriety was chiefly responsible for the changes in her. And it was ironic, I thought, that although Ted publicly applauded her success, he did not know how to react to the new Joan and to the different dynamic in their marriage. Fortunately, Joan was aware of the problem. She wanted to be seen as a strong, independent woman, but at the same time she didn't want to antagonize Ted. On the contrary, she wanted him to care for her, approve of her. It was a difficult position to be in.

"I have to talk to Ted," she said to me shortly after the New Hampshire primary. "I'm worrying my heart sick rehearsing my little speech to tell him about going on '60 Minutes.' He might be mad that I went off on my own. Ted thinks I'm getting out of hand, making decisions without asking his aides."

She practiced her "little speech" with me listening, pretending to be Ted. "Look, Ted, doing the show doesn't mean that much to me. But I can talk about things you can't. I didn't want to bother your staff until after the New Hampshire primary. If you don't want me to do it, I won't. I don't want you to be mad at me. I'll stay out of the press, but doing media appearances is easier than campaigning."

She paused and then said, "You know, I'm not the candidate—I'm not getting brickbats, just flowers. People are feeling guilty because they're not voting for him, so they're running around town saying what a nice lady I am." It occurred to me that perhaps they found Joan so nice that they would feel guilty if they *did* vote for Ted.

Joan's confidence, though growing, was still fragile. After her return from a trip to New York for a fund-raiser dinner, she was upset because she had been placed in a receiving line between Lauren Bacall and Jackie Onassis. When I said it sounded more lively than most occasions, she emphasized her point. "Well, how would you like to stand next to *me* for an hour!" She looked immediately rueful and we both laughed.

After a weekend at the Cape and a terse talk with Ted, Joan decided to cancel "60 Minutes." But she made the call herself and told me that she had indicated, without saying it directly, that it was Ted's staff who thought "60 Minutes" "a tough crowd" and that "they were scared," not she. "I'm still convinced I can do a good job," she said. "One of the producers said I could have a rain check. They think I'm a doll. They said, 'Anytime, sweetheart. We want you to know most people find you a very interesting woman and a personality in your own right.'" The notion delighted Joan. And once again she was happy because she was also pleasing Ted.

For the moment at least, the "Joan Factor" seemed to have diminished in Ted's race for the nomination, perhaps because Joan was proving to be an effective campaigner. But the so-called "character issue" had by no means subsided, and Joan was as annoyed by the way the public continued to perceive Ted as she had been by the way she was perceived. Illinois was the next difficult primary test, and she agreed to go with Ted to Chicago to work on "the character issue." And while we were packing for the trip, Joan said, "I find myself getting mad, frustrated at a lot of the old, old notions of what Ted is like. He's a wonderful guy. He has a sense of humor—even when he's losing. What a human person! He can laugh at himself. People are starved to hear what a nice guy he is."

While I knew she was sincere, Joan's perceptions of Ted seemed almost like campaign rhetoric, rather than her own views from the intimate vantage point of being his wife. And I wondered if Chicago, where they were scheduled to make several appearances together, would change that.

The press would soon begin to acknowledge the qualities Joan spoke of, but for the moment she believed she was the only one who could tell the public what they needed to hear about her husband's character. She admired the way other family members rallied around Ted, such as Ethel "who gives a three-minute speech which never varies," and Ted's nephews "who say their uncle is a wonderful person." "He *is* a wonderful guy," Joan said, "but I want to be the one to say it."

While speech writers developed Joan's material on the character issue for Chicago, the *National Enquirer* was preparing a more sensational collage on the same subject. I was working in my office on the day of the Massachusetts primary in March when Lisa called. "I think the Kennedys may have a deal with the *National Enquirer*," she said.

"What do you mean?" I asked.

"Well, the *Enquirer* agreed not to bug the family, follow David or Caroline, and so forth; and the Kennedys agreed to give them stories from time to time. But the *Enquirer* has to show the story to a press aide first. Next Monday there's going to be a story on Ted's and Joan's marriage with her byline."

Then Lisa explained she had the story at her office. It was essentially material culled by *Enquirer* writers from Joan's TV special and the women's speech, and Lisa said she had edited it, taking out Joan's byline and a quote which said she believed the testimony on Chappaquiddick. Lisa read the article to me and asked if there was anything in it that was not true or would have an adverse effect on Joan. I gave it my OK wishing I knew the extent of our control.

That night Ted's big victory in the Massachusetts primary was celebrated with a party in a large hotel suite for the Kennedy clan, friends, and staff. Tom Brokaw, Walter Cronkite, and David Hartman, with cameras and crew, there to interview Ted, greeted Joan and said they looked forward to seeing her in Chicago. Joan carefully watched Ted's television technique and then spoke in the corridor to some of his staff. "My present stuff has been answered," she said. "They aren't asking about that anymore. What can I say about Ted that will help? And what could I say that would hurt him?" Ted's staff promised to gather examples and anecdotes from their life together for her to use.

The following Saturday afternoon, Joan and I landed at O'Hare Airport in Chicago. Unaccustomed to protection when we traveled alone, we were surprised to be met at the gate by plainclothesmen and four policemen who escorted us through the crowded terminal to waiting cars. Joan seemed nervous and uneasy on the way to the Conrad Hilton where Ted and his staff were already installed. She settled into a bedroom adjoining the living room in Ted's suite, and I was assigned to a small but unexpectedly luxurious suite of my own next door. We immediately changed into bathrobes and spent the rest of that day and evening revising the women's speech for her appearance at Mundelein College the following day. She wanted more emphasis on Ted and his personal attributes.

Our Sunday schedule was crowded, beginning with Ted's interview on "Face the Nation." Dressed in shades of purple from stockings to eyeshadow, Joan arrived at the studio with Ted but they barely exchanged a word. And after the interview when she made an effort to walk near Ted as our group left the studio surrounded by cameras, he again seemed oblivious to her presence.

Next on the itinerary, to bolster the Senator's image among Chicago's conservative Catholics, we traveled by motorcade across the city to a Polish neighborhood where Joan and Ted attended a 12:15 mass at the Church of the Five Martyrs. They sat together on the right side in the front row as TV cameras recorded the rituals of the service—and of their relationship.

The next stop was the International Ballroom back at the Hilton where over a thousand people attended Chicago Mayor Jane Byrne's "Spring of a New Decade" tea party honoring Joan. Ted, in one of his warmest moments toward Joan, introduced her as "the best campaigner in the family." After thanking Ted and Mayor Byrne, Joan read, "Boston may have had the first political tea party when we threw England's tea into the harbor, but this has got to be the biggest political tea party ever—but that's the way you do things in Chicago." Then she turned to the question of Ted's character. "As President my husband will continue to stand, as he always has, for the people who are the heart of the Democratic party. He cares about them. In the eighteen years I have campaigned with Ted I have seen how much he cares—for the elderly, the young, the middle-income families and the poor. For a third of his lifetime he has spoken for all those who have no voice. That is what brought him into this campaign—and that is what sustains him in it. On the wall of our home in Boston there is a print with a line from Albert Camus: 'In the midst of winter, we finally learned that there was in us an invincible summer.' We did have our difficulties and setbacks in the winter of our campaign, but in Massachusetts we found our invincible summer—and I want you to know how happy I am to be here in the spring of a new decade."

It was an affecting speech, and as I stood behind the stage platform with the press, several reporters came over to tell me how much they liked Joan and how well they thought she was doing. One noted, "They're clapping more for her now." Another well-known political commentator said, "I've got a soft spot in my heart for her. I've lost all objectivity when I write about her."

Following Joan's speech, both she and Ted stood in a receiving line with Mayor Byrne, but after thirty minutes they wisely excused themselves from the endless line, and surrounded by Secret Service, moved toward the door. Suddenly, Joan hesitated and looked around for Ted who had stopped to shake more hands. For a moment she seemed lost, and didn't know whether to go back or forward. Then with a look of disappointment she walked on without him. I hurried to join her so she wouldn't be alone.

On the drive that afternoon to Mundelein College, Joan seemed anxious and very tired. Her appearance at the Catholic college, sponsored by the National Organization of Women, attracted an overflow crowd of five hundred people. In a frail voice she delivered the revised version of her women's speech, modified to stress Ted's fine character. Joan described her own struggles to find herself and then talked of Ted, who had been both father and mother to Patrick when she was receiving treatment for alcoholism. Tears came to her eyes as she spoke of her children. Twenty-five times she was interrupted by applause from a captivated audience. The speech was a resounding success, but we did not know if it would translate into votes for Ted.

That night Joan and I sat on the floor of their living room in our bathrobes going over Q and A's for her TV interviews the next day. Ted and Rick came and went while we worked, and Joan seemed exhausted and desperate for recognition, glancing up at Ted from time to time as if expecting him to compliment her. But once again, as had happened so often when they were together, they talked very little to each other. Instead, Ted and Rick bantered back and forth about schedules and politicians and polls, and I wondered if Rick, who appeared so easygoing, felt the same tension from their lack of communication as I did. When they left the room later for a meeting, Joan said, "When I campaign alone I'm approachable. Women talk to me, complain, but when I'm with Ted I'm a Barbie doll." And that role, I knew, she was no longer willing to accept.

The next morning when we arrived with our advance team at CBS, Lee Phillip came out into the hall to greet us. Leading Joan to the set, she said she would ask a question on Chappaquiddick to give Joan an opportunity to "clear it all up." Although we had thought and talked about the subject often, both Joan and I tensed at the prospect. But when the two women sat down on the set for the interview, Joan answered questions with charm and confidence, even difficult questions about Chappaquiddick and the issue of Ted's pro-choice stand on abortion—a source of controversy in many states.

Before Joan's next interview at the same studio with Bill Kurtis, we held a quick conference in a very small and private bathroom. The excitement and glamour of talk shows and TV studios nearly masked the tension of these appearances for both of us. Yet we knew this was serious business and nervously Joan asked me to remind her of how she would use arts education if she became First Lady. Squeezed together in that tiny space filled with men's toiletries and clothes, she fixed her makeup and hair in the small mirror over the sink while I declaimed on how the arts are integral to all learning. Before I was through she stopped me, her raised hand reflected in the mirror, "No! No! I can't say that. It's too boring!"

· ·

Following our trip to Chicago it was difficult to assess whether Joan's efforts to change Ted's image had made a difference. More apparent was the Senator's own ability to change public opinion by the manner in which he handled himself during this often painful campaign. His personal attributes emerged, not through rhetoric, but because of the kind of man he was. Norman C. Miller wrote in the *Wall Street Journal* five days before the Illinois primary: "Senator Kennedy's resilience and perseverance are demonstrating an admirable aspect of his character. . . . Mr. Kennedy has accepted his setbacks with grace and good humor and pressed on with his campaign against lengthening odds. . . . In personal terms he is giving a gutsy performance under very trying conditions. Those who question Ted Kennedy's character should, in fairness, consider that in their judgment."

Three days later in *The New York Times* Anthony Lewis wrote, "In adversity, Edward Kennedy is uncomplaining. He exhibits none of the petulance of a George Bush, the resentment of a Gene McCarthy. To the contrary he is good-humored, patient, never irritable with the press or unfriendly members of the public. He is not fooling himself about his situation. But he seems to have accepted it. . . ." Although welcome words, they came too late to influence Illinois voters. Kennedy lost the Illinois primary to Carter. But the race was not over yet.

Joan, too, received more favorable attention from the press. In the first week of April, *Newsweek* turned over nearly a page to her in an article titled "A Born-Again Politician." "A whole page on me," Joan said, calling me from Hyannis Port, her voice breathy. "There's a big picture and it's all on me, not Ted. And it's not all about my alcoholism."

The story reviewed Joan's history, the fears of Kennedy staff about her participation in the campaign, her separation from Ted, her struggle with alcoholism. It traced her shaky beginning, noted her willingness to talk about being a survivor, and quoted her as saying, "It gives you incredible strength that you never thought you'd have. I think a lot of women feel I've been through a lot and they feel we're talking the same language." In response to the comment that Ted rarely talked to her in public or showed any affection, Joan said that it was just his style, as it had been Jack's and Bobby's. "In private Mrs. Kennedy says her husband is 'adorable.' He calls me up and says, 'Hey, I saw you on television. You were terrific.' And of course I'm just glowing at the other end of the phone." Although the article questioned whether Joan was truly an asset to Ted, she was pleased to have been singled out and taken seriously.

A week later the Star ran its own feature story on Joan and Ted, revealing their "secret pact" to live together again after the election whether Ted won or not. Alfred Fiandaca, Joan's dress designer, was quoted as saying, "They are discovering themselves, and their love for each other, all over again. I'm so happy for them. It's a fairy tale come true." Two campaign workers, whose names I did not recognize, discussed Ted's and Joan's plan to move to Hyannis Port in May. "She's already making plans. May can't come soon enough (for Joan)." The article pronounced their marriage on firm ground, "And that's what really matters, isn't it?" Fiandaca said.

Another report, although less sensational, may have been more accurate. In the Boston Herald American the Eye wrote—and this time she didn't call me to ask if it were true—"Joan Kennedy was spotted getting a lift in the black and silver limo driven by Boston developer—new Atlantic Monthly owner, Mort Zuckerman. Eye say! Maybe she's doing an Atlantic article."

Kennedy's political star rose and Carter's popularity plummeted with the aborted attempt to rescue the hostages in Iran. In the primaries that followed, Kennedy won New York, Connecticut, Pennsylvania, and Michigan, while Carter won Indiana, North Carolina, and Tennessee. Still loyally addressing the "character issue," Joan had traveled to the southern states with Ted on a trip that culminated in Indiana. Sounding very much the political wife, she called me to report, "Suddenly Carter is available to campaign. The press are snickering." But even though Ted's chances to win the nomination seemed better than ever, the possibility of a reconciliation with his wife, the Star to the contrary, remained remote.

After campaigning together, Ted flew to Washington. And I

realized that once again Joan must have been disappointed by his lack of attention, because she arranged to go to Ohio to see Gordon, knowing he would offer her the assurance and affirmation Ted seemed unable to provide.

Disguising herself with a scarf and clear glasses to avoid detection, she left with Gordon after a fund-raiser and they drove several hours to his home. The next day she called again. "He's at work so I get to sleep all day. I'll come back rested," she said. Then she asked me to get together some thoughts for her to use for an interview with *Ladies Home Journal* over the weekend at the Cape.

"If anyone comes looking for me," Joan said, "say I just spent seven days with Ted. Usually he doesn't give a damn where I'm going—I don't blame him, he has so much going on. But this time he said, 'Oh, you're staying over a day?' " She seemed happy that Ted had noticed.

11 CROSSROADS

All my life I've had to get attention by drinking. That was the only time he ever noticed me. Now I'm being good in the campaign and not getting his attention.

—JOAN

On a clear Saturday morning in early May, soon after Joan returned from the Midwest, I drove her blue Impala along Route 3 and the mid-Cape highway, while she sat beside me reading over our agenda for a working weekend at the house in Hyannis Port and the notes for her interview with the *Ladies Home Journal* on Sunday.

When we arrived at the big, weathered, gray-shingled colonial sitting high on a bluff on Squaw Island, we decided it was too glorious to spend the afternoon indoors. Dropping off our canvas totes in the mud room, we crossed the lawn high over the waters of Nantucket Sound, and dashed down the long flight of wooden steps to the beach below. "Come on," Joan called, tugging at my sleeve. She began to jog ahead of me, delighted to be there. I caught up with her, then we slowed to a walk—always talking. Occasionally, I stopped to collect pink and coral scallop shells, scattered on top of the thick dark blanket of seaweed at the water's edge.

Before dinner we began our work in the den, a small family room at the back of the house overlooking an expansive view of the ocean. It was decorated in the blues and greens of the ocean's changing colors, glimmering beyond the sliding glass doors to the patio. The room was filled with sailing trophies, framed pictures of the Kennedy family with friends and world leaders, photos of Jack's presidency and Bobby's term as Attorney General, and on the wall in the small adjoining room was the Irish prayer, "May the road rise to meet you / May the wind be always at your back."

Joan sat in an oversized, blue, upholstered chair with a high back, "the Senator's chair," which was placed at an angle facing the three-screened television set. "I used to be free here and be the boss," she said running her hand over the arm of the chair. "Last winter Ted had this chair recovered and we had a fight about it. Most people would say, 'Look, sweetheart, if that's your only problem . . .' but I was enraged. I'd been sober six months. When I yelled at Ted, he just said, 'It's only a chair.' He didn't understand I felt left out. They keep taking away all my authority. It was the last straw. Nobody even sent me fabric swatches."

I sat on a small blue chair across from her that evening and we talked about our marriages and other relationships we had had with men. Joan spoke about not feeling worthy of Ted and his family and how that had led to brief liaisons. "At least I found out it wasn't me," she said. "It was him. I found out I was still attractive."

As dusk fell and the ocean deepened in color, we went into the large kitchen to get dinner. There were two stoves side by side, two white refrigerators and a water cooler in the corner. Wooden cabinets had been painted pale yellow, and white ruffled curtains hung at the windows. Under the butcher block island, stacks of stainless steel pots and pans competed for shelf space with all sizes of frying pans. Two open wastebaskets with fresh green trash bags and a refrigerator full of single-serving fish and chicken casseroles, soft drinks and a tossed salad were signs that Irene Hurley had been there before us. She owned a restaurant in a nearby town where she lived with her husband, John, and the Hurleys came to Squaw Island as needed to open or close the house, clean, run errands, or shop for groceries.

We ate dinner at the yellow formica kitchen table, still talking about our past experiences. It was at quiet moments like these that I came to understand Joan better, to sense the strength behind her vulnerability, her sheer will to survive. Finally, she looked up at the clock on the wall. "It's only eight," she said. "We still have time to go to a group meeting." We got our coats and purses and rushed out into the foggy spring night.

Joan drove from the island into Hyannis and we were welcomed at the bottom of the stairs to the basement of the Baptist church by a smiling young man. Another man who had been drinking stood unsteadily behind him, also waiting to welcome guests. I shook his outstretched hand, but he suddenly pulled me toward him for a more affectionate greeting. After I managed to extricate myself, behind me and forewarned, Joan took a deep breath and dashed into the meeting room, escaping with a pinched fanny.

There was a stage with maroon velvet curtains and a simple wooden podium at one end of the large room, and when the meeting began, people came up from the audience to talk about how their lives had been transformed after they stopped drinking. A young man just graduating from Brown spoke first and reminded the audience that alcoholism could happen to anyone. Other speakers followed, almost all of them in their teens and twenties, and I admired their ability to accept alcoholism so young. I often wished that someone had told me the signs when I was growing up. I was usually the one in my crowd who drove everybody home because drinking didn't affect me. I didn't know that an unusually high tolerance for alcohol can sometimes be an early signal for a later change: a low tolerance for alcohol and an inability to metabolize it. For the young people in this room alcoholism had not taken the customary fifteen to twenty years to develop; many of them had discovered the problem with their first teenage taste of beer. And although they must have thought they were too young to be alcoholics, by facing it and learning to live without drinking, they would be spared years of turmoil and trouble. The final speaker, a young woman with pink cheeks, red hair, and a liberated sense of humor, stood up and said she was just happy to know who she woke up with in the morning. The audience laughed, all of us identifying with her in our own ways.

After the meeting, Joan and I stopped at Howard Johnson's on Main Street and sat at the counter eating hot fudge sundaes like two teenagers. We laughed at ourselves, sitting on stools on a Saturday night, wondering how we could be having so much fun. But we knew it was because we felt gratitude for our lives, for the pleasure of living without drinking, and for the intense and challenging work we shared.

With the meeting still fresh in our minds, I asked Joan if she had thought about doing something to help women alcoholics. "If you go to the White House," I said, "you could have a great impact. If not, you can find other forums. Let's talk about it sometime."

Joan nodded. "Yes," she said, "but we won't say that now. The subject scares people, you know."

Unfortunately, she was right.

Our conversation then turned to the interview tomorrow, and Joan said she wanted to be "upbeat and come across as a strong woman."

The next morning Joan slept late while I did the mail outside in the sun on the patio. Joan joined me at about 11:30, wearing a light blue terry robe and carrying a glass of Tab. I showed her a sympathetic article from the *Baltimore Sun* which reviewed her life and noted, "You can pick out the most intimate, private subject in Joan Kennedy's life and somewhere you can find an article about it . . . But that's one of the prices you pay for being a Kennedy." Joan, so sensitive to her coverage in the press, read the article and remarked matter of factly, "It's too smaltzy and sweet." We spent the next few hours reviewing Q and A's for the interview and making plans for our upcoming trip through the western primary states. Then Joan went upstairs to dress.

Phyllis Battelle from the *Ladies Home Journal* was driving down from Boston, and when she arrived, Joan greeted her, showed her the house and the view, then led her out to the patio. I plugged in the tape recorder, brought soft drinks, put out an ash tray for Phyllis, then left them alone, remembering my instructions to return every twenty to thirty minutes in case Joan wanted an opportunity to end the interview.

I had planned to return to Boston with Phyllis after the interview, but Joan asked that I stay and go back with her. And late that night, after we had returned to the city, we discussed possible subjects for her thesis in preparation for a meeting with her college advisers the next day. We decided on an arts idea for children's television and began planning a project that we could do together when the campaign was over. It had been a full day for Joan, but a rewarding one. She thought the interview with Phyllis Battelle had gone well. Neither of us realized then what far-reaching repercussions that interview would have.

Even though President Carter was now only 160 delegates short of nomination, Kennedy continued to crisscross the country, seeking support. But as Joan and I prepared to rejoin the western campaign in mid-May, schedulers alerted me to a delicate situation. The Senator had "women friends" on the West Coast, and they were concerned about the logistics of scheduling Ted and Joan together on this trip. I was glad they had forewarned me and appreciated their sensitivity to Joan.

Meanwhile, the Senator was still unable to pluck President Carter from the Rose Garden for a debate. And when one of Ted's aides suggested a debate between Joan and Vice-President Mondale instead, Joan hesitated at first, but finally agreed. Mondale also agreed, and although it would be simply a joint appearance, not a debate, it would become the focus of our western trip. Because Joan's comments would certainly draw national attention, we asked Dick Drayne, the Senator's experienced press aide, to help us. I wanted to have Joan's speech ready and typed on cards before we left Boston, but Dick was so busy traveling and working for the Senator that the most he could provide were some general ideas and a few amusing openers. Joan and I flew to Portland, Oregon, our first stop, without knowing what she was going to say for her most important appearance of the campaign.

The next few days were a maelstrom of limousines, small planes, TV, newspaper and radio interviews, fund-raisers, visits to senior citizen centers and schools, and packing and unpacking in an endless succession of hotel rooms. We moved from Portland to Los Angeles, crisscrossing California, our schedule too frantic and our pace too erratic to hide Joan's growing fatigue. And not all the reporters were kind. After Bella Stumbo from the *Los Angeles Times* accompanied Joan to Disneyland in a rented limousine, she wrote that Joan had said, "I'm just having a marvelous time. And the Senator and I have a wonderful relationship. We are doing this together! I choose to be here, helping him. I'm just so happy with myself. I love whatever I'm doing, it's all just so terrific—I'm fine.

I'm really fine." Stumbo observed, however, that Joan did not look fine, and for someone speaking of absolute happiness, there was nothing about Joan's appearance or voice that indicated it. She went on to say that Joan "has her ups and downs. At times . . . quiet and friendly, other times she is irritable and defensive. She is alternately humble and arrogant. Talking to her can be like walking through a mine field." Stumbo also reported remarks she had made at a luncheon that day: "When Joan quavered her way across the finish line, the audience gave her a standing ovation."

Joan's exhaustion was showing, yet we couldn't stop the momentum of our trip. On Mother's Day we were in San Francisco three thousand miles from our children, and that night our trail merged with the Senator's. He and Joan attended two fund-raisers, after which we all left for San Diego and then Albuquerque where Kennedy gave a moving and powerful speech at an outdoor rally in Old Town Plaza. Ironically, as his hopes for the nomination faded, his audiences reacted with near frenzy. It was frightening to see how difficult it became to control their enthusiasm and move Joan and Ted through grasping crowds of well-wishers that at any time could contain a Sirhan Sirhan or a Lee Harvey Oswald.

During our two-day stay in Albuquerque, several sudden changes occurred. Kennedy held a series of mysterious meetings at the Four Seasons Hotel, where we were staying, which Joan did not attend. Although she did not usually sit in on strategy sessions, this time she felt deliberately excluded. There was a certain secrecy in the air, and soon after several additional young women arrived—I was told they were typists—they, the Senator, and his regular staff left abruptly for Los Angeles. We did not learn until later that the purpose of the meetings had been to prepare for a major address in Los Angeles in which the Senator would offer to give up his candidacy if President Carter agreed to meet him in debate and then beat him in the final round of primaries on June 3.

Confused by her husband's sudden departure, Joan retreated into the nearby luxurious private home of supporters for a day of rest. Her hostess gave her the master suite and took all her meals up on trays. When the volunteer assigned to us drove me over to visit Joan to review our schedule, she was so distraught she didn't want to talk about it. Instead, she handed me an empty prescription bottle and asked me to find some way to get her more lithium, which her doctor had prescribed as a mood stabilizer. The volunteer took on the task and was able to refill the prescription largely because of the magic of the Kennedy name. Meanwhile, I had to tell Joan that another city had just been added to our already exhausting itinerary. Fortunately, she did not suspect that the addition had been made, in part, to keep her occupied while the Senator continued his West Coast campaign without her.

Our new itinerary now included a day and night in Sioux Falls, South Dakota, on our way to the debate with Mondale in Helena, Montana, and I was not sure Joan could endure it. Then we were informed by a frantic call from Washington that Mondale had to cancel the debate. Joan would still be expected to speak, but other than a few more random thoughts provided by Ted's staff, we still did not know the substance of what she would say. No matter where I was, I tried to reach Dick to finish her speech.

In Sioux Falls, Joan did a TV talk show and an interview for the evening news, visited the Senior Citizens' Center, gave a brief speech at the Minnehaha Democratic luncheon, and answered questions for two more TV interviews in our suite. That night, just as we were leaving for the airport to begin our trek to Helena, we heard that Mondale had decided he would debate after all and had requested to speak second. The only part of Joan's speech we had—the openers—were based on the assumption that the Vice-President would speak first. Now even they would have to be rewritten.

The Sioux Falls addition to our trip was so unplanned that no one met us in Denver where we were to spend the night, before continuing on a connecting flight to Billings, Montana, the next day. We found a taxi and two rooms at the airport Hilton. But at midnight, exhausted by the schedule and exasperated by the lack of cooperation from the campaign staff, Joan finally exploded.

"This is terrible," she said angrily, as we stood in our nightgowns in the doorway of our adjoining rooms. "No one thanks me. No one helps. Rosalynn Carter has a huge staff. I'm not going to be able to get my hair done again. No one's done my speech. This is it—the last day. I can't go on. I'm just too tired." She turned back to her unpacked suitcase, found a gift-wrapped box of chocolates under her clothes and began to eat one piece after another.

"The worst part was not letting me in on Ted's L.A. speech," she said. "When I saw him in Albuquerque Wednesday afternoon, I knew I wasn't wanted so I left the room." She held out the chocolates to me and then chose another for herself, until eventually the box was a jumble of empty brown papers.

"All my life I've had to get attention by drinking," she said in an avalanche of emotion as she paced her room. "That was the only time he ever noticed me. Now, I'm being good in the campaign and not getting his attention." She whirled around to face me. "I should have that speech."

Her despair was warranted, and she was so upset that I dialed our advance man, Chris Doherty, who was waiting for us in Helena, and we took turns venting our frustration. At 2 A.M. I put in wake-up calls for 8:30, leaving no time for breakfast before our flight, because sleep seemed more important.

The phone in my room rang at 7:30. I snapped on the light and reached for a pencil. Dick was calling in the speech from Washington, and I sat up in bed, writing as fast as I could in longhand on little Hilton note pads. When our Washington scheduler called at 8:10 to announce that Mondale now wanted to go first, I began again to rewrite the opening.

Joan was relieved to have the speech, even if it was only my handwritten notes, but she was still so exhausted that on the flight to Billings she fell asleep with the notes on her lap.

Chris met us in Billings with a huge blue van fitted out with swivel chairs and a refrigerator. Joan lay down in back to rest, while Chris and I and the driver Bill, a local Kennedy supporter, talked about current concerns in Montana: the depressed wood-products industry, saving the Milwaukee railroad, the coal severance tax, parity, the grain embargo, and the recession in agriculture. As the van rolled along, I wrote down ideas for Joan and added them to the sheaf of notes I already had, most of them legible only to me. Joan came forward to listen and looked through the three-ring issues notebooks Bill and Chris had brought. But it was hopeless trying to figure out my notes for the speech she would have to give in just a few hours.

By midafternoon we finally arrived in Helena at the motel on North Last Chance Gulch. Joan was due in a half hour at a symposium to listen to supporters discuss specific issues, which left her even less time to study the speech. I had to find a typewriter to transfer my longhand notes onto speech cards. A typewriter appeared—and a typist, but when she couldn't decipher my notes, I had to read them aloud, word by word. The phone rang incessantly. One call announced a change: Mondale now wanted to go last.

By the time Joan and I returned from the symposium, most of my notes had been transcribed in big block letters onto speech cards, but with only an hour or so left, Joan wanted to rest a few minutes and then dress. One of Mondale's advance team called my room to say, "The Vice-President will arrive in Helena in half an hour, but he will have to leave early for an engagement in Kansas City and must speak first."

And then, in what seemed like a matter of only a few minutes, another call. "The Vice-President is here," a Mondale staffer announced. "Is Mrs. Kennedy ready?"

I hastily assembled the speech cards and rushed into Joan's room. Her hair still in rollers, she was just putting on her makeup.

"Mondale is here," I said trying to conceal my panic. "Can you take time to read these through?" I held out the cards to her.

Joan shook her head no, one finger poised over an eyelid. "You read them to me."

I sat down in her tiny dressing room, and while she finished her makeup, I read her speech with all the energy and enthusiasm I could summon, even pausing for laugh lines.

Chris knocked at the door—and kept knocking. "Is she ready? Mondale is waiting."

I finished the speech and again held out the cards to Joan who was removing her hair curlers. "Now shouldn't you read it so you'll be familiar with where the words are on the cards?"

"No," she said calmly. "I'll be OK if you just read it again."

I read again, while Joan finished dressing.

"Hurry!" Chris called. "Mr. Mondale has to leave soon."

Minutes later we left the motel, hurried across the cobblestone street and around the corner to the Shrine Temple where the Mansfield/Metcalf Democratic dinner debate was being held. As

Joan walked up the front steps she was given an armload of colorful spring flowers. She handed the flowing bouquet to me to carry,
and then started straight up the long center aisle of the hall. Surprised by her dramatic entrance, the huge audience on the main
floor and in the balconies jumped to its feet and applauded wildly.
Score one for Joan, I thought, as I followed behind her, feeling like
a bridesmaid. When she arrived at the front of the stage, Mondale
walked briskly out of the wings to welcome her with a warm hug
and a kiss. The audience cheered even louder.

Mondale went first. He spoke well and was applauded, but his
talk was a regular campaign speech. Then it was Joan's turn, and as
I watched from the wings, she rose from her chair and walked to
the podium, holding a sheaf of cards for a speech she had never
read, and had heard only moments before. I held my breath.

Joan delivered the speech perfectly, ad-libbing and waiting for
the laugh lines, and yet becoming serious and compelling when she
focused on Ted's stand on specific issues. Mondale did not leave
the hall. He stayed to listen, and when Joan finished, he joined the
audience in a thunderous ovation. No one clapped louder than I
did. Once again, Joan had come through.

Back at the motel, clad in bathrobes, Joan and I joined Chris
and Bill at a card table in the corner of my room to have dinner and
watch her stunning performance on the evening news. And the next
morning, Chris and Bill returned to my door loaded with dozens of
copies of every Montana newspaper—all featuring Joan on the front
page. But there was little time to relish her triumph. We had one
more stop to make in Cleveland and another in Cincinnati before
returning to Boston. And unknown to us, the volcanic ash from the
gigantic eruption of Mount Saint Helens in Washington was drifting eastward. We flew out on the last plane to leave Montana for
the next three days.

12 PRESSING INCIDENTS

*He was in the tub. I went in with my calendar
and sat on the john seat. That's the only time
he ever talks to me.*

—JOAN

Back in Boston several controversial stories surfaced that shook Joan's confidence. She had attended a small dinner party after a fund-raiser in San Francisco, and Herb Caen, the gossip columnist for the *San Francisco Chronicle*, had also been there. As reported in *People* magazine: "First he shouldered aside an already seated guest to put himself at Joan's immediate right at a table for 10 in a chic, wine-only French restaurant. Then, in the middle of the main course, he produced a bottle of vodka from a paper bag, brandished it at Joan—whose struggle with alcoholism has been well publicized—and asked: 'This used to be your favorite, wasn't it?' Joan gracefully let it pass, but the other guests were appalled. 'Perfectly outrageous,' fumed Jell-O heir Jack Victor's wife, Lita." The story was picked up and repeated in other publications across the country.

Caen immediately wrote to Joan, saying he was "stunned" to read the piece in *People*, particularly because he had no recollection of the incident. "If I *did* do anything so hateful, I apologize profusely and endlessly, and can only pray you will forgive me some day." On the other hand if he had not done it, he wished Joan would write a short note to *People* to say the story was incorrect, and he closed with, "Everybody here who was at the dinner that night agrees that the incident did not take place."

183

Joan had no memory of the incident either. She accepted Caen's apology graciously, and there the matter came to rest. I wondered why such a story would have been reported in the first place. It seemed to prove only that Joan was "news," even if that news was untrue. But after twenty years as a celebrity, she had become accustomed to that kind of story.

Another story, however, was not as easy to ignore. *Women's Wear Daily* had attempted to interview Joan for months, but at her direction, I had turned down their requests. Then one day, during a fitting for the beige lacy dress Joan would wear to her niece Courtney Kennedy's June wedding, Alfred Fiandaca, her dress designer, asked her to give an interview to *WWD*, explaining that it would be for their Japanese edition only and would be good publicity for him. Joan told me she had agreed to the interview. "It'll be all right because it will just be read in Japan." Her decision surprised me, because ordinarily she did not attend fashion events or grant interviews to the fashion press.

Joan's unlisted telephone number was given to reporter Susan Watters, who called her directly to make an appointment for the interview, and they agreed to talk on Saturday morning, May 24, at Joan's apartment. Watters came first to my apartment and I directed her to Joan's. I did not attend the interview, but as soon as it was over, Joan called me, worried about what she had said. When I questioned her about it, she hesitated. "I can't remember, but it'll only be for the Japanese edition, so it doesn't matter."

The following Wednesday, Joan's interview with *WWD* appeared in the U.S. edition and the next few days in papers around the country under devastating headlines: "Joan Kennedy rips Rosalynn: I'm better one," "Joan Kennedy: I'm better qualified than Rosalynn." The *WWD* article noted that with less than a week before the crucial California primary, Joan Kennedy was taking swipes at her competition, First Lady Rosalynn Carter. "I'm a very sophisticated lady. I just have so much going for me. And I can make so many more contributions . . . Rosalynn Carter doesn't have a master's. I wonder how many First Ladies there are with graduate degrees? . . . It's terrific if Rosalynn Carter wants to sit in on policy meetings, but I have talents and areas of expertise that don't lie in advising my husband on Afghanistan."

The day the story was repeated in a Boston paper, both phones in my office started ringing early. The first caller gasped, "I just saw the *Globe* story on page six. Is that authentic?" Then an angry caller: "How could she compare herself to Rosalynn Carter? There's no comparison. She's an alcoholic and Rosalynn is on the street working every day." And another: "I hesitated to call you, but I can't imagine her giving that kind of interview. I think Rosalynn has so much going for her. People have felt sorry for Joan and now she is sounding her own horn. Maybe they should muzzle candidates' wives."

I tried to call Joan but the ringing phone kept me from making outgoing calls. "Flaunting her degree!" a man blurted indignantly. "Lots of people have degrees. Who cares if she has a degree? There are plenty of people without a degree. Who cares if she is sophisticated. . . ." The next caller echoed those sentiments, "It put a bad taste in a lot of people's mouths this morning. Sophisticated! I don't care about sophisticated. I want someone who will work, a concerned First Lady." Another man sounded skeptical: "A degree from Lesley College is meaningless in the academic world. I was wondering if someone put it in as a joke."

When I finally reached Joan an hour later she had seen the papers. In obvious distress she said she was going back to bed and wanted to avoid the press for the next few days. "I'll get over it," she said again and again. "I'll get over this."

More than just the tone of the interview was unfortunate. Joan did not have a graduate degree yet and would not for another year. Representatives from her school program called me to register their complaints and to ask how to handle the situation. Since Lisa had resigned, I talked to Joan and then called Washington for advice. Dick Drayne, the Senator's press aide, immediately returned my call from San Francisco where Joan's comments had also received headline coverage. His counsel was that "she will have to eat crow." He recommended that we issue a statement for Joan apologizing for her comments and suggested she say: "I meant no disrespect to the First Lady. Frankly, I'm proud of having gone back to school after some difficult times for me. If I sounded too proud, then I regret it. I'm very enthusiastic, but I certainly did not mean to put too much emphasis on it, and if I caused anyone discomfort then I'm sorry."

Later that day I met with Joan and proposed the apology recommended by Ted's aide. "No," she said without hesitation, "I'm going to deny the whole thing." She had made up her mind and no statement was issued.

Letters continued to pour in, almost all of them negative: "I have never heard or read anything so outrageous . . . you have actually marked yourself as an extremely insecure person," "I never thought you were a detriment to your husband's campaign until now," ". . . no matter how educated, a person can still be stupid."

I did not show the letters to Joan. As much as I wanted to believe she had been misquoted in the article, the words and phrases sounded like Joan's. Even if WWD had violated the conditions of the interview, Joan often expressed her opinions too candidly, unaware of how they might sound to others. Once again she had exaggerated her own accomplishments because she needed approval. Far from being sophisticated, she could sometimes be very unsophisticated, and her remarks, I thought, reflected the grave insecurity she must have felt at this point in her life. It was by no means certain that she would remain Ted's wife, let alone become First Lady. She had been caught at a vulnerable moment, which perhaps could have been salvaged with an apology. But choosing to ignore it was characteristic of Joan. Although she could face some of her problems with the utmost candor, she could deny that others even existed.

Still uncomfortable about the WWD article, Joan left for Cleveland to meet Ted at a rally in the Cleveland Arcade, intending to carefully avoid the press. When it was over she said she suspected that she had been asked to attend the rally only to draw the attention of all three major networks, and feeling confused about her role in the campaign and even more estranged from her husband, she turned for solace to food. While waiting for her return flight to Boston in the Cleveland airport, she heard there would be no lunch served on the plane, and with four police escorts in tow, she searched the airport for a vending machine. She told me that when she finally found one, "I bought six candy bars and sat on the plane eating them all, one after the other." Still feeling uneasy, she left a few days later for Washington to wait out the results of the critical round of primaries on June 3. It was the day that would determine the course of the rest of her life.

When the tallies came in, Carter had won the 1,666 convention delegates he needed for renomination, even though Kennedy had won in New Jersey, Rhode Island, South Dakota, New Mexico, and California. Joining Joan in Washington, Ted declared he would fight on to the August convention in New York and told supporters, "Tonight is the first night of the rest of the campaign. Today Democrats from coast to coast were unwilling to concede this nomination to Jimmy. And neither am I."

Depressed, Joan called me from Washington. "This is such a political city and they all have knives out," she said in anger and frustration. "This town is so jaded—we won five states and all they say is that Carter is over the top. Oh, God, I hate this town." But her real concern was how Ted's losses might affect their future. They had stayed together at their McLean house and Joan said, "After three nights in the same bed I didn't sleep a wink."

By Friday of that week Joan was back in Boston and we decided to go to a meeting. The topic that evening focused on making restitution to family, friends, and business associates for problems we caused while drinking. Joan seemed preoccupied throughout the meeting and afterward wanted to walk home. We strolled through the Boston Common, crossed Charles Street, then walked in the Boston Public Garden. Joan was angry and said the discussion reminded her of the time a social worker had insisted she write letters of apology to Jackie and her mother-in-law even before she had stopped drinking, and how much she had hated doing it. Her anger was so intense I should have realized there was more on her mind than letters and just how much she needed to talk.

When we stopped at an outdoor café for coffee, I reviewed several requests for interviews that had come in from newspapers and magazines. Joan listlessly stirred her coffee long after it was cool and said no to every one. Then just after we arrived at Beacon Street and were still in the lobby, she suddenly told me what was upsetting her. "I'm thinking about a divorce," she said in a rush of words. "My doctor thinks I should divorce Ted right away."

Before I could respond or guide her to a less public place she continued, "I know people who will testify that I'm a fit mother. I'm going to be tough, and I'm going to fight for Patrick."

I stood facing her in front of the elevator doors, thinking that her fatigue might influence her to act rashly. "Are you sure?" I asked as the elevator doors slid open.

Joan entered and leaned against the wall. I followed and pushed her floor number. "He doesn't love me," she said, tears filling her eyes, "and I have to accept it." Brushing away the tears with the back of her hand she straightened up. "My doctor is going to terminate me. If anyone thinks this is his idea or that he's part of the decision, it will weaken my case. He says to get the toughest lawyer—an F. Lee Bailey type—because I'm so sweet and Ted will walk all over me."

I didn't know if these were Joan's thoughts or her doctor's. Throughout the campaign he had supported her and protected her against too much pressure. Now that it appeared the Senator would not be the nominee, it seemed that he was encouraging Joan to make a major move more difficult than any she had undertaken before. But if these were his suggestions, they indicated that he thought she was ready and had the strength to do it.

As we rode up in the elevator, Joan said she hoped Patrick would come to the Boston area to go to school, boarding during the week, and seeing his father and her on weekends. She praised Ted for being a wonderful father, but said he really wasn't home very much. She also hoped Kara would apply to a Boston area school, such as Radcliffe or Tufts, and that Teddy, Jr., would move closer to Boston.

When I asked how Ted would react to the idea of a divorce, she answered the way she had before. "Oh, he'll promise me anything—houses, that I can date or have affairs, anything—if I will stay married."

That evening we talked for nearly an hour about divorce and agreed that if Joan stayed in her marriage to please others, she would be depriving herself of a full life and a long-term relationship with a man. We both knew that women seldom find satisfaction in a marriage where love is not reciprocated. And having affairs would not be enough for Joan. Although the attraction of being married to a Kennedy had always been a powerful one, she had to think about herself and her own future.

But she was worried about her age. "Maybe I'm too old even to think about divorce," she said. "Another birthday and I'll be forty-four."

"It's always painful, no matter how old you are," I said. "But your divorced friends will be your best allies. You have me and lots of. . . ."

"Oh, I know," she sighed, "everyone is divorced."

Joan was also worried about timing. Obviously, she could do nothing about a divorce until after the convention. But while it was still possible Ted could get the nomination, Joan thought it so remote that she wanted to begin planning her life as if he would not win in August.

Unknown to Joan, Ted was making plans of his own that did not include divorce. Rick had called a few days before to talk to me confidentially. "Would you be willing," he asked cautiously, "to consider moving to Washington after the convention? We'll help you, you know."

The request was so carefully worded that I was able to answer yes without making a commitment. But I realized that it could be used to encourage Joan to return to Washington if Ted lost, and to make it easier for her to do so. A divorce could affect his credibility and possibly be a hindrance to Ted's political future. Apparently, he wished to perpetuate the image of a happy marriage created during the campaign.

"You know," Rick added seriously, his tone almost pleading, "you're the only thing that's worked in all these years."

I appreciated his praise, but I knew that Joan was responsible for her own recovery. And her role in the campaign had made her feel useful and needed for the first time in years. Joan was becoming a very different person.

Rick and I agreed to keep our conversation to ourselves. That was important to me for two reasons: I wanted Joan to make decisions without influence from me; and I knew she would be sensitive to the suggestion that she still needed help. If Joan did move back to Washington, it would be on her own terms, I thought, not Ted's. Or if she stayed in Boston, that, too, would be on her own terms. It had not occurred to me then that one of those terms might be divorce.

Speculation about the Kennedy campaign continued to center on two questions: should the Senator stay in the race and if so, how long? Some commentators urged him to continue, others to drop out. Tom Oliphant wrote in the *Boston Globe:* "His campaign impact on the Democratic Party in 1980, on the President's policies and prospects, and on the future course of his own career in public life—all this remains unfinished, and still to be assessed." Also still to be assessed was the future course of the Kennedy marriage.

The public's curiosity about this subject prompted *McCall's* to run a June cover story, "Joan Kennedy: The Truth About My Marriage Now." In an interview with Myra MacPherson, Joan said she loved her life. "One minute I'm at the top of a political win and the next I'm at an A.A. meeting." She denied rumors of a face-lift. "It just so happens that the date given in the gossip column when I was supposedly in the hospital for it, I was out skiing." And she still played the dutiful political wife. Of the campaign she said it had been the most wonderful thing in the world for her "and it's been terrific for our marriage." And when MacPherson suggested that her presence with Ted revealed rather than masked a hollow marriage, Joan was emphatic: "We're being truthful and, if people aren't going to buy it, it's their problem not ours." She was also defensive when talking about Ted's lack of emotion or affection toward her in public and MacPherson wrote, "His actions give rise to the view in Washington inner circles that Joan still loves him and wants the marriage to continue but that he does not." When Joan and Ted were asked about living together in the White House, both said Joan would. When Joan was asked if she would move back to Washington if her husband lost, she answered "Yes." But to the same question the Senator was quoted as saying, "Well, that's something we'll have to talk about."

Now that divorce had entered Joan's thoughts, I suspected they would have a lot more to talk about than Ted anticipated.

• •

In early July, Joan slipped off to Rancho La Puerto in Mexico for a rest and to lose weight, and as soon as the trip was no longer a secret, the press began to speculate that she was drinking again. Whether she had been recognized flying to Mexico or whether her presence at the spa was revealed by someone on the staff we never learned, but AP immediately dispatched a photographer to Mexico. And when the resort denied she was there, that sparked even greater curiosity.

I received numerous calls from Boston, Washington, and New York, and one determined reporter called five times looking for information I would not give him. I was asked, "Are there agents with her?" "Why did she go?" "Has she been there before?" "What other places has she gone?" "Is she under stress?" "Is she overweight?" "Is she in poor health?" "How long will she be there?" To eliminate suspicions and innuendos that Joan was drinking, I said only one thing—that she was in good health. Nonetheless, headlines about Joan appeared all across the country: In the *San Francisco Chronicle*—"Joan Kennedy Resting at a Baja Health Spa"; in the *Cincinnati Enquirer*—"Politics Has Been Hard on Joan Kennedy"; in the *Washington Star*—"Friends tell how campaign strain forced exhausted Joan Kennedy to rest at health spa."

Since Joan could not receive phone calls, we agreed on times when she could reach me in Boston. Just after the July Fourth weekend she telephoned. "I'm standing in a phone booth that I had to walk a mile to get to. This is the middle of the world, it's like a desert." Angry that the press has discovered she was there, she said, "Would you believe that last night when I went jogging, ABC and NBC followed me with cameras?"

She was also annoyed that the spa was being described as posh. "If people are going to write about me here, I want them to know that I get up at 5:30 A.M. to climb mountains! If any reporters call, tell them how rigorous my days are." I promised I would.

We reviewed her schedule after her return to Boston, and Joan also asked me to get as much information as possible about "the Rose Parade," the July celebration of Rose Kennedy's ninetieth birthday. She wanted to know who would be there, what she would be doing, what she should wear. And then she divulged another plan—a trip to Greece right after the convention. "Set up briefings and buy lots of books on Greece. I want to be briefed as if it were a really big thing—like going on 'Good Morning America.' Ted's staff has to help me."

As I was writing all this down Joan remembered Patrick's birthday. "Oh, and could you send a telegram to him to arrive by July 13. Say 'Dearest Patrick, Happy Birthday to my new teenager. Lots of love from your mom in Mexico.' "

Finally she said, "I'm fantasizing about men. What am I going to do?"

"We could go to a summer Pops concert by the river—would you like that?" I asked.

"Yes, and can you get me a date?" Joan wondered.

"I know just the man for you to meet," I said, and promised to arrange it.

When Joan returned she kept up her exercise routine by jogging with me in the mornings. Fellow joggers smiled and waved as we skimmed by in our shorts and jerseys along the river path across from MIT in the direction of Boston and Harvard universities.

On our first morning run Joan took a breath and said, "I'm upset with you, you know."

"Why?" I asked.

"Because you said I was in good health."

I kept running and waited for her explanation.

"It makes people," Joan said, "think the opposite."

I had to agree, in her case at least, that was probably true.

On the Saturday evening of the Pops concert Joan came down to my apartment and admired the picnic basket packed with food, linen napkins, plates, glasses, Perrier, and drinks for the men. She wore a lovely white pants suit and was as excited as a schoolgirl. When the men arrived, both of them longtime family friends of mine, the four of us strolled over the footbridge at Dartmouth and Beacon streets carrying the basket and plaid blankets to the concert by the river's edge. The sky had turned a soft pink, sailboats drifted in a warm breeze, and families of mallards glided near the river bank. As we spread out our blankets near several others in front of the band shell, heads turned when people recognized Joan, perhaps because she was with a man who was obviously not her husband. Even policemen patrolling on foot noticed her, whispered, and looked in our direction. The concert began and we unpacked our picnic basket, but Joan seemed unaware of being watched. She talked, giggled, and sat affectionately close to her new friend. I was frankly relieved when we all returned to Beacon Street. The incident pointed up the very difficult situation Joan would be in if she acquiesced to the arrangement Ted had proposed. Aside from sometimes being uninhibited in public, she was a celebrity, instantly recognizable, who attracted attention wherever she went and even comment in the press. If she had grown accustomed to that, any man with whom she had a "date" or an "affair" might not find the attendant publicity quite so easy to accept.

On Sunday Joan prepared for her walk beside Ted in the Rose Parade in Boston. Similar parades had been scheduled that day in other Massachusetts towns—Hyannis, Lowell, Springfield, Taunton, and Worcester—and the Senator planned to attend as many of them as he could. But Joan felt able to attend only the parade beginning at the Boston Common at 3:30.

The Senator seemed brusque and impatient when he arrived at Joan's apartment to pick her up. With Kara and Patrick, they traveled by motorcade to the common just outside the State House. The temperature hovered near a hundred that Sunday afternoon and the streets were like saunas. Kennedy had already marched in several parades; his light blue shirt was dark with perspiration and his hair glistened in the sunlight. Yet his irritation of moments ago had vanished, replaced by a cordial smile beneath eyes squinting into the bright sun. Joan, in contrast, looked cool and fresh in a cotton sundress. Then the family began the march. Pressed tightly together, shoulder to shoulder, wet clothes against wet skin, the paraders walked a mile and a half in the blazing heat down Beacon Street, past the Parker House to Waterfront Park.

Ted mounted the newly erected platform overlooking Boston harbor to speak in praise of his mother who, because of her health and the heat, had remained in Hyannis Port. Joan was sitting near him on the platform, and when Ted finished and stepped away from the podium, the doctor traveling with the entourage reminded him in a whisper that he had neglected to mention her. Ted went back to the podium and took the mike again to praise Joan. A few minutes later she stepped up to cut a seven-foot birthday cake as the press closed in for pictures. Again, for an important ceremonial occasion, she was at her husband's side.

After a stop at Joan's apartment, the group reconvened a few hours later at the Kennedy Library, a modern black and white structure built on a point of land in South Boston extending out into the harbor. Ted delivered a variation of his earlier speech in praise of his mother and this time included Joan. But at the reception that followed, she seemed restless and distracted. Finally, she told me she wanted to leave before the slide show about her mother-in-law began and to stop briefly at a meeting.

One of the motorcade drivers agreed to take us back to Boston and Ted walked us to the library exit. I slid into the air-conditioned backseat of a sedan parked behind the empty limousine, expecting Joan to follow me. But she and Ted turned away from the car and walked toward the ocean where they stood talking—one of the few times I had seen Ted's attention fully focused on Joan. After several minutes of intense conversation, Ted strode quickly into the library and Joan dashed back to the car and sank into the seat beside me. She was crying. A few minutes later she told me what had happened.

That afternoon after the Rose Parade, when she and Ted were together in her apartment, Joan had decided to talk to him. She was looking for some sign of how he felt about her and wondered how she would fit into his future plans. "He was in the tub," she said. "I went in with my calendar and sat on the john seat. That's the only time he ever talks to me. I told him I was going to stay in Boston and write papers. He didn't bat an eye, he didn't say a word. As far as I'm concerned it's all over."

She began to cry again and fought to regain her composure as the car turned north onto the Southeast Expressway and raced toward the Boston skyline where the summer light was beginning to dim.

"When he says I'm the best campaigner in the family, I know he doesn't mean it—it's just good politics," she said finally, smoothing the skirt of her cotton dress.

"Yes, he means it. Because you are," I told her.

She turned to me, her blue-green eyes flashing, "Well, he said I couldn't go to Greece."

"Where can you go?" I asked.

"I can have weekends with friends, some chic crowds. I'll meet people, but establishing a single identity will take a long time," Joan said wistfully. "He said I could go to Europe in January to give a paper for UNESCO or something like that, and then I can take a side trip, but I can't go now."

The driver stopped near the elegant mansion in Back Bay that housed the Boston Center for Adult Education and we walked up the stone steps into an ornate gold and white ballroom where the meeting was being held. We sat in the back row, Joan with her eyes closed, mascara running down her cheeks, and I knew that, understandably, she was not listening to the speakers.

Later we walked slowly home along the brick sidewalks of Commonwealth Avenue under the glow of gas streetlamps. "Now I'm not feeling so negative," Joan said. "After all the flattering compliments today, the press all over me. But this atmosphere really grounds me. I remember where I came from."

"And nothing ever gets better drinking over it," I said. "I can't think of one thing, no matter how difficult, that would improve if I had a drink."

"I know," Joan said, brushing her hair back from her face. "I'll be OK. I used to feel inferior, the least loved in the family. But now I'm coming to like myself."

I remembered our walk of just a few weeks ago when Joan had announced that she was considering divorce. Obviously, she had not yet spoken to Ted about that. She was still marching with the rest of the family, still the dutiful wife. And I wondered now if she thought a reconciliation was possible, or if she was merely marking time.

13 DARK PASSAGES

*When Ted and I went abroad, I had to get
drunk before I could pack, and it wasn't because I was scared about meeting de Gaulle or
someone like that. Once we got there, I didn't
drink and I was always the lady.*

—JOAN

The two weeks before the Democratic National Convention in New York were a difficult and confusing time for Joan, for she knew she would see Ted again and come face to face with her future. But as if the race for the nomination, as well as her marriage, were already over, she talked endlessly about men—past and present. Our conversations and work sessions were colorful with her fantasies.

"First," she said one day, "there are the powerful men, rich, social, important. With them life's very exciting, but there's nothing to fall back on when the clapping ends. Then there are the dreamboats who are sweet, kind, supportive, and are terrific in bed." Having had a taste of the former with Ted, she was now inclined to favor the latter.

Two men in particular captured Joan's fancy and imagination, one of whom she had met recently at a dinner party in New York. "He's six, four and the best looking thing I'd ever want to clap eyes on. A writer. He's won lots of prizes and he's only thirty-three. I met him two years ago and thought he was divine, but never even thought of him as a possible. Back then I would have picked out a fat, balding man. That's how far I've come. So for the next two years I'm going to date lots of men. I'm well enough to handle the stress of seeing men again. But I want to be hard to get."

If Joan did divorce Ted, she would have to start over again, which could account for her preoccupation with men—and her understandable anxiety. Many women facing divorce wonder where they will fit in or whether they will remarry. But I thought Joan's talk was reminiscent of courtship in the fifties when girls played hard to get and men played hard to get them. Yet in a way that was how she still saw her role in a man's life.

Since I wasn't sure if or when Joan would get a divorce, I said, "If you are going to date, don't you think you should get a legal separation first? Then later if you want to marry, you could get a divorce."

"You're brilliant," she said squeezing me delightedly. "Why am I paying all these Ph.D.s tons of money when you come up with better ideas?"

After a brief rest at the Cape, Joan was ready to think about the convention and called to say, "Get out all the old stuff. It's under the TV or in the chest in my bedroom. The things on what I'd do as First Lady, the article on Mrs. Carter and all that." When she arrived in New York she wanted Kennedy advisers to brief her on the answers to questions she might get on talk shows and in print interviews, and to the spontaneous questions she often got from reporters which we referred to as "microphones in the nose."

I had all the briefing materials ready for Joan's return, and our final preparation for her appearances in New York began. But our work sessions and Joan's requests for more political information continued to be interspersed with daydreams of men.

"Every hour on the hour I'm dreaming of a new way to see men," she said, with a faraway look in her eyes. "I keep thinking of that songwriter in New York." Then we would return to the task at hand.

Joan was prepared with a speech for committed delegates, another for uncommitted delegates, and carefully worded answers to questions on Billy Carter, other candidates' wives, how the campaign had affected her and her family, why delegates should vote for her husband, the rules changes for an open convention, economic policies, and women's issues. She knew the answers to most of these questions, with one exception: what would she do after the convention if Ted lost? Joan was counseled by advisers to answer cautiously—for example, "Talk about immediate vacation plans (e.g., Hyannis). If pressed, talk about plans for completing thesis. You don't know how long this will take."

The day before Joan was to leave for New York, she suddenly became so upset at the thought of the convention and the decisive effect it would have on her life that she retreated to bed in the early afternoon. When I stopped working that night at nine o'clock and went upstairs to see her, she was just getting up and had barely begun to pack. Her open, nearly empty suitcases covered her king-sized bed and the floor. I went over the events she would be attending in the next few days and then helped her pack.

"I've been figuring out my future and reliving the past," she said. "Particularly trips with Ted." Struck with the old terrors, Joan kept up a stream of almost nonstop conversation, as we pulled dress after dress from her closet, Ted's bedroom closet down the hall, and the children's bedroom closets. "I'm going to bring along so many suitcases you wouldn't believe it," she said, handing me two more dresses in clear plastic bags. "Before a trip, Ted always used to say to me, 'Gee, you'd think you were packing for the rest of your life.' He was right. I packed as if I were going to die. Then everyone would find my stuff all neat. I used to call relatives all day, like I was never coming back. When Ted and I went abroad, I had to get drunk before I could pack, and it wasn't because I was scared about meeting de Gaulle or someone like that. Once we got there, I didn't drink and I was always the lady.

"After you left this morning," she went on, "I said to myself, 'Joan Kennedy, you are a sick lady.' I went out and ate three hot fudge sundaes and brought more ice cream home. Once I started, I couldn't stop. It was like having a first drink. And today, driving back from my doctor's appointment, I stopped at my favorite Italian sub shop. Instead of getting my usual two small subs, I bought two huge ones. I ate one in the parking lot and wolfed down the other when I got home. Then I was in a terrible funk and went to bed." Finally, she told me what was troubling her. After weeks of assuming that Ted would lose the nomination, she was now worried about her future if he did, in fact, win both the nomination and the election.

I knew Joan was ambivalent. She had seen the glamour of the White House firsthand and was intrigued with the idea of being First Lady. There was also a part of her that longed for a reconciliation with Ted. Yet at the same time, she was afraid of losing her independence.

"I'm terrified I'll have no freedom," she said. "That's what's bothering me. Just for fun I imagine getting my kicks. I'm figuring ways to get out of the White House because I couldn't get through those boring chores if I weren't meeting a lover at seven."

She went on talking, fantasizing now, about how she would drive the Secret Service agents "mad" by escaping for a rendezvous with a lover. Then she spoke of running off to New York for two days of concerts and the theater in some wonderful disguise, or of returning secretly to her Boston apartment. Finally, she stopped talking and laughed at herself.

I laughed too, but I could not help but feel sympathy for her deep need to be loved, whatever the course of her future.

On Thursday Joan flew to New York to stay at Rose Kennedy's three-bedroom apartment on Central Park South, which had been specially stocked for her with soft drinks, canned creamed chicken, and cottage cheese. She preferred solitude away from the campaign commotion at the Waldorf, the scene of Kennedy headquarters and the hotel where many delegates would be staying. She also wanted to arrive ahead of the others to get settled and rested before convention ceremonies began on Monday.

I flew to New York on Friday afternoon, and setting off the burglar alarm in the process, moved into the brownstone apartment of a friend. Then I left for the Waldorf to meet Joan.

The Senator was staying in suite 16 R at the end of the heavily guarded sixteenth floor corridor. His staff had been assigned small bedrooms along the hallway, and one large bedroom had been converted to a bustling staff room filled with desks, typewriters, telephones, and a small refrigerator. Two floors above, Kennedy campaign headquarters duplicated this scene on a grand scale in a much larger room with banks of telephones and tables displaying issues sheets and information on the Kennedy candidacy. Dozens of volunteers and staff manned the telephones and handled delegates' questions.

When I arrived on the sixteenth floor that evening, I found Joan in a small staff bedroom at a meeting of Washington schedulers. She had changed her mind about the solitude of Rose's apartment. "I'm missing too much," she said. "Could you have my things moved to the Waldorf?" Her suitcases were picked up and brought to the hotel where I helped her unpack in a lovely lavender and white bedroom next to the living room in the Senator's suite.

Joan's spirits were high and her cheeks flushed as she said she was actually looking forward to the next few days. The politics of the convention almost seemed less important to her than being with her family and the people working on the campaign. But once again she was prepared to play her part. First on her schedule was an appearance with Ted the next morning at an NBC-TV interview with David Brinkley and John Chancellor.

When I returned to the Senator's suite that morning, Joan called me into her bedroom and, as she dressed and did her hair, we rehearsed answers to questions she might be asked. We were in the lavender and white tiled bathroom reviewing women's issues when the nozzle on the spray-net can broke. While I shook and pressed frantically, Joan caught a dribble of sticky liquid in both hands and patted it onto her hair until she was sure it would stay in place. Then we hurried to meet Ted.

When we arrived at the Louis IV Room in the Waldorf, we were ushered into the control room and Joan was told that Brinkley and Chancellor would begin with the Senator and she would be invited to join them in the studio halfway. The interview began, and Joan and I stood watching the monitor as the Senator was asked questions he had answered so many times before. Every few minutes Joan patted her hair or glanced in a hand mirror to check her makeup, expecting to be summoned before the cameras. But then, suddenly, the interview was over and she had not been called in to participate. It seemed to have slipped everybody's minds but ours.

Joan smiled sweetly through the handshakes and farewells, and on the way out Ted carefully stopped in the corridor to wait for her so they could leave together. But back in her bedroom, Joan's smile faded. "Can you believe it?" she said angrily. "Here I am more prepared than ever and I didn't get to say a thing! The whole campaign I just tried to get through and now they're not letting me have a chance."

I mentioned how fast the time goes when you're on the air, but I couldn't help wondering if Joan's exclusion had been intentional.

When Joan left to have her hair done at Elizabeth Arden's, I had lunch with Nancy Korman, the owner of a successful public relations firm in Boston. Nancy had worked hard for Ted in Boston and Cleveland, raised a great deal of money for him, and had a close friendship with him as well. We chose a tiny Greek restaurant off Lexington where Nancy handed me a copy of an article she had written for the Sunday, August 3, *Boston Herald* entitled: "Women and the Kennedy Campaign—still so many unanswered questions." Although women's advocates, such as Barbara Mikulski, Bella Abzug, Gloria Steinem, Shirley Chisholm, and Midge Costanza, had endorsed Kennedy and he had worked hard on legislation benefiting women, Nancy's article questioned whether women delegates would back him at the convention. We still did not know.

Then Nancy and I began to talk about the effect the campaign was having on Joan. "She's discovered the women's movement," Nancy said, "and learned that women aren't just pretty or adornments. They have clout. I think Joan has made a major contribution to the campaign and learned to care about the issues."

I agreed. And when Nancy asked what I thought about Ted and Joan's relationship and how Joan felt about Ted, I said, "I think she still cares and wants her marriage to continue."

"Then tell her to go after him and try and get him back," she said.

I respected Nancy, but wondered if she really believed Joan and Ted could revive their marriage after all that had happened to them. Perhaps she was more objective than I was since she knew and had worked with both of them. But she was also aware of Ted's distant behavior during the campaign. And she knew about the other women in his life. Joan herself knew that, and although she had been deeply hurt, she had made an effort to accept it and at times even to joke about it. "There was always an aide who got the women up one staircase and down the other," she once said to me.

Was there any hope that that might change in the future? Nancy and I agreed that Ted's encounters with other women required no love or commitment and allowed him to protect himself from the vulnerability of intimacy. We thought we understood his need for protection after such profound tragedy and loss in his life—his need to create walls around himself. And those walls, we were afraid, would continue to exclude Joan.

That afternoon Joan took a few hours off from her busy schedule to walk with Patrick to the Biltmore Hotel and point out the famous clock where she used to meet Ted for dates. In the same mood of nostalgia, she took Nancy and me on a tour of the Waldorf ballroom to show us where she had made her debut. And that night she was delighted by the arrival of Teddy and Kara.

The entire family attended mass at St. Patrick's on Sunday morning, together for the first time in weeks. But they were surrounded by staff and Secret Service, every eye was on them, and they were mobbed by photographers when they left the cathedral. Did this family ever have any quiet moments together, I wondered? Or was it too late for that, just as it was perhaps too late for a reconciliation between Joan and Ted?

The next major event on the schedule was a musical fundraiser that night at the Shubert Theater: "Broadway for Kennedy—An Evening with Composers and Lyricists," hosted by Lauren Bacall. That afternoon advanceman Mark Brand and I went to the theater to familiarize ourselves with the arrangements. Then we stopped for sandwiches and cheesecake at Lindy's, where we were seated at a small table by old-school waiters no longer impressed by the parade of politicians and famous faces who were their daily clientele.

Suddenly, Mark leaned forward and looked directly at me. "You know we're going to lose, don't you?" he said.

I nodded but I couldn't voice it. So much hope had fueled the campaign that most of us never thought about losing. Still, I was fascinated by how many intelligent, talented people had worked indefatigably and continued to do so in the face of almost certain defeat. My own cause was personal—Joan's welfare and, on a larger scale, her success in defeating alcoholism. But I was curious about what motivated others. Mark was a campaign veteran, much more aware than I of all the people who had given up high-paying and prestigious jobs to devote themselves totally to this campaign. I asked him why they did it.

He thought a moment, then said, "Some people see their name on a door, some like a circus coming to town, some are devoted to the issues, others are devoted to the Kennedy family, and some do it to escape their own problems."

When I asked him if he thought the campaign had been well run, he said, "The problem with this campaign is it's run by too many committees, family committees, state committees, city committees, and there are no big heavies at the top. The talent is all at the bottom. But these people are great, you know. I've never been in a campaign with so little sex."

His remark caught me by surprise and I asked him to explain.

"Well, it's usually the candidate with the advance, advance with Secret Service, and the Secret Service with the wife," he said, shrugging his shoulders.

The subject, which had never occurred to me, could be added to the rest of my political naivete.

That night at seven, Joan and I arrived at the Shubert for the benefit performance and Joan, surrounded by almost the entire Kennedy clan, took her seat in the center section close to the stage. The seat next to her was empty. Because Ted planned to attend the Black Caucus at the New York Statler and visit the Pennsylvania delegation at the Roosevelt, he was going to be late. The program started without him and at the request of a woman from the Washington staff I slipped into the Senator's seat to watch the parade of famous composers and lyricists—Betty Comden and Adolph Green, E. Y. Harburg and Cy Coleman—play and sing their own songs.

When Ted finally arrived, he strode briskly out on stage with Joan at his side and gave a rousing talk to his loyal friends and supporters. Then he was gone again, and during the intermission, Joan and I went backstage to talk to Lauren Bacall and then to Sammy Cahn and Jule Styne who were also on the program.

We stayed in the wings for the rest of the show, and just before Leonard Bernstein went on stage to play "West Side Story," he asked Joan if she would like to sit beside him and turn pages. She accepted but was so nervous that she turned too early or too late and he had to keep reaching up to help her. The audience loved it.

The evening culminated with a cast party at Jean and Steve Smith's on East 62nd Street. On the way, Mark and I accompanied Joan to the National Women's Political Caucus at the Copacabana on East 60th, but at the last minute she hesitated and decided not to go in. Instead, we stopped at Madison Square Garden to take a brief look at the convention hall, then went on to the party at the Smiths. Joan chatted with the famous guests and family members until midnight, but she seemed somewhat ill at ease. Perhaps her thoughts were on the convention, now only a day away, which could either mark a new beginning of her relationship with Ted or the end.

The main floor of Madison Square Garden was divided into seating sections for all the state delegations by signs rising from poles attached to heavy metal supports. The floor was covered with huge root systems of cables and wires for dozens of TV cameramen and announcers. At seemingly unplanned intervals, blizzards of balloons rained down on throngs of delegates lobbying and voting on various issues and platform changes. Wild spontaneous demonstrations broke out, posters and buttons were passed around, and parades of sign-carrying people in straw hats wove among the delegates like circus clowns. Deafening noise often obscured the voice of the speaker at the podium. Organ music, reminiscent of skating rinks, swirled from loudspeakers. Security was tightly controlled in and outside of the Garden, where even celebrities, politicians, and recognizable newsmen had to produce convention passes. The 1980 Democratic National Convention was underway.

The Secret Service protectively guided Joan through the milling crowds on Monday afternoon. She sat with her children in the first row of her box and several other staff members and I were two rows behind her. Political wives, such as Sharon Percy Rockefeller (who grew up three blocks from my home in Kenilworth, Illinois) were escorted over to greet Joan. Shelley Winters sat with us for a while and the Oscar de la Rentas paid a visit. TV cameras focused on Joan continuously while she was at the Garden. It would be the longest sustained performance of her political career.

Coverage of the entire convention was intense; the outcome still uncertain. Three weeks ago a new "Dump Carter" movement had emerged when national polls showed him at historic lows for an incumbent President, and Kennedy strategists believed that if delegates could vote their choice, he might win the nomination. They were gearing up for a fight to pass a proposal for an open convention, a rules change that would release Carter delegates from their commitment to vote for him on the first ballot. At that time Carter had nearly 2,000 delegates, Kennedy 1,250. If Kennedy lost the rules battle, the convention for him would be over.

As Joan watched the beginning of the rules fight, she looked especially lovely and vibrant. There was still a ray of hope. But after hours of heated debate and loud and unruly demonstrations from the floor, Carter defeated Kennedy in a show of voting force. The rules would stand, the delegates remained committed, and they would vote their first ballot Wednesday night. Kennedy had lost, and at the Waldorf later that evening, he announced to his stunned staff, supporters, and press that he was withdrawing from the race. But he reaffirmed his intention to address the convention the next night on the party's economic policies.

Neither Joan nor I had been told of his plan to withdraw. The momentum of the past months had been so compelling that we could barely absorb the idea of defeat. And only with reluctance did the staff wearily acknowledge that their months of intense work had come to an end. They rallied, however, and let off steam in an impromptu party in the staff room down the hall from the Kennedy suite. More than two dozen people exchanged campaign stories and expressed the love and appreciation they felt for one another. Rick joined in the fun and laughter even after he was generously doused with beer, presumably for handing out instructions to so many so often. Tony Podesta, the chief scheduler, also received a beer bath. With beer running down his face and soaking his clothes, he laughingly pointed to his fellow workers and said, "You won't have me to kick around anymore." One of the women who had helped with the press and sent Joan's clippings to her said what many were thinking, "It's sad that he lost, but thank God he's alive."

The final hours and days of the convention were a roller coaster of emotions for Joan. There was the exhilaration of Ted's address to the convention on Tuesday night, a speech which some reporters called a hero's farewell and others a defeated politician's rallying cry for a new beginning. Then there was the deep disappointment the next day when Ted took her to lunch and she discovered that it was just "another media event." Even before the convention ended, her children left for Washington or the Cape and most of the staff made arrangements for their own departures. I helped Joan pack to leave for their Virginia home and the next day I returned to Boston. When I spoke to her again, she told me of the flight from Washington when Ted abruptly abandoned her at Montauk, leaving her to fly on to the Cape alone.

It was the end of Joan's fantasies of becoming First Lady, the end of her dreams about a reconciliation with Ted. His failure to win the Democratic nomination for President had left her with an unwritten scenario: a choice between a lonely and loveless marriage or a possibly frightening divorce. The time for choice had come.

14 CHOICES

*Jackie said not to worry about Ted, that he'll
be fine. She said I should look out for myself.*

—JOAN

Joan was stranded on the Cape. Denied her wish to go abroad, and with no appointments to keep, no interviews to give, and few of the domestic chores that attach many women to their homes and children, she was floating free, once again alone and unneeded.

She called me often during the sultry days of August. I still worked for Joan, handling the press and her correspondence, but there was nothing for her to do, and I thought her frequent calls were probably inspired by her need just to talk to someone who understood her dilemma.

One afternoon I was working at my desk with a light on, as dark clouds gathered for promised showers. The phone rang and it was Joan again. "I feel so lost," she said. "I get up and go for walks, trying to sort things out. I really wanted to just go away for a while."

We talked about her feelings of uncertainty, of not knowing what to do, and I wished I could have told her she must come to Boston for a television appearance, a speech, or even a hair appointment, but as I pulled her August calendar toward me I saw the days were blank. Ironically, they had been kept empty and available for Ted's campaign as the Democratic candidate.

Yet, as Joan continued to talk, I was impressed by her equanimity and acceptance of her situation. "You know, I'm not furious anymore. It's just reality," she said calmly. "I have to concentrate on what I want to do for me. I have to get going to make my own reality. Life is right back to where it has been for the past fifteen years. Ted never mentioned this weekend. Or the next two weeks. Or next fall. I can do anything I want. I always could. It's up to me. Ted's number one advance man is at loose ends, too. He said he could practice law in Miami or go to California to rest. But he doesn't have to go anywhere. I guess that's my problem, too."

Joan did not intend to sit around feeling sorry for herself. I could hear the storm breaking outside as we began to make plans. Ted had promised her the use of his boat for an occasional day's sail midweek and now Joan talked of using it for parties or to entertain a date.

"I want to see lots of men," she said. "One every night. I keep saying to myself, 'You'll die on the vine of loneliness.' "

I cautioned her to wait, even though I knew how lonely she must feel.

She disagreed. "Well, sometimes I say to myself 'What's the rush?' and then I think, 'Why wait?' I'm out of practice except for Gordon. I want to get a few more guys out of my system." Then she began to laugh. "Oh, I know I'm being indiscriminate, but if I'm not, how am I supposed to know when I meet Mr. Right?"

"I understand," I told her, "but I still think you should wait and go slowly."

Still, she was not convinced and recalled the two years she had wasted fantasizing about a certain man. "Then, after all the buildup, when we finally got together after a dinner party of political types and journalists and sneaked back to his house, it was a disaster—all over in ten minutes. Am I asking too much?" she sighed.

"Of course not," I said, recalling that Joan had once ruefully referred to Ted as "the five-minute-man."

"Then, remember, I told you it happened again? Same thing. Only the second time it was in his incredibly gorgeous penthouse apartment. We had it all to ourselves with the chauffeur waiting out front in the limousine, because he didn't want me to spend the night."

"That's just my point," I said. "You can't go anywhere without being recognized. And as long as you're still married, it'll be difficult to see any man."

Outside the storm had intensified and the static on the phone made it impossible to continue our conversation, so we hurriedly completed plans for the first sailing party—a thank you for the staff and Joan's friends who had helped us during the campaign.

The day of the party, excitement and curiosity were high, as people arrived at the Hyannis Port Yacht Club, a small shingled house behind a low picket fence. Dinghies and other small craft lined the walkway out into the water, and larger boats bobbed at their moorings in the calm harbor. When all the guests had arrived, we were taken in shifts by launch out to the Senator's fifty-five-foot sloop, *The Curragh*, anchored in the distance. Many of us hadn't seen each other since the intense days of the campaign and it felt like a reunion.

Kendall, the captain, soon raised the sails and a gentle breeze sent us in the direction of Martha's Vineyard. Irene had prepared tomatoes stuffed with lobster salad, hot chowder, and coffee which I served from below. Kendall talked sailing with some of the guests, as Joan moved from group to group, chatting with her friends, meeting their wives and husbands, and thanking them for their help in the campaign. Her face was lightly tanned from the past days of walking on the beach, and her hair whipped around her head like spun gold. The nautical colors she wore, a heavy navy sweater and white pants, underscored her relaxed manner and ease on the water.

When Kendall called, "OK. It's your watch, Mrs. Kennedy," Joan smiled, waved, and came up to take a turn at the wheel. Even I had to prove to Kendall that I knew how to handle the huge wheel. Finally, he guided the boat into the harbor and the launch took us back to the dock. Everyone had enjoyed the day of sailing and reminiscing—Joan most of all.

I called her the next day from Boston to discuss the party and whether we should change anything for the two others she had scheduled—one for writers and another for media experts. She sounded unhappy and I could hear music blaring in the background. "You wouldn't believe it," she said. "This house is full of people. Kara and Teddy's friends are staying here and everyone in this house is screwing." Then our conversation turned to the boat party and Joan commented on a staff member's husband. "When I was introduced to that guy I said to myself, 'I like guys a tiny bit naughty looking.' There are two kinds of guys—either they are quite a lay or you can bring them home to mother."

We laughed at how much that remark sounded like something men might say, but Joan's laugh was mirthless. Even with Kara and Teddy there, even with a houseful of their friends, she was still lonely. Her older children had grown up without her, and now she felt left out of their lives. When the house was overrun with guests, I knew she usually stayed upstairs in her bedroom, venturing down to the kitchen only for something to eat.

As the late summer days drifted by, an unspoken battle began between Joan and Ted over using the house and boat. Joan wanted to know Ted's exact schedule so she could plan her own activities on certain dates and weekends when she would have the house and boat to herself. "I don't want any surprises," she said emphatically. So I called Rick and then reported back to Joan. As far as I knew, that was the only form of communication between her and Ted.

Joan herself realized that such a situation couldn't continue indefinitely. Divorce, which she had begun to consider nearly two months ago, finally seemed to be the only solution. But she was still ambivalent about it—and just as uncertain about how to approach Ted. "I've been planning what I'm going to say," she said, in another call from the Cape. "I have some phrases ready. Tell me what you think: 'We have to talk.' 'We can't go on like this.' 'I need more from my marriage.' " She paused, then said, "I guess I want a divorce. But then I say to myself, 'You idiot! How many women in the world would give their eye teeth to be married to Ted Kennedy?' And here I am, planning to give him up—along with the whole schmeer. Where's my courage?"

"I know how scary it is," I said. "You've been married more than twenty years."

"You know," she said, "sometimes I think of Bobby's speeches. He often talked of how you can never be happy or have your life improve unless you scramble for what you want. If there's no love in your life, go after it. I remember sitting next to Ted during one of those speeches and wondering if it was too late for us. It's all over, I know that now, but then I think I should put off the divorce and wait." She sighed. "The trouble is I'm flip-flopping. You know, if I were forty-eight or more I wouldn't change horses—I've got lots of things. But I have to convince myself that people don't change."

"For me just making the decision was the hardest part of getting divorced," I said. "But you have changed. And maybe Ted can change, too. Can't you sit down and talk to him before you make the decision for both of you?"

"I don't think so," she said sadly, and then described the times she had tried to talk to Ted over the years and he had closed the door, both literally and figuratively. His rejection felt "like a knife going through me," she said and now she had become numb, her reaction one of indifference. "Not hatred, just indifference. And if I don't do it, if I don't get a divorce, how am I going to see other men?"

"You really can't," I agreed. The old double standard was still casting its shadow. It was known and accepted that Ted saw other women. But for Joan, clandestine affairs would be demeaning and virtually impossible.

At the very same moment that Joan was considering divorce, a reporter from the *National Enquirer* called me to verify its version of the Kennedy marriage, the public one—that the Senator and Mrs. Kennedy had become closer as a result of the campaign. "Is that true?" he asked. "Have their feelings increased? Are they really a team?"

He went on to say that someone who knew Mrs. Kennedy, but asked not to be named, had said that Joan and Ted were as deeply in love as when they first got married and they had buried the hatchet. "Can you think of an anecdote to corroborate this?" he asked.

Unfortunately, I could not.

"Do you think they really love each other?"

"Everyone in the family loves each other," I replied lamely.

Meanwhile, Joan still vacillated, as fantasies about what she wanted for herself played themselves out against what she would have to give up. Finally, she decided to ask for a divorce and called me to describe how she envisioned the scene. She would walk into the den and hand Ted a cold beer, she said, but would be careful it wasn't during the national news. "Then I'll sit down and say, 'I have something to talk to you about.' " She hadn't thought much beyond those words, she told me; they would be hard enough for her to say.

I was relieved that at least she wouldn't be giving Ted an ultimatum. But as it turned out, that is exactly what it was.

Two days later her call came. "What I did," Joan said, "in spite of all my plans, was just walk into the den where he was sitting in his chair. I don't remember if the television was on or if he was reading. I didn't take him a beer. I just walked in and said, 'How are you going to handle the questions?' And Ted said, 'Oh, what do you mean?' and I said, 'Because I want a divorce.' "

A silence followed in our conversation like the one that must have occurred in the den. And I pictured Ted sitting in the blue "Senator's chair," confusion and perhaps disbelief etched on his face. Was he surprised by Joan's assertiveness? Finally, I asked, "How did he react?"

"He didn't say much. Only that he was taking Patrick to Nantucket the next morning at eight and would be away until Friday at six P.M. and that he would think about it on their camping trip." Joan's voice was strong. But then it changed abruptly and she said breathlessly, "Now I'm a wreck. I got it out, but I'm afraid I'll back down. I called my doctor in Boston and he encouraged me. They aren't supposed to encourage you, you know. He said I could do it, but that I'd have a tough year. I'm a wreck thinking about the future. It's like stopping drinking."

Ted may not have been surprised at all by Joan's announcement. She told me that before she spoke to Ted she had called his press secretary in Washington to alert him to her intentions and ask for his cooperation in handling the press. That struck me as a rather curious way to ask your husband for a divorce, but perhaps Joan had grown accustomed to dealing with Ted through his aides.

His response, when it came, was to summon Father English, the family's religious counselor, to the Cape. "He's going to say the same thing for two days straight. He'll encourage us to stay together," Joan told me. And I realized that in addition to family and political pressures, Joan would also be under the pressure of religious dictums and customs to resume living with Ted, to move back to Washington, or at least to maintain the status quo in her marriage. But it would be the status quo of their marital pattern before the campaign and before Joan became sober. I knew she would no longer tolerate living in that kind of limbo. And I suspected that whatever Father English was going to say to Joan and Ted, it would be unrelated to the sad reality of their relationship.

During the next few days and weeks Joan needed repeated assurances from me and other friends that she wouldn't be alone and that she had made the right decision. Just as she had said, imagining the future without Ted was in many ways like imagining the future without drinking—which for some prompts such questions as "How will I ever be able to go to weddings and dinner parties for the rest of my life without having cocktails, champagne, or wine again?" The answer is to live life in small segments, a day at a time or even less, if necessary. No one can imagine a lifetime all at once, but sometimes it seemed as if Joan tried.

She knew that things would be quite different without Ted and the lifestyle and protection he provided. She worried about how she would take care of herself in her Boston apartment and how she would finish her schoolwork. When she asked for my help in writing her thesis, I agreed. That relieved her, but her fears about giving up the Kennedy magic crept continually back into our conversations. She spoke about it to other friends, too, including her sister-in-law Jackie.

"I spent four hours talking to Jackie," Joan told me. "She said she's crazy about Ted, but she's known for years that I should have done it fifteen years ago. She was so supportive. She even suggested I use her New York lawyer. If Jackie recommends him and says he's distinguished, he must be good. Jackie said not to worry about Ted, that he'll be fine. She said I should look out for myself."

Then Joan told me she had asked Jackie about meeting men, and she had offered to introduce Joan to some younger men at small dinner parties in her New York apartment. But she cautioned that meeting someone new would not happen overnight.

"Her best advice to me," Joan said, "was to be relaxed, very relaxed. One thing that men have told her is that if a woman is looking or desperate, they can smell it. It was a real girl-to-girl talk with one of the most sophisticated women in the world."

Joan was relieved and gratified that Jackie had supported her decision. "Jackie also told me," she added, "that she wishes she had given me this advice before and maybe I wouldn't have gotten so sick. But back then, fifteen years ago, I probably wouldn't have been able to take her advice. I had to consider being a Catholic and I really couldn't do anything. But nowadays," she said, echoing a note that she had sounded in the campaign, "women have so many choices."

15 STARTING OVER

That's the story of my life. I've heard about all the big things in this family from the news.

—JOAN

In spite of her fears for her future, Joan continued to press for a divorce to which, according to one insider, Ted offered only token resistance. While he might have preferred to stay married for political reasons, to spare his family the painful publicity that would inevitably surround a divorce, and even, perhaps, to retain the personal protection that marriage afforded him, he may also have recognized the futility of their situation. As long as Joan had requested the divorce, no matter how unpleasant, it would be a convenient way out for both of them. Ted asked, however, that the public not be told of their decision until January, after the inauguration. And Joan, once again, deferred to political expediency.

Meanwhile, press and public alike waited impatiently for a sign, such as Joan's return to Washington, that would fulfill the promises made during the campaign. But as the hot days of August drifted toward the cool days of early fall, Joan remained secluded in Hyannis Port, while Ted went back alone to Washington, to the Senate, and to the campaign trail—this time for President Carter. Except for an occasional appearance together for some political event, they lived separate lives.

In October Joan went with Ted to campaign for Carter in Boston's North End. And as she sat on stage at the Christopher Columbus Community Center, listening to Ted say he would return in

'82, '83, and '84, tears began to roll down her cheeks. A photographer captured the moment and large closeup pictures of Joan's face were again front-page news. But where the public read joy, devotion, and love in her eyes, I saw sadness in her realization that she would not be a part of Ted's future.

As usual, everything Joan said and did was watched and reported, even her efforts to be closer to her children. Fueling speculation that she might return to Washington, she spent a few days there visiting Patrick in October. Three weeks later she went abroad to see her daughter Kara who was traveling on a student ship. They met in Egypt and together saw the pyramids, the tombs in the Valley of the Kings, and had a private visit with Mrs. Sadat, wife of the late Egyptian President Anwar Sadat. Joan then took her long awaited trip to Greece, where a Boston friend had arranged for her to meet a Greek shipping family who generously offered Joan and Kara the use of a plane, a car, a yacht, an apartment in Athens, and a villa outside the city.

When Joan returned to Boston after Thanksgiving, she was in much better spirits and ready to make plans for a future that would no longer include Ted. The Christmas holiday was clouded by the pending divorce announcement. Nevertheless, Joan went to their McLean home and to Lift One in Aspen for the family's traditional ski vacation. Even more candid now about her desire to meet new men, she called from Aspen to tell me about Boston psychiatrist Dr. Gerald Aranoff, whom she had seen on a TV program speaking about the problems of treating pain in America. "He's so handsome," she said. "I'm dreaming and fantasizing about him. How can I let him know I want to see him? I have to be more aggressive than other women, you know."

On January 25, Joan was scheduled to narrate *Peter and the Wolf* at a Cameo concert in Boston and she decided to invite Dr. Aranoff, whom she had met once before briefly, to attend. Over the phone from Colorado we composed a letter complimenting him on his work and inviting him to the concert.

The November elections had brought a landslide victory for Ronald Reagan, and Joan accompanied Ted to the inauguration. It was an emotionally trying time for both of them—for Ted, because he had hoped it would be his own inauguration, and for Joan, because it would be her last public appearance as Ted's wife. She expected the divorce announcement to be made two days later, but Kennedy's office inexplicably issued the statement the next day. Joan was furious when she called from Washington to say she had heard it on the radio driving back from having her hair done at Elizabeth Arden's. "That's the story of my life," she said angrily. "I've heard about all the big things in this family from the news."

Neither Joan nor I had seen a copy of the statement before she left for Washington, although Ted reportedly showed it to her at breakfast before they left for Reagan's inauguration. They and their staffs had agreed beforehand to make no comments and to let the carefully worded announcement speak for itself:

"With regret, yet with respect and consideration for each other, we have agreed to terminate our marriage. We have reached this decision together, with the understanding of our children, and after pastoral counseling. Appropriate legal proceedings will be commenced in due course, and we intend to resolve as friends all matters relating to the dissolution of our marriage.

"In the interests of our children and other members of our family, we hope that the press and the public will understand our wish to decline further comment on this family matter."

I, too, was unprepared for the early announcement, and because Joan was still out of town, Boston reporters with TV cameramen and photographers immediately descended on me. They swarmed outside the building and waited in cars, vans, and on foot, hoping to catch me, or even one of my children returning from school, for a comment. Finally several reporters managed to slip into the building with a local grocery delivery and rang Joan's bell. Kitty, in disbelief and shocked by the news, sent them down to me. When I declined comment, they congregated outside my apartment, set up cameras, and focused on my gray front door, which was later featured on the six o'clock news as a silent symbol of how difficult this story would be to unlock. The next morning, the superintendent summoned me down to the lobby where I found two well-dressed men holding large baskets of fresh flowers with instructions "to deliver them to Mrs. Kennedy in person." When I grew suspicious, they finally admitted they were reporters, gave me the flowers, and left.

Joan intended to keep her promise not to talk to reporters about the divorce. When she returned to Boston, she called to practice what she would say. "I'll tell them it's a private matter. Our statement speaks for itself and it's not appropriate to say anything further." Her silence did not stop the presses, however. Nearly every paper in the country wrote front page stories, editorials, or feature articles, reviewing, interpreting, and analyzing the marriage, the campaign, and the divorce. Father English, spokesman for the family, was quoted frequently. From Washington, he said, "Two people can marry when they're very very young and Joan and Ted did that—and can become in the course of their lives different people. They just don't match that well anymore. . . ." That was the "official" explanation. It was left to reporters to speculate on the far more complex reasons for the divorce—and what might happen next.

Joan's narration of *Peter and the Wolf* would be her first public appearance after the divorce announcement. Because she was afraid the press would follow her to the rehearsal scheduled for Symphony Hall, she rehearsed in the privacy of her own apartment with conductor Harry Ellis Dickson and pianist Myron Romano. And on the day of the performance, although she was nervous, she hoped that her appearance would reassure the public that she was not "poor Joan" anymore. She was also pleased that Dr. Aranoff had accepted her invitation to attend.

That afternoon I helped Joan dress in a royal blue velvet outfit which she called her "lucky suit." And since we now were without drivers, limousines, or security, a friend drove us to the Colonnade Hotel and left us at an obscure side entrance, again to avoid the press. We were met by Dick Gallagher, a Kennedy volunteer acting as advanceman and bodyguard for us that day. He led us on a circuitous route through the steamy kitchen to a holding room upstairs where Joan made her final preparations. Then we paraded back through the kitchen and into the hotel ballroom to join our table of eight guests. Dr. Aranoff rose immediately to his feet, smiled, and greeted Joan.

Jerry, thirty-six and eight years younger than Joan, was an attractive man with brown eyes, a shock of thick curly graying hair, and a lean muscular frame. As Director of the Pain Unit at the Massachusetts Rehabilitation Hospital in Boston, he was highly regarded by his colleagues and dedicated to his work. Joan sat down next to him to talk before the concert began.

Peter and the Wolf followed a piece by Mozart, and Joan walked to the stage to accept a large flowing bouquet of red roses and baby's breath sent to her from Ted. Then Maestro Dickson raised his baton and everyone in the room focused on Joan as the music began. She had narrated the Prokofiev score many times before, yet that afternoon her delivery was somewhat tentative and her words more subdued than usual. But that seemed less important to the audience than seeing Joan and knowing she was all right. Her performance was rewarded with loud applause. When she returned to our table she talked almost exclusively to Jerry, and their meeting, conceived in Colorado, was the beginning of an important new relationship for Joan.

The Kennedys' announcement was soon overshadowed by another event that touched off a national celebration. For the fifty-two recently released hostages as they returned home to the United States, Americans rang church bells, flew flags, held parades, sent up fireworks, and tied yellow ribbons on trees. Seeing a flimsy connection between the two events one columnist quipped, "Now that the hostages have been welcomed home, how about hanging their 'Free at Last' signs on Joan Kennedy's apartment house."

But Joan was not quite as free as the announcement made it appear. She was not free to comment on the divorce to the press. And she was not free of the restrictions or obligations that came with being a public figure and a Kennedy wife. She instructed me to refuse all talk shows and print interviews, and frustrated reporters, noting that she had talked to them when she wanted publicity, suggested that she had "used" the press over the past several months to serve her own ends. Apart from her pledge to Ted, I knew that

Joan was not yet ready to speak out publicly about the divorce or anything else. There were still too many unknowns in her future. But maintaining a good relationship with the press seemed vital to her, and she always requested that I invite every reporter or producer who called to call back in three months. And they did.

For the present, without direct access to Joan, reporters had only one recourse—to follow her on evenings out with Jerry. They were photographed arriving at the Boston Ballet's "Balanchine Festival," having dinner at Rosalie's restaurant in Marblehead, leaving the play *Sweeney Todd*, attending performances at the Boston Shakespeare Company, The American Repertory Theater and the Shubert Theater. Photographers missed them going to and from their weekly ballroom dancing classes—but being ever watchful they didn't miss much else.

Jerry handled the publicity well and responded enthusiastically to inquiries about his relationship with Joan. He told the *Boston Herald American*, "She's a wonderful person—stimulating and marvelous company." Joan, on the other hand, did not mention Jerry to reporters at all. She gave me a statement to use to cover their dates which read: "I love Boston's ballet, concerts, and theater. I'm happy I have so many wonderful old and new friends to share them with." Although I gave it out whenever reporters called to ask about Jerry, I was not surprised that it did not see print.

After the postcampaign doldrums, Joan's life suddenly took on a new momentum. In a typical week she had appointments with one or more of her doctors, her lawyer, her college adviser, her decorator, her hair stylist, her clothes designer, and her masseuse. And in the evenings she went to a concert, symphony, or the theater, almost always with Jerry. Kitty managed the housekeeping and continued to come in at ten on Tuesdays and Fridays, using her own key so she wouldn't wake Joan. She followed the instructions in Joan's notes scattered around on the rug, then cleaned, watered the plants (we later hired a plant waterer), gathered up Joan's clothes from the floor, ordered the canned and frozen groceries, soft drinks, and household supplies, waited for their delivery, put everything away, and then took Joan's laundry home with her.

Since there was so little time left in Joan's schedule for us to meet, she and I also relied on notes. I slipped them under her door several times a day, with important people, dates, and subjects underlined in red, and sometimes she returned them with instructions in the margins, other times I called for her answers. A sample of a partial day's exchange read as follows:

> Do you want Othello tickets? If so, need a check for $136 and I'll send it. (Joan replied, "No.")

> Mike Douglas Show hated to hear the "no," but will repeat the invitation in six to nine months.

> Timothy will come here to do your hair. He has opera tickets that afternoon and offered 11 A.M. or 6:30 P.M. I talked him back to 12:30. If that's not OK, you can negotiate when you see him the 29th at 1. (Joan answered, "Try Mr. Martin at Michel Kazan.")

> Reminder: Call Father Gregory.

> P.S. I didn't have time to get the National Enquirer you wanted today. Will try Friday.

This last request had been unusual. Disguising herself with a scarf and glasses, Joan often went into stores and bought the tabloid papers herself.

As I wrote more and more such notes, I couldn't help realizing how much Joan's life, and therefore my job, had changed. Where once we had both been involved in matters and issues of national concern, I was now becoming a personal or social secretary for Joan. But I had agreed to help her with her thesis, and until that was written I did not want to leave. And I anticipated that we would continue to work together on two other projects which we had often discussed: a television arts series for children and a book on women and alcoholism. The television series became the subject of her thesis.

Joan placed particular importance on receiving her graduate degree, and during the past month we had done most of the research, interviewed experts, and collected materials for two papers and her thesis, due at the end of April. The thesis, a proposal for weekly television segments we called *Artsnews*, was directed to children eight to fifteen, but also designed to appeal to their parents. It was written in a format for us to use later as a presentation to local TV stations, and if it were accepted, it could be the beginning of a career for Joan and the resumption of mine. We finished the papers, and in a last-minute flurry made the deadline for the thesis, which was dispatched in a taxi to Lesley College. Even before it was accepted, Joan optimistically asked me to draw up a guest list for a graduation party, and wondered wistfully if the invitations might be worded as if Ted and the children were giving her the party.

Throughout that spring Joan was featured often in the tabloids and other papers, even though she gave no interviews and continued to refuse comment on the divorce. And in April, the *Ladies Home Journal* published an article titled, "Joan Kennedy Without Ted: Finding Her Own Strength," which contained comments Joan had made in the interview with Phyllis Battelle on the Cape months before. "I'm the tops. I have talent, I know I'm smart," she was quoted as saying. "I got straight A's in graduate school. I've still got my looks. I know I've got all these terrific things going for me. I mean, my God, you are talking to, I think, one of the most fascinating women in this country."

Once again Joan had been caught at a vulnerable moment, and her boastful remarks did not really reflect how she felt about herself when they were made or when they finally appeared. The repercussions were not as severe as when she had compared herself to Rosalynn Carter, perhaps because she was no longer considered a potential First Lady. She was now a mere celebrity—fair game for the press—and the papers continued to print sensational and erroneous stories about her romance with Jerry, as well as her relationship with Ted and her children. An article in a May issue of the *Globe* described "Joan's Agony as Her Children Drift Away," when, in fact, she was trying very hard to stay in touch with her children and to obtain custody of Patrick.

Her mail also revealed a subtle change in the way she was perceived by the public. One woman wrote that she was glad Joan was

going out socially but suggested she "choose an international ty-
coon." A divorced man said that he had read she was one of the
most fascinating women in America and thought it a great coinci-
dence—because he was one of the most fascinating men. He then
went on to tell why in two more single-spaced pages. A sixty-three-
year-old man, "divorced with no dependents" who had stopped
drinking almost twenty years ago, sent her his philosophy of life
typed on little yellow cards and also listed his character references.
And one postcard in a series from the same admirer read: "Greetings Blonde Bomber—while we have met only twice, respectfully
request that you would take me to Miami Beach on TWA at your
earliest convenience."

Lesley College accepted and approved Joan's thesis, and she
was now qualified to receive a graduate degree. Her family gathered
on graduation day, the twenty-third of May, and when Ted and the
children arrived at her apartment promptly at one, Joan was already
dressed in the traditional cap and gown. Then we all were driven to
Boston University where the commencement was to be held, and
not surprisingly the press was lying in wait for us outside the au-
ditorium. The wind on that bright sunny day was so brisk that
Joan's gown flapped and her hair flew as photographers snapped
pictures. Ted, Kara, Teddy, and Patrick ducked inside to their
reserved seats, while I stayed outside a little longer to help Joan
with her hair and the press.

Following the two o'clock ceremony, Joan put on a new white
lacy dress and the bracelet Ted had just given her in order to welcome friends in two upstairs rooms at the Harvard Club. A harpist
played in the background, and Joan instructed the only photographer
allowed inside the club to take "lots and lots of pictures for my
scrapbooks."

Her graduation was probably one of the happiest days in Joan's
life. She had proved something to herself and to her family—and to
the legion of Kennedy watchers who followed her every move. She
was justifiably proud of herself, and when her picture in cap and
gown appeared in *Time* in early June, she ordered dozens of copies
and asked that they be sent to all her friends. But as important as

her graduation was to Joan's self-confidence, it also underscored her continuing ambivalence about her future. Even though she was divorcing Ted, she wanted him to be at the ceremony and at her party. And even though she was involved in a new and rewarding relationship, she was not yet ready to acknowledge it in public by inviting Jerry. He planned his own graduation party for Joan instead.

A similar situation arose two weeks before Jerry's party. Joan was preparing for another narration of *Peter and the Wolf*, this time at Symphony Hall, and asked me to invite guests for three tables reserved in her name. Jerry was not one of them. He was requested to sit alone in the balcony. Then a few days later, concerned that press coverage of her romance might affect divorce negotiations, Joan decided he shouldn't come at all. She asked me to call Jerry to "uninvite" him and to make it seem like my idea. She also asked me to tell him she was worried about the press at his party and might not be able to attend.

I sympathized with her predicament but saw no reason why Joan couldn't call Jerry herself. But she insisted, so I reluctantly dialed Jerry's secretary, Marsha (it was "his Marsha" and "her Marcia"), and Jerry came right on the line. I told him what Joan had asked me to say and when I finished there was a long uncomfortable pause.

"I've tried to be less conspicuous and have gone out of my way," Jerry said finally.

"Yes, I know," I said. "I have Joan's copy of the letter you wrote to your hospital public relations department discouraging attention to your personal life." The divorce was making it very difficult for both of them.

Jerry agreed not to be seen at Symphony Hall and assured me that Joan didn't have to worry about his party. "I've hired two policemen," he said. "There will be no press. Everyone will be screened. There'll be one policeman in front and another walking on the beach. I've been telling people not to talk to the press. But I'll do whatever she wishes, whatever she wants."

After so many years in the limelight, all Joan wanted was time alone. It was not to be. Even then she and Jerry were mak-

ing plans to travel together in Europe at the end of June, and somehow their plans, which they wanted to keep secret, had leaked to
the press. Norma Nathan wrote: "And she has summer plans, to
lecture someplace in Italy on something in late June. . . . Eye-
wronically Aranoff will be in Italy the selfsame two weeks she'll be
there. They've booked separate plane reservations for the same time,
same stations (Venice, Florence, Rome and Turino)." Because
Joan was arranging this sub-rosa trip directly with the travel agent,
this time Norma was better informed than I was.

On a Saturday night in early June, a friend of mine drove
Joan, Gail and her husband, and me to Jerry's party at his home in
Swampscott. Despite the directions that Jerry had given us and
the fact that Joan had been there several times, somewhere around
the Wonderland dog track we took a wrong turn and got lost. The
party had received so much publicity that Joan was nervous about
going, but as Jerry had promised, there were no reporters and when
we arrived, a policeman stopped the car in the driveway. He glanced
into the back seat, recognized Joan, then laughed and waved us
through.

Jerry's huge Victorian house stood high above the beach. It
was sparsely furnished except for a cozy blue-carpeted den overlooking the ocean and his hot tub outside. Most of the guests, in black
tie and elegantly coiffed, were friends of Jerry's from the entertain-
ment and medical fields. Joan, in a simple cotton dress, seemed distracted as they introduced themselves to her. Two hours later we
were on our way back to Boston, wondering if it was any one of the
guests at the party who faithfully reported Jerry and Joan's activities
to reporters. The evening had been a strain for Joan, perhaps because it implied an intimacy with Jerry that she felt was too soon to
acknowledge—even to herself.

Nevertheless, they continued to make plans for their European
trip, changing them frequently to ensure privacy. Joan rehearsed
the narration for Aaron Copland's A Lincoln Portrait with Michel
Sasoon who would conduct the performance at Turin's Teatro
Regio. She went to her dressmaker for final fittings on the long
green chiffon and satin gown she would wear for the concert. But
a few days before they were to leave, she again grew nervous because

of the divorce and press and decided that Jerry should not accompany her to Europe after all. Very disappointed, he again agreed to her wishes and did not go.

Joan's performance in Turin was a success. She was besieged by Italian photographers, whom she charmingly encouraged by saying that American paparazzi were much worse. From Italy, she flew to London where she had planned to stay a few weeks, but she called me several times to say how lonely she was. On her last call before leaving London she said, "I've been to lots of glamorous parties. But I woke up this morning and said to myself, 'I've got to get home.' I'm homesick. Can you meet me at the airport Wednesday with my car? I want to go straight to the Cape and you can take the luggage back to the apartment. This whole week I've been very lonely. I dragged it out until I was really miserable."

"Did you have any fun at all?" I asked.

"Well, yes. Michael Caine and Jack Nicholson fought over me. And I've done my shopping. I'm the toast of the town. But I'm tired. I almost came home last week. I feel mixed about the divorce. When you come to the airport bring me a note with Ted's weekend schedule. Have Kitty unpack me and take things to the dry cleaner and have Jerry come to the Cape, but he'll have to leave by the weekend."

I could hear the homesickness in her voice, but I thought she should know about an unpleasant incident that had occurred during her absence. "Jerry called me about a bomb threat, and he received a note that said, 'What a mess you've gotten yourself in with Joan. Leave $5,000 at 3 A.M. for keeping me quiet tonight.' " I told her he had hired police protection and a team of dogs, but he had been very uneasy until it was over.

"Poor Jerry," Joan said, sounding more lost than ever.

Two days later she was back in Boston and on her way to the Cape and a brief reunion with Jerry. On weekends she usually drove back to her apartment, leaving the Cape house free for Ted.

Joan's and Ted's schedules were planned so they would not see each other. Ted was supposed to stay at his mother's when they were there together, but he was often in and out of their house for meals and to see the children. Their meetings were "amicable," according to Kitty, who traveled to the Cape to work for Joan that summer. But the divorce put a chill on the relationship between Joan and Rose who, again according to Kitty, appeared to blame it all on Joan.

Joan turned to her own family for the security she was losing with the Kennedys. It had been five years since she had seen her father and she invited him and her sister's son, Dochie, to spend a week with her and Patrick at the Cape in the middle of August.

A handsome, pleasant man, Mr. Bennett was recovering from a stroke and spent much of his time alone reading, as Joan, unaware that this was to be her last visit with him, continued her usual round of activities. Then just before his scheduled departure he suddenly suffered a severe heart attack and was rushed by ambulance to a hospital in Boston for intensive care. Joan followed him to Boston and then immediately requested special arrangements be made for putting a bed aboard a commercial flight so her father could go home to Louisiana. Two days later he died.

Now both of her parents were dead, she was divorcing her husband of twenty-three years, her children were increasingly independent. Except for a few close friends, Joan was very much alone.

16 GOING

FORWARD

The most important thing that I can share with you is the personal knowledge that decisions are not irrevocable, that choices do come back, sometimes in different forms and in different ways, but they can be remade.

—JOAN

The death of her father magnified Joan's anxiety about the future and an even more immediate concern, the divorce. It was being handled by lawyers in New York, and from what Joan told me, I knew the negotiations were acrimonious.

In an attempt to focus her attention on something else, I suggested we pursue our arts education project for children's television and retrieved Joan's thesis from my files. We reread it, reviewing its purpose and our particular roles, which were similar to the way we had worked together during the campaign: Joan would be on-camera while I assisted behind the scenes with ideas, writing, and production. Then I made an appointment in the last week of August to present our idea in person to the station manager of WBZ-TV, known for its interest and work in the arts. We both felt excited and a little nervous going to the station, and even more so when we found the station manager's office filled with people. The program director and several assistants had joined the meeting to listen and question us during our presentation. They appeared interested and we left, agreeing to talk again.

But Joan's thoughts soon returned to the divorce and to the financial settlement in particular. Taken for granted during all the years of her marriage, money now became her major worry. "I've been dreaming," she told me. "They aren't dreams—they're so real. I dreamed that Ted's counteroffer came back and it wasn't as much as I asked for. Then my lawyer tells me I'd better take it, and I say, 'You're fired.'" Then with conviction she added, "I'll go to court and ask for three times that amount and I'll get every penny."

I did not know just what amount Ted's lawyers had proposed, but I did know that if Joan were going to battle the Kennedys, it would require as much effort and self-assertion as she had displayed to become sober. She would have to fight, and fight hard.

Meanwhile, she spent most of her evenings with Jerry, delighted to have someone to talk to, to share her interests in the theater and music. They tried to avoid the press, but that merely intensified curiosity about their relationship and the divorce. From my desk in the front hall I fielded the same questions over and over: "Is she planning to remarry?" "Is the reason the divorce papers haven't been filed because she's asking for part of Ted's trust funds?" "Is she teaching?" "Could you, at least, just tell me what she's doing now?" In keeping with Joan's wishes I answered none of those questions.

In the absence of real news, the press manufactured its own stories. In October, after Joan attended temple with Jerry the night before Yom Kippur, the *National Enquirer* wrote: "A tormented Joan Kennedy is facing the most agonizing decision of her life— whether to cling to her Catholic faith and risk losing the Jewish man she loves, or convert to his religion and risk alienating her beloved children." An article in the *Globe* announced: "If Joan converts to the Jewish faith, she would no longer face the disapproval of the Catholic Church over divorcing Kennedy, who is also reportedly seeking an annulment to leave him free to marry again."

Juxtaposed with sensational and fictionalized tales of Joan's romance were stories of Ted's "red-hot love triangle" with Helga Wagner, a thirty-nine-year-old jewelry designer, whom he had known several years, and actress Susan St. James. Accustomed as Joan was to tabloid journalism, even she believed and was distressed by some of these stories. One, which speculated that St. James might make a likely wife for Ted if he ran again for President in 1984, was illustrated with a picture of her with Ted and Patrick in Hyannis Port. Infuriated, Joan pointed to the newspaper she had left open on her sofa. "How could he! How could he have women there with Patrick?" she said, showing me the picture. "I've been so careful. Jerry has never been around when the kids were."

Again I tried to turn her attention to our television project, but when we met to talk about it, her original enthusiasm had cooled. She told me she didn't really want to work. I was very disappointed, but I still hoped I could count on her participation in a second project: a book on women and alcoholism which I had started with another friend and for which Joan had agreed to write the foreword. A few days later, when she told me she didn't want to do that either, I was again let down. But until the divorce was finally settled, perhaps it was unrealistic to expect her to make commitments she might not be able to keep. Joan had so much to contribute, but it was not my role to influence her decisions. She no longer needed me. We both realized it was time to go our separate ways. In the months ahead, however, each time we set a date for my departure, Joan extended it and I agreed to stay. Disentangling our lives would not be easy for either of us.

The divorce made it extremely difficult for Joan to maintain normal family ties. For the usual Thanksgiving dinner at the Cape, she made plans for the menu and asked for films and a projector to be brought over—watching movies at home was a Kennedy tradition. But she was disappointed when Ted went to Palm Beach to be with his mother and flew Patrick and his cousin Dochie to Florida to join him. Teddy, Jr., was in Paris, and only Kara dined with her mother. Saddened, Joan reacted by overeating, but this time it was with more self-understanding, derived, at least in part, from attending behavior modification classes at McLean for weight control. "I was so upset that I ate twelve pieces of toast," she told me. "I was either anxious, bored, or lonely."

She was, in fact, all three. In spite of her relationship with Jerry and new insights into herself, Joan was still unhappy. Shortly after Thanksgiving, Hazel called me one evening. She had just spent some time with Joan and was very concerned. "Joan doesn't know what she'll do," she said. "She told me she wanted to do something of value and that you were encouraging her. But, Marcia, you know she's not Eunice. At this moment, Joan's main concern is herself. She's obsessed with the divorce, wants another lawyer, is grandstanding about taking Ted to court and getting half his fortune. She's spinning her wheels about losing affinity with the Kennedys. She thinks she's in control, but it's fantasy and illusion."

Both Hazel and I agreed that Joan was facing an uncertain future. But there seemed to be very little we could do to help her through this latest ordeal in her life. She was struggling to find her way, and she would have to do that herself, just as she had overcome alcoholism.

As the Christmas holidays drew closer Joan was once again made aware that the divorce was isolating her, not only from the Kennedy family, but from her own children. She was determined to fight back. "Ted thinks it would be better if I didn't go to Washington for Christmas," she said, during one of our work sessions in early December. "But I'm going anyway." She leaned back in her chair and watched me put dates on her calendar and make notes for plane reservations. "And he doesn't want me in Aspen this year either. So I booked myself into a place across the street. When he heard that, he made plans to stay with a bachelor friend—so he'll have all the comforts and lots of women. So now I'm staying with the kids and he's feeling sorry for himself."

In the contest for their children's affection, Ted appeared to have all the advantages, and Joan's reactions were, understandably, bitter. She was angered in particular by a series running in the *Boston Globe* by Harrison Rainie on the Kennedy children. Called "The Third Generation," it portrayed Ted in a very favorable light, and part four of the series told the story of how he had helped his son, Teddy, Jr., through his battle with cancer. "He was always there when I needed him," Teddy, Jr., was quoted as saying. "He was the one who gave me strength to go on at times when I didn't think I could. . . ." Joan showed me the article and said, "The more Ted does things like this, the tougher I'll get."

One day, shortly after Christmas, Joan led me into her kitchen and announced wistfully, "Pretend I'm a bride and very poor. Make out a gift list of things that will last the rest of my life." Then she grew serious and said she and Jerry had cooked noodles for dinner one night. "But I had nothing to drain the noodles in." She wanted a complete inventory of everything she would ever need.

Down on my hands and knees, opening cupboards and drawers, I discovered that where most people put pots and pans, Joan had rows of purses—leather, lizard, gold lamé. Where other women might store casseroles or dishes, she had shelves of shoes—several of each style in a rainbow of colors. And in drawers normally used for cooking utensils, she had her collection of bathing suits—prints, solids, one-piece, two-piece, three-piece, most with matching caps.

"And don't forget a toaster oven or Jerry can't have his bagels in the morning," Joan reminded me. "Why don't people think of these things? You know, Ted did me a disservice all those years. We had so much staff I never learned to do anything. Jerry can't believe it—I'm so helpless."

When my list was complete, it had grown from colander and toaster oven to cookie sheets, measuring cups, an electric mixer, roasting pans, and muffin tins—a fully equipped kitchen for a woman who never cooked. But soon after inventory day Joan proudly announced, "I'm learning to use the microwave. Jerry's teaching me." And she also learned to cook Kitty's recipe for chicken breasts—in a sauce of dry onion soup mix, bottled Russian dressing, and apricot preserves—which she served at her first small dinner party with Jerry as host. The evening was a success and she was delighted with her accomplishments.

When Jerry moved some of his clothes into Ted's closet, Joan was happier than I had seen her in months—energetic, high, and fun to be with. While we were driving to the Cape together to conduct another inventory at the house there, she talked enthusiastically about their new arrangement.

"It's so much fun. Jerry stays from Sunday night to Friday morning. He gets up before I do to leave for the hospital. It's so comfortable, and I don't have to worry about how I look."

"What does he do when you're with Patrick on weekends?" I asked.

"Oh, he reads and writes, sees friends, does his mail and runs errands." She tilted her head toward me. "You know, I like Jerry, but I don't think I really love him. Besides," she added with a laugh, "I want to have lots of affairs in the next five years. Then, when I'm fifty, maybe I'll settle down with someone for companionship. With someone a little bald and plump, but cozy. Jackie and her friends used to say that your first marriage should be for lust, your second for money, and your third for companionship."

When we arrived at the Cape house Irene was there to help us. She had already gone to the drugstore for Joan, and in a voice deep from years of smoking, she said that she had had to pay $2.71 in cash for her purchase because the unpaid drugstore bill was up to $2,000.

When Joan heard that she immediately went to the yellow wall phone in the kitchen and called the woman in Washington who handled family plans and problems. "Just send me that bill and he'll be very sorry in court he didn't pay it," she said. "I'm sorry, Joanna, this is just so irritating and it's not fair. If it were you, you wouldn't think so either."

After Joan hung up, she told Irene and me that Ted "sees red" on two subjects: department store bills and drugstore bills. Then she began to talk about the financial settlement, which was the source of so much contention. To determine her living allowance, the lawyers were averaging her expenses of the last four years. Joan felt that the past year was a more realistic one, but Ted's lawyer pointed out that people spend more during a campaign year. Joan told us she had countered by saying, "It is very difficult for a lady who is incarcerated in hospitals to buy clothes, have her hair done, buy food, entertain, and fix up her apartment."

After dinner we set to work on another kitchen inventory and drew up a schedule of repairs and improvements that Joan wanted made to the house. Walking through each room she decided what should be done—remodeling, painting, slipcovering, new carpeting, cabinet work—and I followed, making lists. When we had finished, we returned to the den to talk late into the night. Joan sat in the "Senator's chair," her blond hair tossed against its bright blue fabric.

"Ted ignored me," she said, remembering all the years they had lived together in this house. "I never knew where I stood with him or his family or the kids."

But that was in the past. Now Joan knew exactly where she

stood. In her battles with Ted she may have been both difficult and demanding, but she would no longer be ignored.

Within weeks of our visit, the Cape house and Joan's Boston apartment were full of workmen: painters, carpenters, plumbers, carpet cleaners. Both her bedroom and bathroom were remodeled and her kitchen was newly stocked with electrical appliances, Waterford glassware, bone china, and even cartons of light bulbs in every shape and wattage she would ever need. For a future office in her apartment and the secretary she eventually intended to hire, the back rooms bulged with dozens of boxes of engraved stationery, note pads, paper, file folders, rolls of stamps and Scotch tape. Joan made appointments with her designer for new clothes, and shopped in department stores for even more. She bought cosmetics by the case. Boxes began to pile up all over the apartment until finally, when the torrent of things had grown beyond us, trucks were sent to the Cape carrying mattresses, towels, stainless steel kitchen sets, sterling silver, new blankets and sheets, and all sorts of household supplies to be stored in the attic of the Cape house and indexed with elaborate maps so Joan could find things there over the years.

In her own way, she was trying to create some security for her future. And as the divorce negotiations dragged on, Joan herself moved at a whirlwind pace. She supervised the workmen in her apartment and at the Cape, demanding that they work overtime and on holidays and weekends, in order to finish their many projects, she admitted candidly, while Ted was still paying the bills. She was equally demanding of me and of Kitty. "I'd walk in the front door and there would be twenty notes of things for me to do on top of my regular chores before I got to the kitchen," Kitty recalled, "then there would be more notes lined up on the fridge. She told me she wanted the window sills clean enough to eat scrambled eggs on." Kitty admitted ruefully that she had found it much easier to work for Joan when she had been drinking.

Kitty and I and Joan's other friends understood that she was going through the final and perhaps the most traumatic episode of her marriage. In fact, Joan was puzzled by her own behavior. "Everyone thinks I'm crazy," she said. "And I know something is wrong.

I'm back to eating six bowls of cereal with two inches of sugar in the middle of the night. And buying several pints of ice cream at a time."

Joan grew even more upset when Ted's lawyers requested an explanation for some of her extraordinary bills. Just before Valentine's Day her lawyer flew in from New York for a consultation, and when I saw Joan the next morning she looked pale and tired. The meeting with her lawyer, she told me, had increased her anxiety to such a pitch that "I yelled at Jerry last night and told him to sleep in Ted's room." Feeling remorseful, she said that he had never seen her behave that way before. "I'm the pretender, always the smiler. Jerry couldn't understand. If I'd had pills I would have thrown them all down my throat. In fact, I would say, 'So long world,' if I didn't feel needed by Patrick. Ted is just waiting for me to make a mistake: take a drink. The day the divorce is done, I could go to outer Siberia and stay for a month. Yesterday I would have drunk a whole bottle of vodka, but I don't have that option."

I heaved an inner sigh of relief. Joan was aware of the temptation to drink, but knew it would be no more than a temporary escape that would only compound her problems. Even under these trying conditions, or perhaps because of them, her sobriety seemed strong.

She also seemed to be much more at ease in her relationship with Jerry, and when she told me they were planning a secret trip to Mexico, I decided to advise caution. "You're in the middle of a highly publicized divorce, easily recognizable," I said. "Shouldn't you tell your lawyer about the trip?"

"Another friend told me the same thing," she replied. "Maybe I shouldn't go at all because of the publicity."

Nonetheless, Joan and Jerry flew to Cancun for a long weekend. They evaded the press, but the trip was a disappointment. "Oh, it was terrible," Joan said. "Not romantic at all. You wouldn't believe it, I was tired and mad at Jerry. He was sunburned and sick the whole time. Then I got Montezuma's revenge. Can you believe it—a trip with a lover and on the plane I'm in my kerchief and shades and feel so faint I want to lie down on the floor."

Joan returned to see more favorable press for Ted. An article in *People* titled "Ted Kennedy Reflects on His Life, His Family, and His Political Future at 50," celebrated his devotion to public service, his famous family, his handling of setbacks, and the possibility of his running again for the presidency in 1984. Joan was barely mentioned—as if "family" no longer included her. If Kennedy image makers were gearing up for Ted's run for reelection to the Senate that fall, it may have seemed expedient to brush Joan and the pending divorce under the Kennedy carpet. Joan reacted angrily. "I'm going to stick this out until I get what I want. He thinks I'm too nice to fight, but I'll play my trump card: what his immediate family thinks of him and what I know of him. I'll say, 'He throws millions at the poor, but he's stingy with his wife.' He wants this over before the Senate election next fall, but I'm in no rush. They are treating me like an alcoholic who is still drinking and I won't let them."

Joan was, however, mentioned prominently in a highly critical book published that spring. In *The Kennedy Imprisonment: A Meditation on Power*, Garry Wills wrote: "The exceptional Kennedy in-laws married the brothers who were murdered. . . . Joan Bennett Kennedy was not in the league of these tough ladies. . . . Try as she would, she was on the outmost rim of the concentered Kennedy family. The nucleus was the father. Around him circled the sons, near the point of disappearing at times into this center of family gravity. Outside that tight ring came the women Kennedys, wife and daughters. Outside that, the male in-laws. . . . Outside that ring, the female in-laws—but even here Joan was not equal to the other two; she came in a distant third, farthest from the family's animating center—till she spun out, alone, into darkness."

Joan asked me to buy the book for her, but if she read it, she kept her thoughts to herself. Being a Kennedy—for better or for worse—had been the core of Joan's identity all her adult life. Finding an identity of her own was the most difficult problem she now faced. To me it was ironic that some people thought she had never really been a Kennedy at all.

When I arrived at her apartment one Friday morning for a work session to plan a series of four spring cocktail parties, Joan was up and making coffee in the kitchen. She came out to greet me, but looked pale and drawn. I knew that Sally had returned to the hospital, there was nothing doctors could do now, and that Joan had visited her earlier in the week. "Sally died last night," she said softly. Sally was our age, the mother of four children, and she had been devoted to Joan. No one would forget her courage and her capacity to love. She had been the Senator's cousin's wife, and also Joan's last link to the Kennedy clan.

Joan and Ted's greatest source of contention in the divorce was the Cape house, which he wanted to keep because it was near his family's compound. Joan was not only determined to have it, but also wanted Ted to pay the upkeep. As we walked along the beach in front of the house one day that spring, she told me she had turned down an offer of another house anywhere else on the Cape and had instructed her attorney not to yield. Shortly after, she requested a litigator, suggesting that if Ted were not "generous" with her she would take him to court just before the Senate election. Years of pain and humiliation were fueling Joan's fight for a fair divorce settlement.

Unfortunately, the anger that she had so long repressed sometimes spilled over on her friends and the people who worked for her. As devoted as she was to Joan, even Kitty finally decided to leave, but she continued to work for the Senator at his small apartment three blocks away on Marlborough Street. After Joan postponed my departure from June 1 to August 1, and again to November 1, I hired several other women to complete as many projects as possible before I left. Together we worked down the list: gathering a supply of wedding and birthday presents, planning that year's Christmas gifts, redoing six categories of address books, setting up an office for a future secretary in Joan's apartment, composing and indexing model letters for every conceivable purpose, to be used by the next secretary. As the list grew, I realized that my departure was now included among Joan's many other anxieties. With me, as with Ted, she was trying to prepare for every eventuality in a still uncertain future.

While I worked in Boston that summer Joan was at the Cape and we talked often by phone. Even there, at the place she loved best, among those whom she loved best and who loved her, she was tense and unhappy. "It's been awful," she said. "I want to swat the older kids. I'm yelling at all of them. And I have to leave the house for two weeks around the Fourth and two weeks at Labor Day so Ted can have it." The divorce had now been prolonged for over a year and with no end in sight, Joan still had no real control over her life.

We continued working together on various projects throughout that summer and into the fall. I hoped the divorce would be settled by the time of my departure in November, but it was not until a month later that Ted issued a formal statement announcing he would not be a candidate for the Democratic nomination in 1984, and soon after he and Joan filed for divorce in Hyannis Port. As much as they preferred to keep the results of their long negotiations private, articles speculated that Joan's settlement was in the area of $5 million with an annual alimony of $175,000. She also got the house on the Cape.

It was over at last. Joan was free from her past, free to face her future. And that same month, as if to make up for the years she had missed with him, she and Patrick went to Israel and afterward appeared together on "Good Morning America" to talk about their trip. "We've been getting to know each other in a way that I couldn't when things were worse," Patrick said. "Now it's just like the old days. We've caught up on a lot. . . . My mother and I kind of discovered each other on that trip."

In the spring, Joan and Jerry, uncertain about the future of their relationship, decided to go their separate ways. Although she made several public appearances for narrations and benefits, she seemed content to spend most of her time at the Cape or in Boston, seeing friends and attending plays and concerts. Yet her activities, no matter how ordinary, continued to make news. If she was no longer a Kennedy, she was the only defector from America's royal family, and the only Kennedy woman to make herself available to the media. In the spring and summer of 1983, articles about her appeared in such magazines as the *Ladies Home Journal, Good Housekeeping,* and *McCall's.* In one of them I was especially pleased that she talked of future career plans, including television and the arts for children. In another, she spoke candidly about her alcoholism and advised: "If you think you have a problem with alcohol, please don't wait for things to get worse—don't wait until you've lost the love of your family or the respect of your friends. Alcoholism is known as the disease of denial, the lonely disease, and the most difficult thing about it is that you first have to admit that you have the problem and be willing to ask for help. . . ."

At the end of the summer Joan celebrated her forty-seventh birthday at the Cape house. She and her children invited longtime family friends, some of Ted's aides, and close personal friends like Hazel. It was a balmy night. Loud and lively music from a combo playing out on the lawn, high above Nantucket Sound, set an upbeat mood, and the finale came when Kara carried into the dining room a dark chocolate cake in the shape of a baby grand piano. In many ways the party was like a second debut for Joan. Behind her now was the rancor of the divorce, ahead a future that would include her children, strong ties with Kennedy family friends, and many lasting friendships of her own. She was pulling all of the threads of her life together, strengthening old relationships and open to new ones.

Joan was beginning to reap the benefits of her recovery. She had now been sober for nearly four years. And she had maintained her sobriety through a grueling political campaign and an emotionally wrenching divorce. It was such a remarkable achievement that whatever else she chose to do with her life, her example would serve as an inspiration to countless others. Far from idle, she lent her name to a variety of cultural causes and events, and then in the spring of 1984 traveled to China with an Earthwatch research team and several of Boston's art experts to study contemporary Chinese music, dance, and film.

Joan's life came full circle on May 20, 1984, when she delivered a moving commencement address at her alma mater, Manhattanville College, and was given an honorary Doctor of Humane Letters degree. Gone were the black habits of the nuns, and probably very few of the three hundred graduating young women had ever worn a pair of white gloves. Looking out over her audience, Joan told them, "It is much harder for you today than it was for us. Yet life has its own way of taking unexpected turns and, even for me, the settled life I thought I had embarked upon through an early marriage has taken me in directions I could never have imagined at the age of twenty-two." She went on to say, "The most important thing I can share with you is the personal knowledge that decisions are not irrevocable, that choices do come back, sometimes in different forms and in different ways, but they can be remade. And there is time, time to shape a balance between family and friends, work and career. Life is not only knowing what you want but what you'll settle for."

There were further commendations for Joan when *Time* reprinted a quote from her address along with her picture, and a week later a feature article in the *Boston Globe* commented that she felt "like a graduate herself—filled with a sense of being on the brink of a new stage in life where almost anything is possible."

And now for Joan, almost anything is possible—her life has taught her that. By will, drive, and hard work she managed to survive alcoholism, an unhappy marriage and a painful divorce. Capable of setting her sights, engendering support, pushing past barriers no matter how inhibiting or intimidating, she eventually reached her goals.

During the decades of her marriage, marked equally by glamour and tragedy, Joan lost her sense of self as she struggled to become a Kennedy. Yet, it was in her final effort to please others, to join her husband in his pursuit of the presidency, and to measure up to the Kennedys' expectations that she chose sobriety. And from the miracles that spring from sobriety, she became self-confident and strong enough to make other difficult choices. It took enormous courage for Joan to give up the position, wealth, and power of being a Kennedy, but she wanted more for herself. She had to find her own identity, and in making those choices, she discovered the person she could become, emerging from the darkness into her own path of light.